C is for Control
A Laboratory Text for Hardware Interfacing with C and C++

John Blankenship
DeVry Institute of Technology

Prentice Hall

Upper Saddle River, New Jersey   Columbus, Ohio

Library of Congress Cataloging-in-Publication Data

Blankenship, John
    C is for control : a laboratory text for hardware interfacing with
  C and C++ / John Blankenship.
      p.   cm.
    Includes index.
    ISBN 0–02–310742–1
    1. C (Computer program language)   2. C++ (Computer program
  language)   3. Computer interfaces.
  QA76.73.C153B584   2000   99-21067
  005.13'3—dc21   CIP

Publisher: Charles E. Stewart, Jr.
Copyeditor: Marianne L'Abbate
Production Editor: Rachel Besen
Design Coordinator: Karrie Converse-Jones
Cover Designer: Rod Harris
Cover Image: Stock Market
Production Manager: Matt Ottenweller
Marketing Manager: Ben Leonard

This book was set in Times Roman and was printed and bound by Banta Company. The cover was printed by Phoenix Color Corp.

©2000 by Prentice-Hall, Inc.
Pearson Education
Upper Saddle River, New Jersey 07458

Printed in the United States of America

10 9 8 7 6 5 4 3 2 1

ISBN: 0-02-310742-1

Prentice-Hall International (UK) Limited, *London*
Prentice-Hall of Australia Pty. Limited, *Sydney*
Prentice-Hall of Canada, Inc., *Toronto*
Prentice-Hall Hispanoamericana, S. A., *Mexico*
Prentice-Hall of India Private Limited, *New Delhi*
Prentice-Hall of Japan, Inc., *Tokyo*
Prentice-Hall (Singapore) Pte. Ltd., *Singapore*
Editora Prentice-Hall do Brasil, Ltda., *Rio de Janeiro*

Contents

Preface

C is one of the most versatile and powerful computer languages ever written, not only because of its raw power but also because of its ability to evolve, adapt, and conform to the challenges of change. C compilers range from large, component-based, Windows development systems to public domain, small C compilers targeted at embedded controllers with many variations in between.

There are many texts explaining how C can be used to handle problems in inventory control or calculate the numbers that must be printed on payroll checks. The power of C, however, is not limited to business applications. Throughout industry today, C is used to implement robots for manufacturing, automated testing systems for quality control, and intelligent diagnostic equipment to aid in the repair of many consumer products. Much of the need for these highly intelligent systems stems from the fact that our products are getting smarter.

Consumer products today are very likely to have embedded microcontrollers determining their capabilities and their personalities. Our automobiles are prime examples. They no longer have only a single embedded processor and have become so complex that a separate computer system is needed for diagnosing problems when they occur.

Don't make the mistake of thinking that computer control is limited to large, expensive products. Nearly any product today is a candidate for an intelligent implant. You'll find microprocessors in telephone answering machines and in microwave ovens. Even your computer's mouse probably has its own internal computer, and many of these computers are programmed in C. It is also likely that the quality control computers that monitor the manufacturing process and the computerized diagnostic equipment for this new breed of consumer products are also programmed in C.

In the past, many of these applications required assembly language because of its efficiencies in both speed and memory requirements. Today's high-speed processors and dropping memory prices coupled with improved compilers and escalating salaries for programmers are making C the language of choice. With competition dictating that products be delivered in shorter and shorter time-to-market schedules, the advantages of C over assembly language become more apparent every day.

This text is about those applications. It's about interfacing the computer to the outside world. You'll see how to control motors and displays and how to collect external data, both digital and analog. You'll learn how software can generate waveforms and how pulses can be measured and edges detected. You'll see how software can replace hardware in order to cut costs and how port pins can be shared to cut costs even further. And we'll have a lot of fun while we do it.

Part I of this text will keep things simple while we're getting started. You will learn about I/O ports and how they are used to interface a computer with its external environment. We'll develop methods and tools that will ensure that the examples can be used in almost any hardware/software environment. It won't matter if you are using an Intel based PC or a Motorola 68HC11 based controller. All of the code in my examples has been designed to work with nearly any version of the C language you wish to use.

Exercise 1 will explore how programs can be constructed as a system of hierarchy-based programming modules. Don't take this material for granted. It will demonstrate the approach taken by the entire text and make it easier for you to comprehend what is to follow.

Part II eases you into more complicated programs and slowly develops your skills by showing you how simple programming modules can be viewed as building blocks or tools that can be used to form more complex systems. As we proceed, you will see that the explanations will become more general in nature and begin to focus more on the principles involved and less on any particular device or technology.

The general nature of Part II is designed to provide tremendous flexibility. I don't want you to be limited to my examples. I do want you to be able to apply this material to other knowledge that you've acquired and to that which you will acquire later. For example, when an interface is discussed, you should feel free to implement it with discrete TTL gates, programmable logic devices (PLDs), or anything else that you have studied. When we examine A/D and D/A conversion, I don't want you to feel that you are limited only to the devices that I mention. In fact, when you are forced to apply the principles of my code to a device or circuit of your choosing, you will enhance your knowledge and understanding far beyond anything you could get from passively reading a book.

In Part III, you will see how complex solutions can be synthesized by combining many of the principles and subsystems discussed in Parts I and II. Your critical thinking skills will be enhanced because you are expected to understand not only the systems being studied but to modify them so they provide new capabilities. Don't be intimidated by this idea. If you make sure you understand each exercise before proceeding to the next, I think you'll find the increasing rigor rewarding as well as challenging.

Remember, this text is not about using *my* programs to control *my* designs. Engineering is about solving real-world problems and this text is about preparing you to work in the real world. As you would expect, all this flexibility will increase the demands on you. When you implement these exercises using parts you've selected, you will have to locate and study the data sheets and application notes for those parts to determine exactly how to proceed. As you search for what you need, you will be getting a real taste of what engineering is all about.

By the time you reach Part IV, you should be ready to apply your skills and knowledge to totally new situations. To help you test your abilities, eleven application projects are discussed and suggestions are given for how to get started. But you must establish the specifications for a project you choose to tackle and you must decide how to implement a solution. You must develop an algorithm, test its capacity to succeed, and break it down into smaller components that can be used as tools for constructing the final product.

It sounds like a lot of work and I would be lying if I said it wasn't. But, I ask you to proceed with all the enthusiasm you can muster. I'll make the adventure as exciting as I can. And if the thousands of students whom I've had before you are any indication of future success, then when this trip is over you will be pleased with our destination.

Acknowledgments

I would like to thank Mike Miller (DeVry Institute of Technology Phoenix); Guoliang Zeng (Arizona State University), and Barbara Johnston (Albuquerque TV/I) for offering valuable feedback during the early stages of manuscript preparation.

Part I
Getting Started

This section sets the stage for the rest of the text. A review of C (Appendix A) is suggested for novices of the language. The first exercise discusses proper program organization and explores the concept of a program monitoring and controlling events external to the computer. Later exercises in this section familiarize the reader with input/output ports and introduce interfacing concepts that will be necessary throughout the text. The need for hardware and software compatibility is addressed and solutions are suggested that should allow the examples in this text to run on a large variety of platforms and compilers.

Exercise 1
Program Construction

PURPOSE: The purpose of this exercise is to illustrate the method of program construction used throughout this text and to introduce the reader to hardware interfacing.

OBJECTIVES: After the completion of this exercise, the reader should be able to:
- Describe the advantage of a hierarchy-based program design methodology.
- List the reasons why the C language is valuable for control applications.
- Understand how a C program can control a simple elevator system.

THEORY: If you examine the world around you in more detail than a casual observer would, it is easy to see that computers are controlling far more than you might have thought. Computers are no longer just on the desktop. You'll find them in your telephone, your burglar alarm, your car, your microwave oven; your TV remote is probably a programmed computer chip.

Even your computer has computers. Chances are your modem and your mouse have single-purpose computers (controllers) embedded in them to gather data or perform actions for the main processor. As we improve our understanding of our computers and ourselves, we will see more and more embedded processors making our life easier and safer. Soon cars will be able to stop themselves if we don't apply the brakes fast enough. Research and development is already underway with human embedded processors that can control our hearts, our insulin, even our muscles when our own systems no longer function properly.

While debate continues as to whether all these changes are really good for society, the fact remains that they are happening and they will probably continue to happen no matter what we think or feel about them. Many programmers in the future will no doubt spend their lives writing programs for printing payroll checks or sorting inventory lists. I'm glad so many programmers find that type of work exciting because we will always need those types of programmers. Future programmers, however, have many more possibilities. Their programs do not have to manipulate data only inside the computer. Instead, programs of the future will be able to gather information about the world we live in and contribute to our lives by interacting with their environment.

The use of embedded processors in today's products requires programs that can read data from and manipulate external devices. But that is just the beginning. Because products now contain embedded processors, they need highly automated assembly plants that can perform complex quality control tests during production and that means computer controlled assembly lines. Even after the products reach the consumer, the need for automated testing continues. It used to be that many automobile owners could diagnose their tune-up needs and perform much of the standard maintenance required by their car. Today's mechanics use sophisticated computers to analyze the data held in your car's memory and run diagnostics to determine the functionality of the sensors as well as of the engine itself. These sophisticated pieces of diagnostic equipment are nothing more than dedicated computer systems with the ability to gather data from the devices being tested. Dedicated and embedded processors may be large or small but they always have one thing in common—someone had to program them. In some cases, especially very small control processors used for simple applications, the need for assembly language still exists. Today, however, control applications involving embedded processors often use C for programming needs.

Why C? First, standard C is more of a high-level assembler than it is a conventional high-level language. C provides the power of assembly language—the power to read ports for interfacing the outside world and to manipulate data easily and efficiently at the bit level. Even though C has the power of assembly language, it offers tremendous advantages over assembly language. C programmers are far more productive when writing and/or debugging code than assembly language programmers. Furthermore, a C programmer can easily write code for embedded processors from different manufacturers without becoming an expert of the assembly language for each of the processors.

Modern C++ compilers increase the productivity even more by providing better methods for maintaining a library of routines that can be reused. Normal C library functions can greatly improve productivity, especially for small applications such as microwave ovens or automobile dashboard controllers, but the classes and objects of C++ are essential in large-scale applications that must be maintained and updated regularly.

Visual languages such as Microsoft's Visual C++ and Borland's C++ Builder take productivity to new heights by allowing the compiler itself to create much of the code needed for your application. Today's visual languages extend the class format to a complete component architecture that greatly enhances productivity.

This versatility is the real beauty of C / C++. It has very few limitations and a great deal of variety. There is a version of C or C++ appropriate for nearly any programming project you can imagine. For that reason, if you had to learn only one language system, I would recommend C / C++.

This text is not designed to teach the fundamentals of C. There are many good books that can do that for you and I recommend having one available as a reference. A short tutorial is provided in Appendix A for those who need a refresher or who have programmed in other languages and just want an overview of the basic C syntax. Actually, most of the examples in this text should be easy to follow for even novice C programmers. Many people learning C get confused by the screen and keyboard functions such as **printf( )**, **scanf( )**, **puts( )**, **getch( )**, **cin**, **cout**, etc. None of these functions are required or used in this text because all of the I/O will be handled through devices and routines developed herein. Another reason the examples are easy to follow is that this text does not delve into exotic techniques or advanced methods and algorithms. What it will do is show you how to use C to interface with the environment outside the computer and it will do so in a manner that will help you understand how to design and organize programs properly.

Most control applications are presently written in C, not C++ or a visual C++, so this text will use conventional C for nearly all of the examples. Most examples should run properly using nearly any standard C or C++ compiler. With minor modifications, the examples should work with visual C compilers or even public domain, small C compilers for controllers based on Motorola's 68HC11 or Intel's 8051.

Properly structured modular C code is easy to convert to a C++ class architecture. This text contains a few class examples so that readers who know C++ can see how the techniques described can be applied to an object-based environment (but this is not a book about object oriented programming).

If you are using a Windows 95, 98, or NT compiler you will need a third-party driver or component to enable C to access I/O ports. This is necessary because Windows 95, 98, and NT prevent I/O port access from application software. I have used TvicHw32 (distributed as shareware, http://www.entechtaiwan.com/tools.htm) and have found it easy to use and compatible with most Windows 95, 98, and NT based C compilers.

Now that we have established why C is the language of choice for this text and have assumed that the reader has at least an introductory background in the C language, it is time to get started. It has been my experience that many students of programming often have little real understanding of how programs should be constructed. All too often, introductory programming texts examine the structure of a program with the eye of an analyst rather than the mind of a designer (assuming, of course, that the introductory text examines *any* programs of sufficient size to make the program's organization truly relevant).

Programs, at least programs of any reasonable size, should be designed and organized with a well-defined hierarchy. Examine the triangular shape in Figure 1.1.

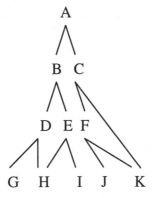

Figure 1.1: Companies and programs can have similar organizational charts.

Notice that the structure in Figure 1.1 looks similar to a corporate organizational chart, with the president at the top and the workers at the bottom. Between the top and bottom levels would be vice-presidents, department heads, etc. It is the responsibility of the president to set the overall goals and objectives of the company. The president might, for example, decide what products the company will make and what customers will be targeted. Company presidents will not make these decisions alone though. They might have a vice-president of manufacturing and a vice-president of marketing (B and C in the diagram) who can gather information to help them make better decisions. In addition, the vice-presidents can oversee the implementation of a president's directives.

The vice-president of manufacturing, for example, might need to ensure that the product is not only built but also tested to ensure its quality. In addition, the vice-president of manufacturing might also be responsible for packaging and shipping the product. Rather than dealing with all of the decisions directly, we would expect the vice-president to oversee various department heads who can concentrate their efforts on problems associated only with their specific goals. If the product is complex enough, for example, there might even be several department heads overseeing the assembly of various parts of the final product. As problems arise, the department heads should be able to handle most situations on their own so that the vice-presidents don't have to get involved. When a problem is too complex or when it involves other departments, a department head can inform his or her vice-president, who can then address the problem by gathering information from other department heads and make a decision that will allow the entire company to run more smoothly.

Let's examine the department-head level. You would not expect the department heads to build any of the products made by the company. Instead they should hire and manage a work force that can do the job. Again, it is the responsibility of the work force to handle most problems for which they were hired. Only when they cannot handle a situation should they report it to their supervisor or department head, and only when it cannot be handled at that level should it be reported to a vice-president. When properly designed, this hierarchy-based structure requires the entities at each level to solve their problems without having to worry about those elsewhere in the organization. It suggests that decisions can be made at the top about *what* needs to be done without having to worry about *how* it will be accomplished. For example, when the president decides to add a new product to the line, he or she might have to acquire the required funding, but he or she would not have to assume responsibility for actually interviewing and hiring the required workers. It would also be unreasonable for the president to have to deal directly with a problem such as a worker that habitually shows up late. If the president could not delegate those kind of tasks, he or she would not be able to perform a president's duties effectively.

While most people can see the logic in the above example, they often fail to see that the organization of a program should follow the same plan. Programs should be organized as a hierarchy of modules so that the modules at the bottom do much of the actual work. Most of the modules in the middle of a program are simply overseeing the work and making decisions that cannot be handled at a lower level.

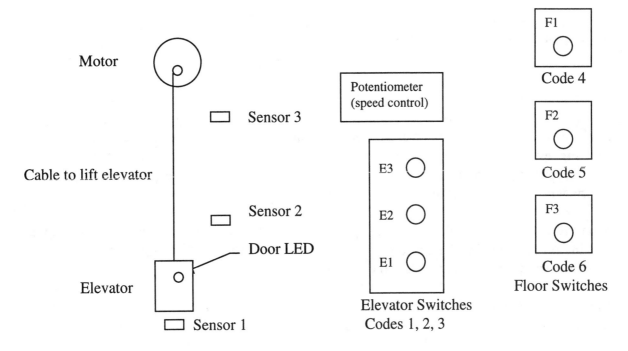

Figure 1.2: The hardware for a simple elevator system.

Furthermore, this type of organization makes it easier for program designers to switch hats as they try to anticipate the possible problems that might arise in a particular module. This is true because the programmer does not have to worry about the details associated with other modules. Let's look at a real, although simplified, programming example to make this clearer.

Let's assume that we want to write a C program that could control a toy elevator such as the one in Figure 1.2. Before we start designing the program, let's examine the characteristics of the elevator itself.

The basic idea is simple. The elevator is a box that can be lifted by a motor winding a string on a spool. As the motor turns one way, the elevator will rise; the opposite direction causes the elevator to descend. Three sensors can provide information about where the elevator is. For now, the exact nature of the sensors is not important. They could be simple mechanical switches that close when the elevator reaches a particular floor or they could be something more elaborate such as a detector of an infrared beam that is broken when the elevator arrives. There are three switches in the elevator (E1, E2, and E3) and a single switch on each floor (F1, F2, and F3). Pressing a floor switch should call the elevator to that floor. Similarly, pressing elevator switches should cause the elevator to move to the requested floor. A single LED serves to indicate if the elevator door is open or closed. (We could, of course, create a real sliding door, but the purpose of this example does not warrant such complexity.)

The C program mentioned earlier must monitor the switches and sensors and decide when the motor needs to be turned on, in which direction it should rotate, and when it should be turned off. In addition, this example will require that each time the elevator moves to a requested floor, it will determine the position of the speed control potentiometer and use that position to decide how fast the elevator should move. Think of this potentiometer as an adjustment to be made by a service representative of the elevator company.

It has been my experience that most students who have had only an introductory C course have little idea of how to design a C program to control an elevator as described above. Even so, I suggest that you try to write such a program or at least prepare a flowchart or an outline of how you might approach such a problem before you continue reading. Compare your efforts with the discussion that follows.

What follows is a description of one design approach to the elevator problem described above. It is important to realize that this answer is not the *only* answer. It is, however, an answer that is indicative of what to expect from the rest of this text.

Based on the previous discussion, you might expect that a program to control this elevator might be complicated. If it is poorly organized, it might be complicated, but with a systematic approach, it certainly doesn't have to be. Remember that the president of a company can decide what has to be done without having to worry about the details of how everything will be accomplished.

Many programmers have learned to organize their thoughts about how a program should be written by using flowcharts. For that reason, I will provide flowcharts for each section of code in this exercise to allow all readers to get a good start. After studying this example though, I think you will see that the code for programs organized as small hierarchy-based modules is just as easy to follow as the flowcharts. Because of that, other exercises in this text will not utilize flowcharts.

The main portion of a program to control our elevator should act like a CEO or other high-level executive in a company. It should only issue orders about *what* has to be done. Other portions of the program should handle the details of *how* to accomplish the designated tasks.

The flowchart in Figure 1.3 shows what the executive portion of our program should do. The first action in the flowchart is to perform an initialization procedure. For our elevator, this means that the elevator must be moved to the first floor so that it starts in a known position. Other sections of the program will assume that the elevator started on the bottom floor and will update its location whenever it is moved.

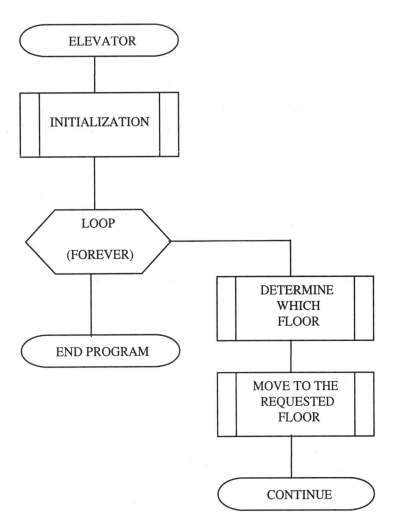

Figure 1.3: The executive portion of the elevator program is very simple.

The elevator is controlled by two functions that are repeated continuously. The elevator must first wait until someone presses one of the six switches to determine which floor has been requested. Once it knows where to move to, it must then move to that floor.

The **main( )** section of the C program should implement the flowchart of Figure 1.3. It is shown in Figure 1.4. Notice that, because this section of code is small and uncomplicated, it matches the flowchart in a very straightforward manner.

This is probably a good time to discuss terminology. Programming modules are often referred to as subroutines or subprograms. Furthermore some programmers call a module that does not return a value a procedure and a module that does return a value a function. This text will not make such a differentiation and the terms *procedure*, *module*, and *function* will be used interchangeably.

```
void main(void)
    {
    int floor;       // create an integer variable called floor
    initialization( );   // moves elevator initially to floor 1
    while(1)             // loop forever
        {
        floor = which_floor( ); // waits for switch press and returns the floor to move to
        move_to(floor);       // moves the elevator to the floor indicated by the
                              // argument
        }
    }
```

Figure 1.4: The **main**( ) module for the elevator program is deceptively simple.

I hope your first impression is that this code is not very complicated. On deeper examination, I hope your second impression is that this portion of the program is not going to require much debugging (at least so far) because there is not much chance that it will not work properly. It is true that the above code is simple only because we have assumed that there are functions such as **initialize**( ), **which_floor**( ), and **move_to**( ) that know how to do their job. But that is the point. Just as the president of a company would not be able to deal with the real issues facing the company as a whole if he or she had to worry about the details of implementation, the **main**( ) in our C program should not be concerned with *how* all of the tasks it calls are implemented.

Of course, as programmers, our job is far from complete. We need to turn our attention to the modules called from **main**( ). The advantage is that we don't have to look at all of them at once. By being able to concentrate on just one aspect of the entire program at a time, we can focus our attention and not be distracted by details associated with other sections of the code. Let's start by looking at the **which_floor**( ) module.

Based on the information in Figure 1.2, we know that there are six switches in our system and that somehow they generate codes 1–6 as indicated. We can see that a code of either 1 or 4 indicates the elevator should move to floor 1, a code of either 2 or 5 implies floor 2, and a code of 3 or 6 implies floor 3. Again, since we don't want to get bogged down in the details of how things are to be done, let's assume we have a module called **keycode**( ) that will wait for a key press and return the code for that key. With these assumptions in mind, it is easy to draw a flowchart and write the code for **which_floor**( ).

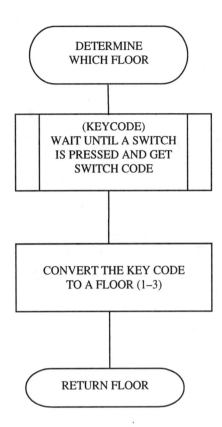

Figure 1.5: This module determines which floor is being requested.

The code that implements the flowchart of Figure 1.5 is shown in Figure 1.6. It assumes that **keycode( )** can only return a valid button code, that is, a number between 1 and 6 inclusive.

The logic of this module looks as simple as that of **main( )**. As long as **keycode( )** performs as expected, we should have no trouble with this module. We will discuss **keycode( )** in more detail later. For now, let's turn our attention to the module **move_to( )**. A flowchart describing a possible implementation of it is shown in Figure 1.7.

```
int which_floor( void )
    {
    int x;
    x=keycode( );
    if(x<4)
        return x;
    else
        return x-3;
    }
```

Figure 1.6: This function returns 1, 2, or 3, indicating to which floor the elevator should move.

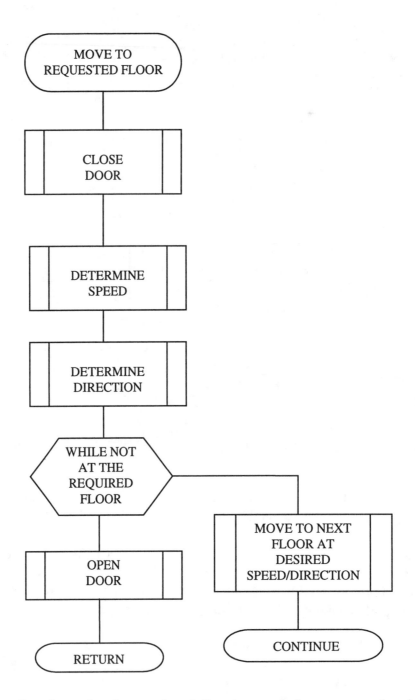

Figure 1.7: If we first determine the speed and direction needed, we can reach a desired floor by moving toward it, one floor at a time.

Let's examine Figure 1.7 and see how the elevator moves to a requested floor. To make this module easy to write, we will assume that we have a module that can move to the next floor, either up or down. Furthermore, assume that all we have to tell this module is the speed and the direction in which we wish to move. Once we assume this ability, the rest is easy.

The first thing we have to do before we move the elevator is close the door. Next, we need to determine the speed and the direction in which we want the elevator to move. Finally, we continually move one floor at a time toward the correct floor at the preselected speed. When the correct floor is reached, the loop will terminate, the door will open, and the module returns.

Now that we have gotten a taste of flowcharting, we need to emphasize an important point. When the flowchart in Figure 1.7 was first mentioned, it was referred to as a *possible* implementation. It is very important for you to realize that this is only my way of solving the problem. Many other methods could be used. For example, it would work just as well to determine the speed and direction and then close the door. It is also feasible to assume that the module that moves to the next floor has the responsibility of determining its own speed instead of having it determined in advance.

All we are trying to do with the flowchart is to describe a series of actions that *could* accomplish the desired task. It is important that we don't get bogged down trying to figure out every detail of *how* everything will be accomplished. For example, this flowchart does not explain how we will actually close the door or how we will determine what speed should be used. Instead, we simply assume that we have other modules (or employees, if we wish to continue with our company analogy) that can handle those tasks for us.

When you are attempting to design a program to solve a particular problem, you should not expect that the first flowchart you draw is the best method to use. Your initial flowchart, however, provides something concrete to help you visualize an abstract solution. As you study a flowchart of a first attempt at solving a problem, you will see errors in your logic or ways of making it more efficient. For many people, it is easier to visualize different solutions using flowcharts than it is using programming statements. It has been my experience that as programmers become more fluent in the language being used, they find that it is just as easy to think in the code itself as it is using flowcharts.

Let's return to the flowchart in Figure 1.7. It should be easy to see that these actions would allow the elevator to move to a floor requested. You should also realize that the reason this solution is easy is because we have assumed that other modules will be available to handle the complicated things that have to be done. Figure 1.8 shows how we can determine what speed to use.

Remember, the original specifications for our elevator stated that a potentiometer could be used to adjust the speed of the elevator. Figure 1.8 simply assumes that we have a module that can read the value of that potentiometer. For the sake of example, let's assume that we can describe the potentiometer's position as a number from 0 to 255.

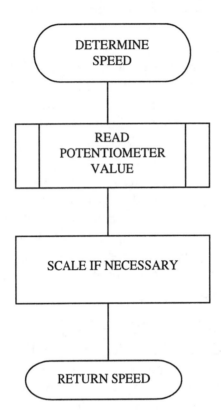

Figure 1.8: The speed that the elevator will move is determined by the position of a potentiometer.

If the motor's speed can be specified using the numbers 0–255, then we use the potentiometer's position to represent the speed. A more likely occurrence, though, is that the value needed for the speed will be different. For example, if the motor had 128 speeds (0–127) we could convert the numeric value of the potentiometer to an appropriate speed by dividing it by two.

Figure 1.9 shows how we can determine which direction the elevator should move. In order for this module to work, we must keep track of where the elevator is. Since we initially moved the elevator to the first floor, we can keep track of the elevator by setting a variable to 1 and adjust it as we move the elevator from one floor to another.

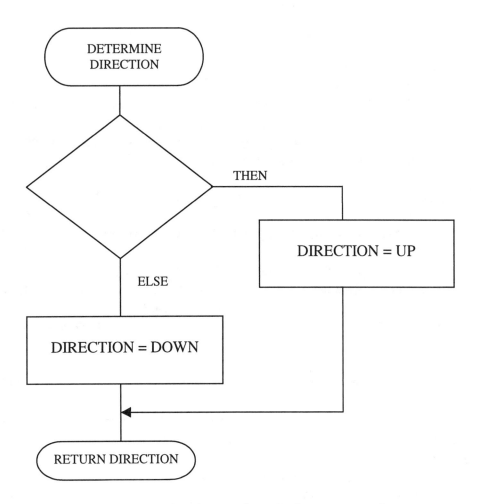

Figure 1.9: As long as we know where the elevator is and where we want it to go, we can determine the direction in which it should move.

Figure 1.10 shows the code necessary to implement a module that can move the elevator to any floor specified. Notice that the code does not match the flowcharts exactly and it doesn't have to. The purpose of the flowchart is to help us decide what has to be done and in what order. If you compare the flowchart to the code, you will see that this goal is accomplished. (People that want flowcharts to match exactly with the code generally want to use flowcharts as a way of *documenting* the program. Personally, I see flowcharts to be much more valuable as a design tool than as a means of documentation.)

Actually, the flowchart differs from the code only in minor ways. For example, the flowchart assumed that the speed and direction would be established using external modules. When these tasks had to be converted to code, it became apparent that they were simple enough that the actions could be performed right in the **move_to( )** module itself. The final implementation of the code requires only two new modules, one to read the position of the potentiometer and one to move the elevator to the next floor.

```
void move_to(int destination)
    {
    static int present_floor = 1;
    int direction, speed, pot;
    door(CLOSE);        // turns off the door LED to indicate the door is closed
    pot = readpot( );    // use a module to read the potentiometers position
    speed = pot/2;       // divide by an appropriate scale factor to convert to speed
    if(present_floor < destination)
        dir = UP;
    else
        dir = DOWN;
    while(destination != present_floor)  // loop until we get to the destination
        {
        move_one_floor(dir, speed, MINIMUM_TIME);
        present_floor = present_floor+dir;  // keeps track of where the elevator is after
        }                                              // each move
    door(OPEN); // turns on the door LED to indicate the door is open
    }
```

Figure 1.10: Moving to a specified floor is easy if you can easily move one floor up or down.

This module also assumes that several constants have been defined globally so that they can be used in other modules as well as here. These constants are UP, DOWN, and MINIMUM_TIME. The actual values of UP and DOWN are somewhat unimportant because we only need something to represent each direction. If we use the values +1 and −1 for UP and DOWN, though, we will be able to simplify portions of our code. We'll see why in a moment. The value for MINIMUM_TIME should be the length of time that the motor is permitted to run before the program checks the sensors. This time needs to be long enough to move the motor slightly, but not long enough for the motor to move past a sensor without us detecting it.

In the code of Figure 1.10, the *static* variable **present_floor** keeps track of where the elevator is presently located. Unlike normal variables, static variables retain their value even after a module ends and is recalled. The value of **present_floor** is initialized to one indicating that the elevator is assumed to start at the first floor. Because of this assumption, the **initialization( )** routine is required to move the elevator to the first floor before any other actions are taken.

After the speed and direction have been established, the **while( )** loop checks to see if the elevator is at its requested destination and if it is not, continues to move the elevator one floor at a time, in an appropriate direction and speed, until the proper floor is reached. Notice that each time the elevator is moved, the value of **dir** is added to **present_floor**. You should see now why the values of +1 and −1 were chosen for UP and DOWN. The value of **present_floor** is decremented or incremented depending on whether the elevator moved up or down. The final action in this module is to open the door. Even though this code gets more involved with determining how to solve a particular task, many of the details are still delegated to subordinate routines.

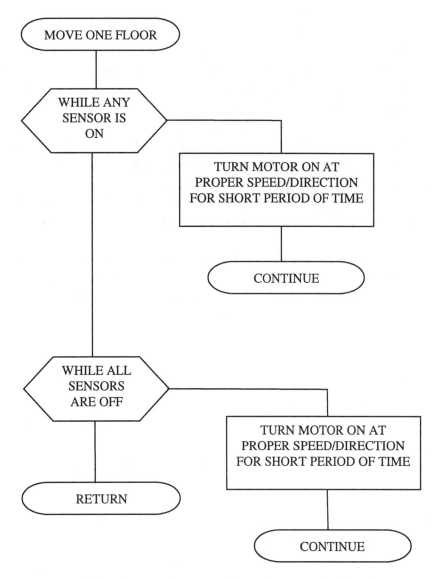

Figure 1.11: The movement of the elevator between floors is controlled by the sensors.

Let's turn our attention to the **move_one_floor**( ) routine. Figure 1.11 shows the flowchart that describes what has to be done to move the elevator to the next floor.

Skip the first loop for a moment and turn your attention to the second loop in Figure 1.11. It moves the elevator toward the desired floor until a sensor activation is detected. This action is really what this module is trying to accomplish. The need for the first loop in Figure 1.11 is probably not obvious. We should normally expect that when the elevator is stopped at a floor, the sensor at that floor should be ON. This is true because the elevator got to its resting position by being moved until a sensor was activated. Of course, the elevator could have coasted past the sensor, but we'll look at this possibility in a moment.

If the elevator is resting with the sensor ON and if we had only the second loop in Figure 1.11, then the loop would immediately terminate without the elevator moving at all. The purpose of the first loop is to move the elevator until the sensor at the present floor turns OFF. The second loop can then take over and move the elevator until the next sensor activates. Since this module is called repeatedly by the **move_to**( ) module, the elevator will eventually reach the desired floor.

Let's examine the potential problem mentioned earlier. What if the elevator coasted past the sensor switch when it stops at its present destination? Fortunately, this presents no problem. If the sensor is not on, then the first loop in Figure 1.11 will test FALSE and will terminate before it starts. The second loop will then perform its job of moving the elevator to the next floor. The code to implement the flowchart of Figure 1.11 is shown in Figure 1.12.

Again, this module is easy to implement because it assumes that other modules will be available for actually controlling the motor and reading the sensors. We will discuss both of the modules shortly. Right now, let's examine the flowchart for the initialization module shown in Figure 1.13.

```
void move_one_floor(int direction, int speed, int min_time)
    {
    while( read_sensors( ) != 0)
        move_motor(direction, speed, MINIMUM_TIME);
    while(read_sensors( ) == 0)
        motor(direction, speed, MINIMUM_TIME);
    }
```

Figure 1.12: Moving up or down one floor requires two loops, one loop to get off the present sensor and another to get to the next sensor.

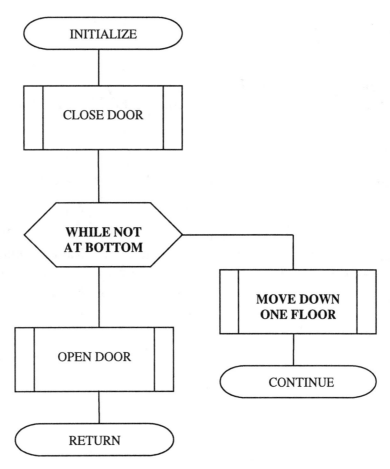

Figure 1.13: The initialization module must ensure that the elevator starts on the bottom floor.

It is important to realize that the **initialization**( ) module cannot use the **move_to**( ) module to move the elevator to the first floor. If you go back and examine the previous figures, you will see why. The **move_to**( ) module assumes that the elevator is at the first floor the first time it is called. This means that we must keep calling the **move_one_floor**( ) module until we reach the first floor.

The code for the **initalization**( ) module is shown in Figure 1.14.

```
void initialize(void)
    {
    door(CLOSE);
    // assume BOTTOM_FLOOR has been defined as the sensor code
    //  for the bottom floor
    while( read_sensors( ) = = BOTTOM_FLOOR )
        move_one_floor(DOWN, read_pot( )/2, MINIMUM_TIME);
    door(OPEN);
    }
```

Figure 1.14: This module moves the elevator to the first floor and opens the door.

If you examine the figures for the elevator program, you will see that only five modules are not fully defined. These modules are shown in Figure 1.15. These modules, and only these modules, are responsible for actually interfacing with the elevator hardware. Understanding, designing, and implementing modules such as these are what much of this text is about. (For example, we will develop a **keycode**( ) module in Exercise 6, a **read_pot**( ) module in Exercise 9, and a **DCmotor**( ) module in Exercise 10.)

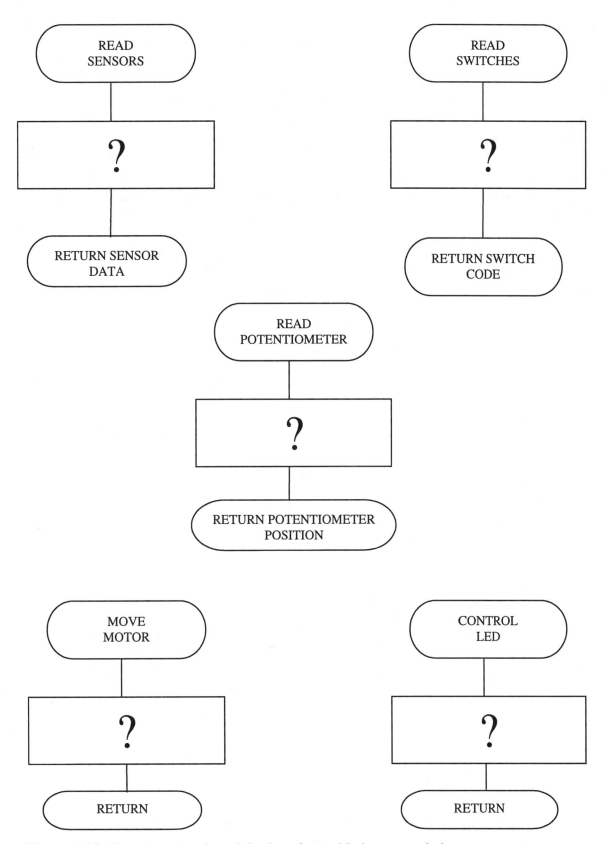

Figure 1.15: These low-level modules interface with the external elevator components.

Knowing how to build the low-level tool functions that do all the work is only part of what we want to accomplish with this text. We also need to understand how they can be combined to solve problems such as controlling an elevator. In order to understand better the significance of this, look at Figure 1.16. It shows a hierarchy-style chart for the elevator modules. Unlike a flowchart, it does not show the order of execution. Rather, it is similar to the organizational chart shown in Figure 1.1 and shows which modules are used by or are subordinate to other modules.

If you examine Figure 1.16, you can see that the main elevator program makes use of only three subordinate modules that perform the functions **move-to-requested-floor**, **initialize**, and **determine-requested-floor**. Further examination will show additional relationships. For

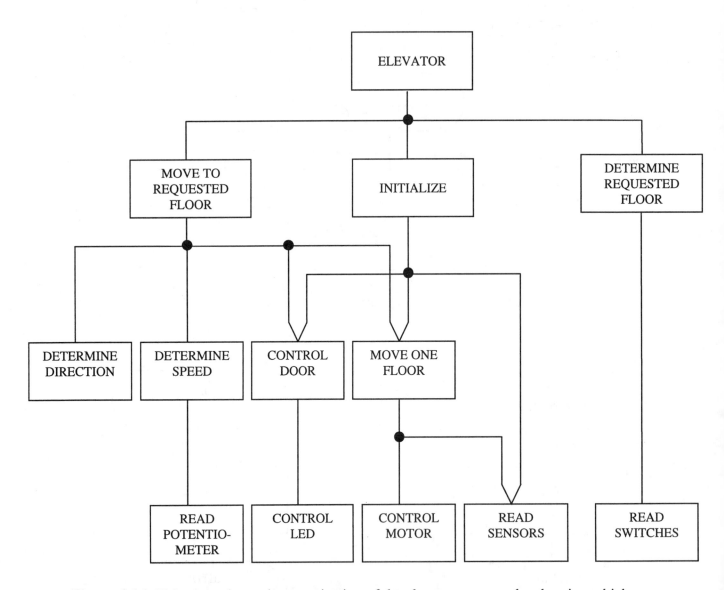

Figure 1.16: This chart shows the organization of the elevator program by showing which modules are used by other modules to accomplish their goals.

example, we can see that the **initialization** module only uses **move-one-floor** and that **move-one-floor** requires **control-motor** and **read-sensors** to accomplish its goals.

What may not be apparent is the value of this type of organization. If you examine the actions taken by each block in the chart, you will see that all of the *actual* work is performed only at the lowest level. This is not to say that modules above the bottom level don't accomplish any goals. It just means that they perform their job by asking subordinate modules to handle much of the details for them. Modules at the top of the chart don't have anything to do with how any of the details are accomplished. They simply decide what has to be done and delegate the responsibility to lower level routines. Those routines either perform the needed work themselves or, if the job is complicated, break it down further and pass it on to someone else to handle. As mentioned earlier, this mirrors the activity in a large corporation.

The first goal of this text is to show you how to create low-level programming modules that can perform the actual work of interfacing with devices outside the computer. As we progress through the text, you will see how to combine these functions to create more intelligent modules that can handle larger problems. These new modules can then be used as building blocks for even larger, more intelligent routines. This cycle continues until a module is created that is capable of accomplishing the desired task. The elevator program is a good example of what you should be able to accomplish by the time you complete this text.

After studying the modules for the elevator program, you should have a *reasonable* understanding of how to write a program that can control the elevator. If you find yourself a little confused, don't be alarmed. At this point it is to be expected. The objective here is not to understand every aspect of this example. Your ability to absorb the material in this text, however, will be greatly enhanced if you have a good overview of what we are trying to accomplish, and the purpose of the elevator example is to provide that overview. Most texts begin with small examples and build larger programs as the reader's knowledge and skill increase. This text certainly uses that approach. As we proceed, though, I think you'll find more significance and value in each exercise if you can see its relevance to our overall goals.

As mentioned earlier, even though this text will concentrate on C rather than C++ code (because C code is generally more applicable for control applications), a few object-oriented examples will be provided to aid readers that prefer the class format. After seeing the examples, readers who are familiar with object-oriented programming should be able to implement the modules as classes in situations when objects are desired. Figure 1.17 shows the elevator example as it might appear as a class implementation. Classes provide the syntax for encapsulating all of the functions and variables relating to a set of tasks—such as those associated with the control of an elevator. If you are familiar with class structures and understand the previous examples, then the code needs little if any explanation. If you are not familiar with class structures, then ignore this example and concentrate on the previous examples.

```
class Elevator
    {
    private:
        int present_floor;
        void door(void);
        void move_one_floor(int);
    public:
        Elevator::Elevator( )
            {
            door(CLOSE);
            while(read_sensors( ) ! = BOTTOM_FLOOR )
                move_one_floor(DOWN, read_pot( )/2, MINIMUM_TIME);
            door(OPEN);
            present_floor = 1;
            }
        int which_floor(void);
        void move_to(int);
    };




int Elevator::which_floor(void)
    {
    int x;
    x=keycode( );
    if(x<4)
        return x;
    else
        return x-3;
    }
```

Figure 1.17: The elevator functions can be implemented as a class.

```
void Elevator::move_to(int destination)
    {
    door(CLOSE); // turns off the door LED to indicate the door is closed
    int direction, speed, pot;
    pot = read_pot( );
    speed = pot / 2;
    if(present_floor < destination)
        dir = UP;
    else
        dir = DOWN;
    while(destination ! = present_floor)
        {
        move_one_floor(dir, speed, MINIMUM_TIME);
        present_floor = present_floor + dir;
        }
    door(OPEN); // turns on the door LED to indicate the door is open
    }


void Elevator::move_one_floor(int direction, int speed, int MINIMUM_TIME)
    {
    while(read_sensors( ) ! = 0)
        move_motor(direction, speed, MINIMUM_TIME);
    while(read_sensors( ) = = 0)
        move_motor(direction, speed, MINIMUM_TIME);
    }


void main(void)
    {
    Elevator number1;
    int floor;
    while(1)
        {
        floor = number1.which_floor( );
        number1.move_to(floor);
        }
    }
```

Figure 1.17: (continued)

Readers familiar with class structures will notice many identical sections of code demonstrating how easy it is to convert *properly organized* C code into a class format. In all fairness, this design for the elevator class could have been improved, but the goal here was to show both examples in a way that made comparing them as easy as possible. As with the C code in this exercise, some minor items, such as **#defined** constants, have been omitted.

ASSIGNMENT: Manually trace through the code and/or the flowcharts for the elevator until you have a full understanding of how they operate. Try using a simple model of the elevator to help you see how the modules work. Physically move the elevator when directed to do so. You don't need anything elaborate; a book can be the elevator and bookshelves can serve as the floors.

I realize that, because there is no actual programming in this exercise, many readers will not take it seriously or perhaps even skip it altogether. I hope you don't make this mistake. The time required to trace through the elevator examples manually will reap huge benefits when we start dealing with real code.

REVIEW QUESTIONS
1. Why will the examples in this text be coded primarily using C rather than the class structure of C++?
2. What are the advantages of designing a program using a hierarchy-based structure?
3. What is the significance of the constant MINIMUM_TIME and how is it used in the program?
4. In this simplified elevator system, the switches E1 and F1 both cause the same action to take place. What other switches also act in this way? Explain your answer.
5. Based on the code in this section, if the speed-controlling potentiometer was moved while the elevator was moving, would the speed change? Explain your answer.
6. Why is it impossible to use the **move_to**( ) module to move to floor 1 when the elevator is initialized?
7. How many modules in the elevator program open or close the elevator door? What are their names?
8. Which modules in the elevator program must determine the state of the sensors? Explain why each module that you listed needs to know the state of the sensors.

Exercise 2
Introduction to Ports

PURPOSE: The purpose of this exercise is to create a generalized set of port-access functions to be used throughout this text. This will ensure compatibility with various PC hardware configurations as well as other types of computers. Typical input/output (I/O) port configurations will be discussed, as well as specific details about using the standard PC printer port for generalized I/O operations

OBJECTIVES: After the completion of this exercise, the reader should be able to:
- Describe the pertinent aspects of I/O ports in general.
- Describe the function and capabilities of each of the three ports associated with the PC parallel printer interface.
- Describe the syntax and function associated with the bit manipulation capability of the C language.
- Understand how the C language can be used to build tools that can read data from and write data to the PC printer interface and other I/O ports.
- Understand how to buffer a port to decrease the possibility of damage to the port from external devices.
- Utilize the appropriate hardware and software to interface switches and LEDs to a computer using I/O ports.

THEORY: In order to control external devices with a computer, the computer must be equipped with some form of input/output (I/O) interface. In general, an I/O port is similar in many ways to a memory location. We can certainly say that an I/O port is basically a register made up of flip/flops. The only way to manipulate the flip/flops associated with a memory location is to write data to that memory address. With an input port, however, the flip/flops that make up the port can be set or cleared by external devices such as switches or sensors connected to the set and reset inputs. By reading the values of the flip/flops in a port, a program can determine the state of the external devices (i.e., is a switch open or closed?).

Output ports can be viewed using a similar analogy. Programs can set or clear the bits in either a memory location or an output port by writing data to the proper address. In the case of an output port, however, imagine that the outputs from each of the flip/flops in the port are physically wired to a terminal so that they can be connected to external devices. This means that when the flip/flop in a port is set or cleared (by writing data to it), the output signal from that flip/flop can be used to control the on/off state of an external device such as an LED or motor.

As mentioned in Exercise 1, this text will make every effort to ensure that the material being covered can be applied to a wide variety of hardware and software. So let's look first at several

DATA REGISTER

D7	D6	D5	D4	D3	D2	D1	D0

CONTROL REGISTER

X	X	X	C4	C3	C2	C1	C0

STATUS REGISTER

S7	S6	S5	S4	S3	X	X	X

Figure 2.1: The PC printer interface is composed of three registers.

options for the PC. Then we will explore ways of implementing those options in a generic way that could apply to many other hardware/software configurations.

Many I/O port cards are available, as options, for IBM PC and PC compatible computers. Many of these interfaces are based on the 8255 peripheral interface chip from Intel, but the available options are far too numerous to list. Nearly all PCs have, as standard equipment, a printer interface that is composed of three ports. For that reason, let's begin by examining how to use the standard printer port to gather information from, or send data to, external devices. The typical size for a PC port is eight bits, but only one of the three ports used in the standard PC printer interface is a true eight-bit port. The other two ports are organized as eight positions, but not all of the positions are active. Refer to Figure 2.1 for more detail.

The first of these registers is the DATA register, which is normally used to send the data to be printed to the printer. All eight bits of the DATA register are implemented as outputs.

The CONTROL register is also an output port that is normally used to send control information to inputs on the printer that perform actions such as initialization and telling the printer when to read information in the DATA register. Only the five lower bits of the CONTROL register are implemented. The most significant of these bits, which is labeled C4 in Figure 2.1, is used by the internal hardware to control a printer interrupt function. This leaves four bits that can be used normally for output functions.

The STATUS register is an INPUT port that normally allows the printer to send the PC bits that indicate such things as the printer is busy printing previously sent data or that the printer is out of paper. There are five bits in this port available to be used as inputs.

Each of the three printer ports can be *addressed* by using a port address (or port number). The base or starting address varies for different PC configurations and models. If we assume that the base address is n, then the DATA port is at address n, the STATUS port is at $n + 1$, and the CONTROL port is at $n + 2$. We will see how to determine n later in this exercise.

Each data bit is available externally on the printer DB-25 connector. When information is sent to the DATA port, it appears on the output connector in its true or noninverted form. Some bit positions for the other two ports, however, internally invert the data passing to or from the PC.

BIT	DB-25 PIN NUMBERS	INVERTED	IN/OUT
D0	2	no	out
D1	3	no	out
D2	4	no	out
D3	5	no	out
D4	6	no	out
D5	7	no	out
D6	8	no	out
D7	9	no	out
C0	1	yes	out
C1	14	yes	out
C2	16	no	out
C3	17	yes	out
S3	15	no	in
S4	13	no	in
S5	12	no	in
S6	10	no	in
S7	11	yes	in
GROUND	18-25		

Figure 2.2: The printer ports are accessed through the printer port connector.

Figure 2.2 shows which bits are inverted. It also shows which pins on the printer port connector are used for each bit.

Most C compilers provide functions that allow *bytes* (8-bit chunks of data) to be sent to output ports and to read bytes from input ports. Unlike most C functions, the functions used to interface with ports have not been standardized. In Borland's DOS oriented C products, for example, the byte-oriented I/O functions are **inportb()** and **outportb()**. Other C compilers should have functions of similar names, such as **inp()** or **outp()**, that operate in much the same manner.

Many smaller processors (such as the 68HC11) map their I/O ports into the normal memory space and use the byte memory access functions **peekb()** and **pokeb()** for reading from and writing to a port. In nearly all cases, the syntax for these access functions is very similar. Note: The trailing **b**'s in these functions indicate that the functions access *bytes*. The Borland functions **peek()** and **inport()**, for example, access 16-bit chunks of data referred to as *words*. Refer to the manual for your compiler to get any details you need for these exercises.

The function **inportb**(*portaddress*) returns the integer value of the bits applied to the port whose address is specified by the argument, *portaddress*. The function **peekb**(*address*) operates in exactly the same manner as **inportb**() except that it returns the value stored at the memory address specified or of an I/O port mapped onto that memory address.

The function **outportb**(*addr*, *data*) sends the data specified to the port specified. For processors that use memory-mapped I/O, the function **pokeb**(*addr*, *data*) operates in the same manner on either memory locations or memory-mapped I/O ports.

We can use the above functions to transfer data to and from the ports. Before we start any major experiments, however, we need some means of determining if the ports are actually working. One way to check would be to place LEDs on the output ports and switches on the input port. The LEDs could provide visual indication that the correct data arrived at the port pins. The input port could be tested by reading the port and comparing the received data to the on/off conditions of the switches.

When external components are connected to the PC printer port, care must be taken to ensure that the voltage and current limitations of the port are respected. Since the individual bit positions for the printer ports are compatible with TTL signals, we can use any TTL gate to act as a buffer.

Figure 2.3 shows how to use inverting gates such as the 7404 as the buffers. Inverters were chosen here simply because they are readily available. You could just as easily have used noninverting gates for the buffers. Buffering the port in this manner is certainly not required and

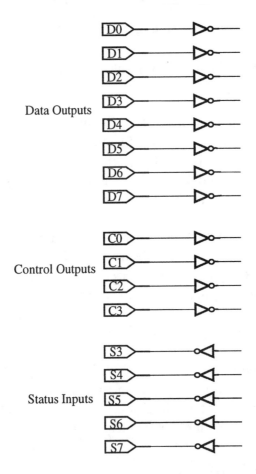

Figure 2.3: The printer port should be buffered to reduce the possibility of damage to the PC.

it does not guarantee that external equipment cannot damage the PC. It does, however, significantly reduce the possibility of damage and is highly recommended. Future exercises in this text will explore additional means of buffering the port pins.

Using inverters to buffer the port does mean that the data for every bit will be inverted. Since some bits are already inverted internally, the inversion from the buffer returns those signals to a normal condition. In order to prevent the signals from the other pins from being inverted, we could send them through two inverters or we could choose a noninverting gate to act as a buffer for those pins. We will see shortly, however, that we will be able to handle all the appropriate inversion with software regardless of whether the pins are inverted. This means we can simplify the hardware by using only a single buffer on every input and output pin.

Figure 2.4 shows how we can interface LEDs to the output pins and switches to the port connections. In the case of the PC printer ports, these connections will include the buffers.

Sections A and B of Figure 2.4 show possible ways of connecting an LED to an output pin. Section A turns the LED on when the inverter's output is low. Inverters used in this way are said to be *sinking* current. Section B, on the other hand, requires a high from the inverter to light the LED. In this case the inverter is *sourcing* current.

In general, since TTL gates can sink more current than they can source, the method shown in section A is preferred. In low-current applications, such as driving an LED, it really doesn't matter which method we use, except for the fact that the ON/OFF condition of the LED is reversed for any given output. As mentioned earlier, reversing the logic of such situations is easily done in software, so the method chosen for connecting the hardware is not critical.

Section C of Figure 2.4 shows how a switch can be used to send either a high or a low to an input pin. The pull-up resistor ensures that the voltage being applied to the port buffer is high unless the switch is closed. Without the resistor, the input voltage of a TTL gate typically *floats* at a

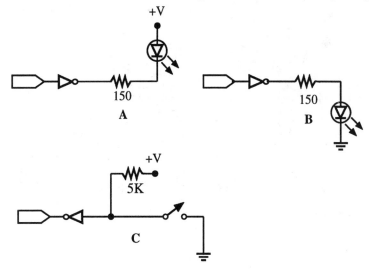

Figure 2.4: Interfacing switches and LEDs to port pins is easy.

voltage of about 2.5 volts. Although this voltage level will usually be seen as a logical 1, it is not high enough to ensure that a logical 1 will always be recognized. Adding the resistor also reduces the possibility that the input pin will be oversensitive to external noise.

Figure 2.5 shows one method for connecting a PC printer port to a solderless protoboard that holds the inverting buffers as well as the LEDs and switches. The cable used is easy to make because it uses press-on connectors on both ends. One end uses a male DB-25 that mates to the printer port on the PC. The other end consists of two 16-pin DIP headers, which can be plugged into the protoboard. Only 25 of the 32 wires coming from the DIP headers actually mate with the DB-25 connector. The other lines can be cut off and left unused. The correlation between the pin numbers on the 16-pin headers and the DB-25 pins will depend on which wires you decide to leave unused. Trace your connections and verify them with an ohmmeter if you decide to build a cable in this manner.

A common four-position DIP switch provides an easily assembled input device, although it allows testing of only four of the five inputs at a time. Just move the switch one position left or right to test the other input pin. Of course, it would be ideal if you can obtain a five-position switch, but they are often hard to find.

Single LEDs can be used as output indicators, but their size can sometimes make it difficult to physically place them in adjacent pins on the protoboard. A DIP version containing 10 LEDs is available from most parts stores and makes assembly quick and easy.

After this exercise, the DIP switch and LEDs can be removed and the appropriate pins on the protoboard can serve as connection points for later exercises.

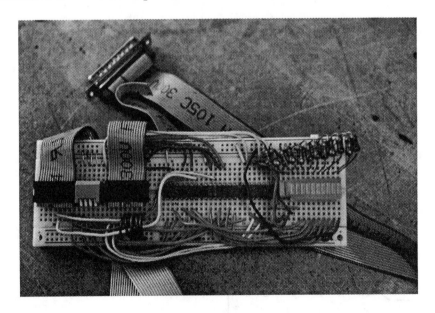

Figure 2.5: An interface for buffering the ports.

Now that we have a way to see data sent to the port, let's see how we can use C to do just that. The **outportb**() function (or an equivalent function), discussed earlier, can easily send data to the 8-bit data port as long as we know the base address for the printer port. Unfortunately, all PC compatible computers do not use the same base address. In most cases, the printer port space starts at hex 378. Fortunately, though, there is an easy way for C to determine the base address. Memory location hex 408, on all PC computers, holds the base address of the primary printer port. Actually, since the base address is a 16-bit word, it is stored in locations 408 and 409.

Figure 2.6 shows a simple program to input data from the status port and write that data to the 8-bit data port. Connect switches to the input port to make entering data easy and LEDs to the output port so that the state of the lines can be easily monitored. The second line inside the function **main**() uses a **peek**() to read a 16-bit word from location 408 (hex) and to store that value in the variable **base_address**. Notice that this **peek**() has an extra argument to specify the segment portion of the address. If you know the address of the printer ports on your machine, you can replace this line with something like

base_address = 0x378; // note how hex numbers are entered in C

Once **base_address** has been initialized, it can be used to access the correct port. The first line inside the **do** loop of Figure 2.6 reads the information present on the input pins of the status port (base address + 1) and stores it in the variable **data**. The next line writes that data obtained from the switches back out to the 8-bit output port. This input/output process will continue as long as the switch connected to the MSB of the input port supplies a *low* to the port. (Recall that the MSB of the status port internally inverts the data being read from the external pin, so with the inverting buffer, the input is true.) Toggling the switch connected to the MSB will make the number being read large enough to terminate the loop and thus the program.

When you run this program, an output light should toggle its state each time you change the position of an input switch. Remember, though, the data being sent to the port will be inverted by the inverting buffers, so the state of the lights will not necessarily match the state of the switches. Furthermore, the action of the MSB should be backward when compared with the other four active bits of the input port, since only the MSB is inverted internally. Finally, since the three least significant bits of the status port are not used, we cannot predict reliably the state that will

```
void main(void)
   {
   int base_address, data;
   base_address=peek(0x408,0); // address 408 hex in segment 0
   do {
      data = inportb(base_address+1);
      outportb(base_address, data);
      } while(data < 128); // while MSB of the status port is 0
   }
```

Figure 2.6: This program sends status port data to the 8-bit output port.

be read for those positions. We could alter the method of connecting our LEDs or just translate everything in our head—but we have a computer at our disposal. We can easily let it handle the transpositions for us by letting the software invert some of the bits.

The C language uses the ^ character to indicate a bitwise exclusive OR (XOR) operation. When a bit is XORed with a **1**, that bit is inverted. There is no effect on bits that are XORed with a **0**. To invert all the bits in an 8-bit word, we would need to XOR the data with binary 11111111, which is FF hex or 255 decimal. The statements below show two methods of outputting the inverse of a variable called **data** to the 8-bit printer port.

```
outportb(base_address, data ^ 0xFF);
outportb(base_address, data ^ 255);
```

As mentioned earlier, hexadecimal numbers are represented in C by preceding them with **0x**, so both of the above statements are identical—at least they will compile to identical code. In the above examples, the original value of **data** is not affected because the altered value was not stored back into the variable. If we want to invert the value of **data** itself, we can use the following statement.

```
data = data ^ 255;
```

If we want to invert only the lower four bits of the variable **data**, we can use the following statement.

```
data = data ^ 0x0F;
```

If we want to send **data** to the 4-bit control port, we can use **base_address+2** as the first argument in the **outportb()** function. If we send data to the control port, though, we have to remember that some of the data bits are inverted by the port's internal hardware. It is also important to make sure that the four most significant bits of the data being sent to the control port remain low because some computers could use those bits internally for other functions.

Remember from Figure 2.2 that bits C3, C1, and C0 are inverted internally. Since the external buffers we added invert all bits, we need to invert only bit C2. We can do that by XORing the data with binary 0100, which is decimal 4. To make sure that the four most significant bits of the byte sent to the port are 0, we need to form a bitwise AND operation with the data and binary 00001111 or decimal 15. In C, the double character symbols && and || are used to represent logical AND and logical OR, respectively. The single character symbols & and | represent bitwise AND and OR operations, respectively. Bitwise ANDing data with 0's can be used to clear bits while bitwise ORing data with 1's can be used to set bits. This means we can write data to the control port in the following way.

```
outportb(baseaddress+2, (data^4)&15);
```

The proper bit will be inverted automatically and the upper bits will be cleared. Obtaining data from the **status** port and making it appear *normal* is slightly more complicated. We can obtain raw data using the following statement.

data = inportb(base_address+1);

All bits of the incoming data are inverted by the buffers. Since bit S7 is inverted by the internal port hardware, our software should invert bits S6, S5, S4, and S3. This task can be accomplished by XORing with binary 01111000, which is decimal 113 or hex 78. Doing so will make sure each bit will be acquired in its normal (uninverted) form, but the positions of the bits are not ideal. It would be better if the five input bits were shifted to the right three bit positions so that the data appeared in the least significant positions.

The C language uses >> and << to indicate shift operations. The following statements show examples of how to shift data.

Example	**Explanation**
y=x>>4	The data in x is shifted right 4 times and stored in y.
x=x<<2	The data in x is shifted left 2 times and stored back in x.

If we combine the above principles, we can see that the following statement can be used to read the control port as if it were a normal 5-bit number.

x = (inportb(base_address+1)^113)>>3;

Even though the above examples show how to access the ports of the printer interface, we can make the task even easier by creating a group of functions (tools) that can be used to access the ports for us. Figure 2.7 shows how to create the necessary functions and demonstrate how they can be used.

```
int base_address;  // global variable so all functions below can use it

void out8data(int data)
    {
    outportb(base_address, data ^ 255);
    }

void out4data(int data)
    {
    outportb(base_address+2,(data^4)&15);
    }

void inputdata(void)
    {
    return (inportb(base_address+1)^113)>>3);
    }

void initialize_ports(void)
    {
    base_address = peek(0x408,0);
    }

void main(void)
  {
  int data;
  initialize_ports();
  do  {
     data=inputdata( );
     out8data(data);
     } while(data ! = 0x01F );
  }
```

Figure 2.7: This program demonstrates functions that can access the printer ports using Borland style I/O instructions.

The function **initialize_ports**() sets the global variable **base_address** to the address of the printer interface ports. Each function uses the **base_address** to access the proper port. Each function also assumes that all the port lines are buffered with inverters and makes the necessary corrections. Furthermore, the data bits obtained from the status register are shifted so that they appear in the lower 5 significant bits.

After the main program initializes the ports, a **do-while** loop executes as long as the data obtained from the input port does not become all 1's (now in the lower 5 bits). The interior of the loop transfers the data read to the LEDs as in our earlier example. As you change the state of each switch, the lights should reflect that change properly. When all the switches are open, 5 1's are sent to the port, causing the program to terminate.

If you prepare and test the above port access functions and place them in an include file, then they can be added easily to any program you write. Since I am assuming that many readers will use the readily available printer interface ports, all of the examples in this text will need no more than 1 5-bit input port and 2 output ports (one 8-bit and one 4-bit).

Of course, it is possible that some readers will have another I/O interface card available and might not want to disconnect the printer each time a port program is used. Let's assume for a moment that you have an I/O interface card built around a popular interface chip, the 8255. The 8255 has three general-purpose I/O ports called A, B, and C. It also has a control port that, depending on the data written to it, can make any of the three data ports operate as either input ports or output ports. Figure 2.8 details the function of each of the bits in the control byte.

The 8255 has additional features in modes other than zero (selected by bits 2, 5 and 6), but they will not be needed for anything in this text so they will not be discussed here. If we also assume that the I/O card is installed at some base address (probably using dip-switch settings on the card itself), then ports A, B, and C and the control port will be at the base address plus 0, 1, 2, and 3, respectively.

The code in Figure 2.9 duplicates the I/O routines provided in Figure 2.7. Ports A and B of the 8255 are used as output ports and port C serves as the input port. Notice that the initialization routine writes to the control port to set up the direction (in/out) of each of the ports. Notice also that these functions assume that there are no buffers added externally to the card. The routines are simple because they do not have to invert or shift any bits. These routines also have the advantage of being able to transfer a full 8 bits to and from any of the ports.

BIT	FUNCTION
7	Must be 1 to enable changing the lower 7 bits
6	Must be 0 to select mode zero (used throughout this text)
5	Must be 0 to select mode zero
4	Controls direction of Port A: 1—input, 0—output
3	Controls upper 4 bits of Port C: 1—input, 0—output
2	Must be 0 to select mode zero
1	Controls direction of Port B: 1—input, 0—output
0	Controls lower 4 bits of Port C: 1—input, 0—output

Figure 2.8: The bits in the control byte control the direction of the other 3 ports.

```
int base_address;

void out8data(int data)
  {outportb(base_address, data);}

void out4data(int data)
  {outportb(base_address+1,data;}

void inputdata(void)
  {return (inportb(base_address+2);}

void initialize_ports(void)
    {
    baseaddress = 0x220;  // or whatever the base address is for the card;
    outportb(baseaddress+3, 0x89); // makes A and B output, C input
    }
```

Figure 2.9: These routines provide access methods for an 8255 I/O chip.

Let's assume that the above routines are saved as a file named **IOport.cpp**. If that file was included with the **main**() from Figure 2.7, we would get the program shown in Figure 2.10. This new program will perform the same functions as the one in Figure 2.7 except that the new program will interface with the switches and LEDs through the 8255 ports rather than the printer interface ports.

If your computer has other I/O capabilities, it should be a straightforward task to create a set of routines similar to these that can access the ports you have available. You will have to refer to the manual on your I/O card to find out how to use its ports and their locations. You will also have to determine if you must use alternatives, such as **peekb**() and **pokeb**(), instead of **inportb**() and **outportb**(). Once you have your routines working, save them as **IOport.cpp**. Future exercises in this text will assume you have created and tested such a file.

```
#include <IOport.cpp>
// note: include path above if needed

void main(void)
  {
  int data;
  initialize_ports();
  do  {
    data=inputdata( );
    out8data(data);
    } while(data ! = 0x01F );
  }
```

Figure 2.10: This program uses the routines in the include file to interface through an 8255.

All of the examples in this text will access ports using the functions **out8data**(), **out4data**(), and **inputdata**(), so the access routines that you create should use these function names. This method should allow the material in this text to be used easily with many different hardware/software configurations. It won't matter if you are using the printer interface ports, 8255 ports, or any other ports that might be available on your system as long as you have created an appropriate include file. In fact, if you have to run your programs on two computers with different configurations (for example, at home and at school or work), all you will have to change is the include statement to select the appropriate file.

ASSIGNMENT: Connect LEDs and switches to an appropriate interface circuit, create an include file that contains the appropriate port functions for your system, and test the hardware and software by using a program such as the one shown in Figure 2.10.

REVIEW QUESTIONS
1. Which bits in which ports of the printer interface are inverted?
2. In general, why should port pins be buffered?
3. Write an **if** statement that will be TRUE if the 2 least significant bits of the status port are both **high**. The value of the other bits should be ignored.
4. Write an **if** statement that will be TRUE if the 2 least significant bits of the status port are both **low**. The value of the other bits should be ignored.
5. Write an **if** statement that will be TRUE if the 2 least significant bits of the status port are **different**. The value of the other bits should be ignored.
6. Why are pull-up resistors used with switches interfaced to input pins?
7. What are the advantages for implementing the port interface functions discussed in this exercise?
8. Compare an I/O port to a memory location.
9. Why does the printer interface need three ports? Give examples of how each of the ports is used when connected to a printer.

Exercise 3
Creating Sounds

PURPOSE: The primary purpose of this exercise is to get the reader started with an interface project that is simple enough not to be intimidating, exciting enough to be motivating, and complex enough to reinforce the hierarchy-based design principles discussed in Exercise 1.

OBJECTIVES: After the completion of this exercise, the reader should be able to:
- Explain the operation of the hardware needed to interface a speaker or headset to an output port.
- Explain how to create a basic tool for producing tones on an external speaker or headset.
- Describe how a basic tone module can be used to create sounds that are more complex.
- Implement a simple library of sound tools that can be used in any program.
- Create a program that can demonstrate the functions in the sound-tool library.

THEORY: Exercise 1 established that programs should have a hierarchy-based design and that C has many advantages when used to control external devices. Exercise 2 introduced I/O ports and demonstrated the fundamentals of how to use them. Now it is time to put these principles to use by writing a real application. Since this is the first real application in this text, it should be interesting without being too complex. After a lot of thought, I decided that using the computer to generate various sounds meets all of these qualifications.

For the computer to generate sound, we will need to interface a speaker or headset to an output port. As long as we don't mind having a limited volume, the circuit in Figure 3.1 will work just fine.

The gate in Figure 3.1 can be a 7404 inverter, but nearly any gate will do. All we need is a way to buffer the port so that we don't draw more current than the port can supply. Since the 100-ohm resistor limits the current, most interface cards should be able to handle this load even without a buffer. Since this text is trying to be as general as possible, however, there is no reason to take chances. This circuit provides plenty of volume when a headset or earphones are used and it will perform reasonably well even if a small speaker is substituted.

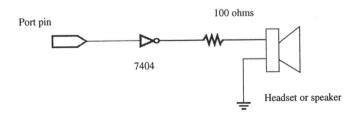

Figure 3.1: This circuit allows your programs to create sounds.

```
void mydelay(int t)
  {
  long int i,k;
  k = 25;   //vary k as indicated in the text
  for(i=0;i<k*t;i++)
     ; // terminates the empty for loop
  }
```

Figure 3.2: The variable k can be used to calibrate this delay routine.

To create a simple tone on the speaker, we need to turn the port pin on and off at the desired frequency. This means we need to delay for an appropriate period of time each time the port pin is changed. To create a full range of frequencies, the delay we need could range from 5 milliseconds (100 Hertz) to 50 microseconds (10,000 Hertz). Even though many C compilers have a built-in delay function, they generally do not provide control at the microsecond level, so we will have to write our own. Figure 3.2 shows how we can create the delay function we need.

The function **mydelay**() shown in Figure 3.2 wastes time by cycling through an empty **for**() loop. The amount of time is based on the argument passed and the value of the constant **k**. The value of **k** should be adjusted to calibrate the routine for use on different machines. Later exercises in this text will require delay routines that are more precise. In this case, however, we just need a delay that is reasonably accurate. On a Pentium-class machine, **k** might need to be 25 or more. On a 486-class machine, **k** will probably be about 5. There will be plenty of chances later in this text to get involved in detail. For now, just relax and have fun. The short program in Figure 3.3 can get you started.

```
#include <IOports.cpp>

// include your mydelay( ) here

void tone(int freq, int dur)
  {
  int i,j;
  float k1=100;
  for(i=0;i<dur*k1/freq;i++)
    {
    out8data(0xFF);       // turn on all 8 port pins
    mydelay(freq);
    out8data(0);          // turn off all 8 port pins
    mydelay(freq);
    }
  }       // note: the delays above control the on and off times


void main(void)
  {
  initialize_ports( );
  tone(100,300);    // high freq. for 1 second
  tone(300,300);    //  low freq. for 1 second
  tone(100,900);    // high freq. for 3 seconds
  }
```

Figure 3.3: This program produces 3 tones.

Before you run the program in Figure 3.3, connect a speaker or headset to *any pin* on the 8-bit printer port as shown in Figure 3.1. Of course, you can use an 8255 port or any other port you have available, as long as your include file, IOport.cpp, contains the drivers described in Exercise 2. When the program executes, you should hear 3 tones. The first argument passed to **tone**() controls the frequency of the tone. The second argument controls the duration. Depending on the speed of your computer, the first 2 tones should last approximately 1 second each. The last tone should have a duration of approximately 3 seconds. If the tones are longer or shorter, adjust the variable **k** in your **mydelay**() function to get the proper time periods. This simple calibration will ensure that the remaining examples in this exercise will operate properly on your computer.

Let's look at the function **tone**() to see how it produces the tones for us. The basic algorithm is simple. The speaker pin is turned on when 0xff is sent to the port and off when 0 is sent to the port. Notice that, since all 8 pins are being turned on and off simultaneously, you may connect the speaker circuit to any of the pins. The on/off time period is controlled by the argument **freq**, which is sent to the function **mydelay**(). The longer the delay, the lower the frequency of the tone produced.

The **for**() loop in the function **tone**() controls the number of cycles of the tone that will be produced. If the **for**() produced only **dur** cycles, then higher frequency tones would be shorter than lower frequency tones of the same specified duration. The reason, of course, is that the time period of a high-frequency cycle is shorter than the time period for a low-frequency cycle. To compensate for this problem, the **for**() needs to produce a number of cycles proportional to the duration and inversely proportional to the frequency. Assuming that you adjusted the **k** in **mydelay**() properly (**k** really calibrates the frequency of the tones), then a **k1** of 100 in **tone**() means that a duration of 300 will translate to about 1 second.

The variable **k1** provides a means to fine-tune the actual total time period for the tone should you want the duration parameter to have some specific meaning. In Figure 3.3, a duration value of 1 translates into 3.3 milliseconds. In a similar analysis, a frequency parameter of 100 creates a tone of approximately 300 Hertz. Specifying a frequency of 300, on the other hand, generates a tone near 100 Hertz. The inverse relationship occurs because the frequency parameter is really a delay time. Increasing the delay decreases the frequency.

It is important to notice the hierarchy-based design of this example. This example program could have been written entirely in **main**() using no other modules. Doing so, however, would make the program difficult to follow and understand, and even more difficult for future programs to make use of portions of the code. In this case, however, it is easy to understand that **main**() produces 3 tones, and it is just as easy to imagine being able to produce tones in any program by using these routines.

If we look deeper, it is just as easy to see that **tone**() itself is easy to follow because we don't have to get involved in the *details* of **mydelay**() to understand **tone**(). It also makes it easy for other programs to take advantage of the functionality of **mydelay**() because it is separated into a distinct function. In addition, remember that **tone**() also makes use of the I/O routines previously prepared and saved in **IOports.cpp**. I don't mean to belabor these points, but their importance is too great to leave any possibility that their value will go unnoticed.

Since one of the major advantages of this type of program organization is the creation of reusable modules, let's save both **mydelay**() and **tone**() in a file called **sound.cpp** so that it can be included in other programs that might need the sound capability.

Let's continue to extend the hierarchy of our tone system while seeing how to use **sound.cpp**. Figure 3.4 shows how to build and use a function that can produce a tone that changes in frequency over time. The first two arguments indicate the starting and ending frequencies. If the first argument is smaller than the second, then the tone will decrease in frequency over time. If the first argument is larger than the second, then the tone will increase over time. The third argument specifies how much the frequency should increase or decrease for each change, and the fourth argument specifies how long each change should last.

```
#include <IOports.cpp>  // must be included first because sounds uses IOports
#include <sounds.cpp>

void changetone(int start, int finish, int step, int dur)
 {
  int i;
  step=abs(step);  // fix if the user thought they needed neg. step
  if(step==0)      // if the user sends a zero, the program will lock up
     step=5;
  if(start<finish)
     {
     for(i=start;i<finish;i+=step)
         tone(i,dur);
     }
  else
     {
     for(i=start;i>finish;i-=step)
         tone(i,dur);
     }
 }

void main(void)
  {
  initialize_ports();
  changetone(100,400,10,10);
  }
```

Figure 3.4: This program demonstrates the function **changetone**().

The internal operation of the function **changetone**() is fairly straightforward. One of two **for**() loops is used, depending on whether the tone to be produced increases or decreases in frequency over time. Each time through the loop, the tone function does all the work.

It may occur to you that, since any program that needs **sounds.cpp** will always need **IOports.cpp**, we might want to include **IOports.cpp** from inside **sound.cpp**. It is a great idea, but we do have to prevent a potential problem. Let's assume that we include **IOports.cpp** in **sounds.cpp**. Let's also assume that we accidentally include **IOports.cpp** at the beginning of our program too. Having two copies of the same source code will produce many errors when we compile the program. Fortunately, there is a simple solution, which is shown in Figure 3.5.

```
#ifndef IOPORT_STUFF                    #ifndef SOUND_STUFF
#define IOPORT_STUFF                    #define SOUND_STUFF
   // place the IOport.cpp code here        // place sounds.cpp code here
#endif                                  #endif
```

Figure 3.5: These two examples show how to prevent files from being included twice.

The compiler directive **#ifndef** checks to see if the specified item has been defined previously. If not, then it continues compiling. If it has, then everything is ignored until the **#endif** is encountered. For example, the first time the IOport.cpp is included, IOPORT_STUFF will not be defined so the code will be included, which will define IOPORT_STUFF, thus causing the code to be ignored on subsequent includes.

Now that we have the routine **changetone**(), it is easy to create other, more complex sounds. Figure 3.6 shows how **changetone**() can be used to build a siren and a phasor module. The sound of a siren should be obvious. The phasor sound will be similar to those you might find in a video game. The argument for **siren**() specifies the number of up/down cycles that will be generated. While the same is true of the argument for **phasor**(), I find it easier to think of the phasor's argument as a duration.

Notice that the only difference between a phasor and a siren is the overall range of frequencies to be used and the size of the steps between frequencies. When you implement these programs, try varying different parameters to see what effects you can create.

```
void siren(int t)
  {
  int i;
  for(i=0;i<t;i++)
     {
     changetone(100,350,3,5); //down
     changetone(350,100,3,5); //up
     }
  }

void phasor(int t)
  {
  int i;
  for(i=0;i<t;i++)
     {
     changetone(150,250,30,5);
     changetone(250,150,30,5);
     }
  }
```

Figure 3.6: Once we have **changetone**(), it is easy to build more complex sounds.

```
#include <sounds.cpp>

void main(void)
  {
  phasor(10);
  siren(4);
  }
```

Figure 3.7: Properly built include files can serve as toolboxes that can make programming easier.

You will probably want to add these new routines to the end of the **sounds.cpp** file. After doing so, you can include the file in any program and be able to create tones, sirens, and phasors with minimal effort. To make the **sounds.cpp** file stand alone, it should also include **IOports.cpp** and you should add **#ifndef**, etc., as shown in Figure 3.5. Figure 3.7 shows how this include file can be used.

ASSIGNMENT: After studying the examples in this exercise, create the file **sounds.cpp** and use it along with **IOports.cpp** to demonstrate various sounds. Try creating your own sounds and add your own modules to your **sounds.cpp** file. As an example, try creating telephone sounds such as ringing or a busy signal. Creating any strange sound can be interesting and therefore motivational, and that is certainly part of the goal of this exercise.

REVIEW QUESTIONS

1. Explain the basic principle for creating a tone using a computer program. How are the frequency and duration of the tone controlled?
2. What is the advantage of using the IOports.cpp routines to access the I/O ports for your machine?
3. Draw a hierarchy chart, as described in Exercise 1, that shows the relationship among all of the functions discussed in this exercise.
4. Discuss the use of and need for the **#ifndef** directive.

Exercise 4
Interfacing a 7-Segment LED

PURPOSE: The purpose of this exercise is to show how to use the port library routines developed in Exercise 2 to control the number displayed on a 7-segment LED. Even though many consumer products have replaced LEDs with LCDs, the simplicity of an LED makes it an ideal device to learn about interfacing and control. The control of LCDs will be addressed later in this text.

OBJECTIVES: After the completion of this exercise, the reader should be able to:
- Identify the hardware and software problems associated with interfacing a 7 segment LED.
- Describe the translation process required to translate numbers to be displayed into the 7-segment code needed by the hardware.
- Implement a tool function for displaying any HEX digit on a 7-segment LED.
- Utilize the tool function described above in simple applications such as a counting display.
- Modify the count application described above so that the user may alter aspects of the counting process while the program is running.

THEORY: In Exercise 2, we learned how to create a set of routines that would allow programs to access I/O ports. Exercise 3 demonstrated several functions that create both simple and complex sounds on a speaker or headset interfaced to a port. In this exercise, we will turn our attention from sound to light and interface a 7-segment LED.

Figure 4.1 shows the hardware required for the interface. Since I have no way of knowing if you are using the printer interface ports or some other system, Figure 4.1 shows that buffers have been added. If you are using the printer interface ports, there will be 2 buffers in series. At least for this exercise, use the double buffering. By the end of this exercise, however, you should know how to alter the software so that it will operate properly without the extra buffers. Remember that the buffers help prevent high voltages and currents from reaching the port itself. It is a lot easier to replace an external inverter than to remove the case to your PC and troubleshoot its internal circuitry.

Since the LED in Figure 4.1 is a common anode, each buffer must output a *low* to turn on its corresponding segment. Using a *low* rather than a *high* for the driving condition is preferred here because TTL gates can sink more current than they can source. The resistors ensure that the current does not exceed the maximum rating for the LED.

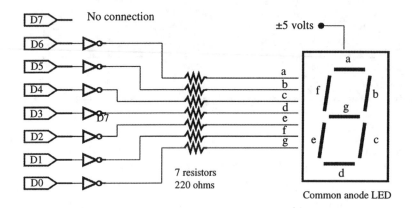

Figure 4.1: The hardware required for interfacing a 7-segment LED is minimal.

The software for this project must supply the correct binary code to turn on the proper segments. In keeping with our *tool* philosophy, all of the details associated with supplying the code should be placed in a procedure that can provide the desired functionality. The prototype for the function could look like this:

void led(int *number*);

The number passed to the function should control what is displayed on the LED. For example, to display a **4**, we should be able simply to pass the number **4**. The function's internal code should decide what binary pattern to use to light the proper segments on the LED. Since a 1 must be sent to a port pin to turn on a segment (because of the inverting buffer), the correct 7-segment pattern for the number **4** is HEX 33 (abcdefg = 0110011). One easy way to select the proper binary pattern is to use an array. For example, let's assume we have an integer array called **display_code**[ ]. If we initialize the array so that **display_code**[0] holds the pattern for a 0, **display_code**[1] holds the pattern for a 1, etc., then the following line can be used to display any *number* from 0 to 9:

out8data(display_code[number]);

Figure 4.2 shows a nearly complete listing for the **led**() module. The only thing you have to do is fill in the remaining 7-segment codes for the array. Notice that the array was established as a *static* integer so that it is only initialized the first time the function is called. If you include this function with your programs, all you have to do to display a number on the LED is pass it to **led**( ). It is assumed that **initialize_ports**() was called earlier in the program before any calls are made to **led**( ).

```
void led(int num)
    {
    static int display_code[16] = {0x7E, 0x30, ········ , 0x47};
    num=num&15;   // accept only the lower 4 bits in num
    out8data(display_code[num]);
    }
```

Figure 4.2: This module displays any number passed to it on a 7-segment LED.

You might be asking yourself why we didn't use a **7446** 7-segment display driver as part of the interface hardware. Doing so would have eliminated the need for translating the number to be displayed to its code, but it would also mean giving up some flexibility. The **7446** can only display the decimal numbers **0** through **9**. With our translation array **display_code[]**, our software can easily display, not only **0** through **9**, but also the HEX numbers **A** through **F**. The codes for these letters should be stored in the array at positions 10 through 15. Actually, a 7-segment LED is rather limiting when it comes to displaying letters, so when displaying the hex digits, the letters **B** and **D** are best done in lowercase.

Another hardware option for generating the appropriate 7-segment codes would be to use a programmable logic device (PLD). If this were a hardware text, then such an exercise would make sense. This being a text on C, however, means the emphasis should be on how programming can be used to solve problems. Even so, however, the tradeoff between hardware and software deserves a little more attention.

If we assume that adding either a 7446 or a simple PLD to a consumer product might add 25 cents to the final production cost, we might conclude that such a small amount might be inconsequential. To prevent you from jumping to such a shortsighted conclusion, let's look at two plausible situations.

Imagine that the product in question is a child's electronic toy based on an inexpensive PIC microprocessor and that the total production budget for each unit is only a few dollars. A price difference of 25 cents on such a product could mean the difference between a product that gets to market or one that does not or, assuming the product gets to market, the difference between it selling well or not.

Another example could be a product that is expensive enough to absorb the extra cost but one that is expected to sell in high volumes. Let's assume sales of 600,000 units a year. In such a case, the extra cost of only 25 cents translates to a savings of $150,000. The point is this: In today's cost-conscious economy, if a feature of a microprocessor-based product can be implemented in either hardware or software, the choice will almost always be software. Typically, the only reason for choosing a hardware implementation would be speed considerations. Although software is the low-cost, flexible alternative, hardware is always faster.

After the **led()** function of Figure 4.2 has been implemented, it is easy to write a main program to display any number entered by the user. The program in Figure 4.3 shows how to use the **led()** function to display hex numbers entered by means of switches (see Exercise 2) connected to the input port. The program continually reads the value of the switches and displays the value of the lower 4 bits (the lower *nibble*) of the port on the LED. If the switch connected to the fifth bit sends a 1 to the port pin (making the number greater than 15), the program will terminate.

```
#include <IOports.cpp>

// include the function led() here

void main(void)
    {
    int num;
    initialize_ports();     // found in IOports.cpp
    do
        {
        num = input_data();    // found in IOports.cpp
        led(num&15);           // sends only the lower 4 bits to be displayed
        } while(num<=15);
    }
```

Figure 4.3: This program demonstrates how to display hex data entered from switches connected to the input port.

Another example application would be to have the LED continuously display a count from **0** to **9**. The code fragment in Figure 4.4 demonstrates the basic principles of a counter. A switch connected to the LSB of the input port can be used to terminate the program. Notice that the input port data is ANDed with 1 to *mask* out all bits except the LSB (bit 0). If the switch position was the third bit from the right, we would need to mask the data with 4 (100 base 2).

Without the delay function in Figure 4.4, the display would change too fast to be legible. If we had a **delay1ms**() routine that delays a specified number of milliseconds, then we could easily create a one second delay. Assuming you have calibrated the **mydelay**() function from Exercise 2, the code in Figure 4.5 not only shows how to create a **delay1ms**() function, it shows how to check its accuracy. Notice that the code assumes that the **led**() function has been placed in an include file. The sounds.cpp file has been included so that we don't have to rewrite the **mydelay**( ) routine.


```
int i;
while(input_data()&1)   // Terminate if the LSB is low
    for(i=0; i<=9; i++)
        {
        led( i);
        delay1ms(1000);  // delays 1000 milliseconds
        }
```

Figure 4.4: This routine counts repeatedly from 0 to 9.

```
#include <sounds.cpp>
#include <led.cpp>

void delay1ms(int t)
  {
  int i;
  for(i=0; i<t; i++)
     mydelay(75);   // change this number to calibrate your routine
  }

void main(void)
  {
  initialize_ports();
  tone(300,20);
  delay1ms(5000);
    tone(300,20);
    }
```

Figure 4.5: Even the delays have a nested hierarchy.

The program in Figure 4.5 produces a tone and then waits for 5 seconds before producing the second tone. Measure the time between the tones with your watch and adjust the number 75 in **delay1ms**() until you get the expected time of 5 seconds. The accuracy for the **delay1ms**() routine is limited by this calibration method, but it works better than you might imagine.

Some of the later exercises in the text will require much more accuracy, so we should examine a better method for calibration. Look at the code in Figure 4.6. The program turns on all the pins of the 8-bit port for 1 ms and then turns them off for 1 ms. This produces a 500-Hertz square wave on all pins of the 8-bit port. The program will continue until a 0 is applied to the LSB of the input port. Use an oscilloscope to display the waveform and adjust the number passed to **mydelay**( ) until the correct frequency is observed.

```
void main(void)
{
initialize_ports( );
while(inputdata( )&1)
    {
    out8data(0xFF);
    delay1ms(1);
    out8data(0);
    delay1ms(1);
    }
}
```

Figure 4.6: The delay1ms( ) routine can be calibrated precisely using this code.

Now that we have a calibrated delay routine, let's improve the counter of Figure 4.4. Look at the code fragment in Figure 4.7. It allows a second switch connected to bit 1 of the input port to control the direction of the counter. The variable **max** controls the maximum number in the count cycle. Initialize **max** to 15 to create a hexadecimal counter. Change the value of **tm** to change the speed of the count.

You may have trouble understanding some of the examples in this exercise until you actually try them on your computer. Seeing and hearing them in action should add to your understanding of this material.

```
void main(void)
    {
    int count = 0, max = 9, tm=500;
    initialize_ports( );
    while(inputdata( ) &1)
        {
        if(inputdata( ) &2)
            count++;
        else
            count--;
        if(count>max)
            count = 0;
        if(count<0)
            count = max;
        led(count);
        delay(tm);
        }
    }
```

Figure 4.7: This program counts up or down depending on the position of a switch.

ASSIGNMENT: After trying the examples in this exercise, write and test the following programs.

1. Create a program that will count repetitively from **0** to **9** (or **0** to **F**, if you prefer) on a 7-segment LED until a switch is pressed. Each number should be displayed for approximately ½ a second or for 1 second, depending on the position of a second switch. Your program should use the value for the second switch to determine how long to delay each pass through the counting loop.
2. Modify Assignment 1 so that a third switch can control whether the count sequence is in decimal or hexadecimal.
3. Refer to Assignment 1. If you happen to run the program with the switch in the *wrong* position, the program will terminate as soon as it starts. Modify any of the above assignments so that the program will start regardless of the switch position. Once the program has been started, it should run until the switch is moved to the other position. Hint: Read the switch as soon as the program starts and store the state in a variable. Terminate the loop only when the switch does not match the stored state.

REVIEW QUESTIONS
1. What character would be displayed if 0x70 were sent to the port hardware in this exercise?
2. What are the advantages of using software to replace the functions of a 7446 chip?
3. What codes should be sent to the port to display the characters 1, 3, and F?
4. Why should the hexadecimal digits B and D be displayed in lowercase?
5. How can an oscilloscope be used to calibrate a delay routine?
6. What is the advantage of using the variable **max** in Figure 4.7 instead of using a number such as 9 or 15?

Part II
Interfacing Displays, Keypads, Sensors, and Motors

This section shows how basic components such as displays, keypads, sensors, and motors can be interfaced to a computer. Subroutines (tools) are developed that provide methods for controlling or accessing these devices. The reader is forced, in some cases, to perform a little research to decide what chips to use and exactly how to implement portions of the solution. This approach has been adopted to foster critical thinking skills that will be necessary later in the text.

Exercise 5
Multiplexing 7-Segment LEDs

PURPOSE: The purpose of this exercise is to demonstrate how to time-multiplex data between two 7-segment LEDs. In addition, this exercise will examine subjects such as refresh timing, look-up tables, and code conversions.

OBJECTIVES: After the completion of this exercise, the reader should be able to:
- Identify problems and advantages associated with time-multiplexed displays.
- Describe the hardware necessary to time-multiplex data between 2 7-segment LEDs.
- Utilize C's manipulation capabilities to separate a number into its decimal and hexadecimal digits.
- Utilize the principles learned from the **led**() module in Exercise 4 to implement a 2-digit, time-multiplexed display.
- Create a counter with two LEDs that displays from **00** to **FF** or **00** to **99**.

THEORY: In Exercise 4, we implemented an **led**() function that could display any single hexadecimal digit that was passed to it. In this exercise, we want to improve on that function so that we can easily display any 2-digit hexadecimal number from **00** to **FF** or decimal number from **00** to **99** on 2 7-segment LEDs.

After completing the last exercise, the most obvious solution to the problem of connecting 2 7-segment LEDs to a computer is to attach each LEDs to its own output port. While such a solution is feasible with 2 LEDs, imagine the problems associated with interfacing, for example, a 6-digit display. Implementing 6 output ports can be expensive. In some cases, as with our use of the PC printer port, the hardware ports available for our use is dictated by standard PC configurations, making 6 ports unavailable.

A better solution for displaying data on multiple LEDs is to have the software alternately illuminate each LED with its portion of the data. For example, if we want to display the hexadecimal number **4A** on 2 LEDs, the program can display **4** on the left LED for a short time and then turn it off and display the **A** on the right LED. If this sequence could be repeated over and over, at a fast enough rate, then the human eye would perceive that the LEDs were both on simultaneously. This sharing of data between 2 LEDs is referred to as *multiplexing*.

Figure 5.1 shows the hardware necessary to multiplex 2 LEDs. Notice that only 1 port is used to control both LEDs. Just as in Exercise 4, the lower 7 bits of the 8-bit data port supplied the 7-segment code. In this case, however, the 7-segment code is supplied to both LEDs. If the anodes for these LEDs were connected to 5 volts, as in Exercise 2, then both LEDs would display the same information. What we need is a way to control which LED is getting the 5-volt power.

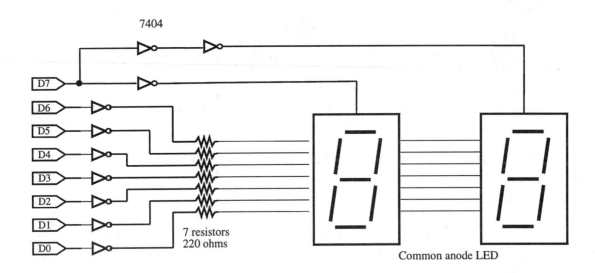

Figure 5.1: This hardware allows a single port to control 2 7-segment LEDs.

The three inverters connected to the MSB of the port determine which LED is active. When the port pin is high, the right LED will be given a logic 1, turning it on, while the left LED will be given a 0 turning it off. When the MSB is low, the reverse is true. You might wonder if the 2 inverters driving the right LED are necessary, since *logically* they can be replaced by a wire. They cannot be eliminated because they act as a buffer. Without them, a logical 1 on the MSB would be applied directly to the anode of the right LED. The current drawn by the LED could load the MSB so that it will appear as a logical 0 to the remaining inverter, causing the left LED to turn on too.

The next step is to write software to place the appropriate 7-segment codes on the lower bits of the port and then turn ON the correct LED for the proper amount of time. To prevent the human eye from perceiving flicker, each LED should be turned on about 60 times per second.

Let's assume that our software will take the form of a module called **display_hex()**, to which will be passed a number from **0** to **255** decimal (**00** to **FF** hexadecimal). The module must separate the number passed into the left and right digits to be displayed. The left and right values must each be converted to 7-segment codes and sent to the port with the MSB either set or cleared so that the display will appear on the proper LED. Figure 5.2 shows the code necessary to implement such a module.

It is assumed that the ports have been initialized and the array **display_code[ ]** contains the 7-segment codes associated with each digit to be displayed. This array of codes will be used as a look-up table to convert a numeric value into its equivalent 7-segment code.

The upper and lower nibbles of the number passed are isolated and stored into the variables **left** and **right**. The 7-segment code for the left digit is sent to the left LED and the **delay1ms()** routine from Exercise 4, Figure 4.5, makes sure it stays ON for 8 milliseconds. When the 7-segment code for the right LED is sent to the port, the MSB is set high by ORing the actual data

```
void display_hex(int num)
    {
    static int display_code[ ]= {  // insert 7-seg codes here };
    int right, left;
    right = num & 0xF;   // keep only the lower nibble
    left = (num & 0xF0) >> 4;   // keep only the upper nibble
    out8data(display_code[left]);
    delay1ms(8);
    out8data(0x80 | display_code[right]);
    delay(8);
    out8data(0);
    }
```

Figure 5.2: This module displays a 2-digit hexadecimal number on 2 LEDs.

with hexadecimal **80**. After waiting another 8 milliseconds, the last line in the function makes sure all segments of the LED are turned OFF before terminating. If the segments are not turned OFF, then the right LED remains ON while the main program is performing other tasks. If this time is significant, then the right LED could be noticeably brighter than the left LED. The 2 8-millisecond delays cause each LED to display its number approximately 60 times per second. If the delays are made longer, the display will flicker. If the delays are shortened considerably or even removed completely, the numbers may still appear on the LEDs, but they will be very faint because the duty cycle ON time will be small compared to the time spent in the rest of the program (such as the overhead of calling the function). Ideally, we want the delay for each LED to be as long as possible without causing flicker.

Although the routine in Figure 5.2 is usable, it lights each LED only once before terminating. This means that the routine must be called repeatedly to keep the LEDs lit. We can increase this tool's usefulness by giving it the capability to multiplex the data to the LEDs by itself. We must, however, provide a way for the calling routine to regain control so that data can continue to be processed. Figure 5.3 shows a new display routine with such capability.

```
void display_hex(int num, int dur)
    {
    static int display_code[ ]= {  // insert 7-seg codes here };
    int right, left, t;
    for(t=0; t<dur/16; t++)
        {
        right = num & 0xF;   // keep only the lower nibble
        left = (num & 0xF0) >> 4;   // keep only the upper nibble
        out8data(display_code[left]);
        delay1ms(8);
        out8data(0x80 | display_code[right]);
        delay1ms(8);
        }
    out8data(0);
    }
```

Figure 5.3: This improved module allows a duration to be specified.

The code in Figure 5.3 is almost identical to that shown in Figure 5.2. The new argument **dur** allows the calling routine to specify a duration, in milliseconds, for the LEDs to remain illuminated. We will see how this new capability can be used in an application in just a moment. Before we do that, however, we need to examine one more aspect of the tool.

The function listed in Figure 5.3 works fine if the number passed is to be displayed in hexadecimal. If we need a decimal display, we can easily create a new function **display_dec**() that is nearly identical to the original. The only difference is the variables **left** and **right** need to be calculated as shown in Figure 5.4.

The left digit is formed using the integer divide, which returns the quotient. The right digit is the remainder from that division, which is obtained using the C modulo operator %.

Once the routines **display_hex**() and **display_dec**() have been written, tested, and debugged, they can be placed into an include file called **LEDS.CPP**. The *include* file should include any files needed. For example, it should include **IOPORTS.CPP** to provide access to the ports. With this completed, a counter can be easily built that displays in hexadecimal or decimal. One method of doing so is shown by the code in Figure 5.5.

```
left = num / 10;
right = num % 10;
```

Figure 5.4: Make these changes to Figure 5.3 so that it will display decimal numbers.

```
#include <leds.cpp>
void main(void)
    {
    int count, n=99, sw, tm=1000;
    initialize_ports( );
    sw = inputdata() & 2;
    while((inputdata() & 2) == sw)
        {
        for(count=0; (count<= n)  && (inputdata() & 2 == sw) ; count++)
            {
            if(inputdata() & 4)   // set the speed
                tm = 1000;
            else
                tm = 500;
            if(inputdata() & 1)   // determine the display mode
                {
                n = 255;
                display_hex(count, tm);
                }
            else
                {
                n = 99;
                display_dec(count, tm);
                }
            }
        }
    }
```

Figure 5.5: Three switches control the count displayed by this program.

Examine the code in Figure 5.5 carefully and you will see that 3 switches connected to the lower bits on the input port control how the count proceeds. One of the switches determines if the program counts in hexadecimal or decimal. Another switch controls the speed of the count. Finally, the last switch causes the program to terminate when it is toggled from its original position. Think about which switch (which bit position) does what; some of the questions at the end of this exercise will deal with this program.

ASSIGNMENT: After studying the information in this exercise, perform the following.

1. Verify that all the examples in this exercise operate properly. Create tool (include) files as necessary.
2. Modify the counter program given in Figure 5.5 so that an additional switch can be used to control whether the count sequence will be up or down.
3. Modify the function **display_dec**() so that leading zeros will not be displayed on the LEDs. Verify that it works by using it with the program in Figure 5.5. You should have to alter only the **display_dec**() function. Nothing else in the program should require modification.

REVIEW QUESTIONS
1. Discuss the advantages and disadvantages of multiplexing LED displays instead of using a separate port for each LED.
2. Refer to Figure 5.1. How does the hardware and software select which digit is to be enabled?
3. Refer to Figure 5.5. Three switches connected to the input port were used to control the count sequence. Which pins on the port were used for each switch? Explain how you arrived at your answers.
4. Assume you need to multiplex 4 7-segment LEDs instead of two. Draw the interface circuit that would be required. (Hint: Use one port to control the segments and a different port to select the digit.) Show how to modify the function **display_dec**() so that it will work with your hardware design. Explain how you chose the delays for your function.
5. Refer to Figure 5.1. Assume that the LSB, not the MSB, was used to control which digit is enabled. The 7 most significant bits would drive the segments of the LED. Discuss the changes that you would have to make to the **display_hex**() function for it to work properly with the new hardware.
6. Explain how the program in Figure 5.5 detects when a switch is toggled. How does the code in this example compare with your code from Assignment 3 in Exercise 4?
7. Discuss why the code in Figure 5.3 is more useful than the code in Figure 5.2. How would the code in Figure 5.5 differ if you had to use the function in Figure 5.2 rather than the one in Figure 5.3?

Exercise 6
Matrix Keypads

PURPOSE: The purpose of this exercise is to introduce the principles involved in determining which key is pressed on a simple matrix keypad.

OBJECTIVES: After the completion of this exercise, the reader should be able to:
- Identify the tradeoffs associated with hardware and software keyboard decoding.
- Describe the basic algorithm used for scanning a matrix keypad.
- Implement a C function that can return a unique code for each key pressed on a matrix keypad.
- Analyze the operation of a **getnum**() function that can enter integer data into a C program through a matrix keypad.

THEORY: To communicate with a computer, humans need methods of handling the input and output of data. Previous exercises have shown how computers can display numeric data on external 7-segment displays. This exercise will show how the computer can obtain keystroke information from external switches arranged as a simple matrix keypad.

Let's assume that we have a computer keypad composed of 16 switches and that we wish for our computer to be able to determine which of the switches has been pressed. One solution, of course, would be to design a hardware encoder that can convert the 16 switches into a 4-bit code that can be entered into the computer by way of an input port. Another alternative would be to replace as much of the hardware as possible with software. Software will typically be slower than hardware, but software has the advantage of being far more flexible than hardware designs and often much cheaper to implement.

Let's see how software can be used to read information from a keypad. Assume that the 16 switches are connected as a 4-by-4 matrix, as shown in Figure 6.1. Each circle in the diagram represents a switch that, when closed, shorts one of the vertical wires to one of the horizontal wires. We need algorithms that can determine *if* a switch is pressed and, if so, *which* switch is pressed.

Notice that the vertical wires in Figure 6.1 are connected to the output port and that the horizontal wires are connected to the lower 4 bits of the input port. The 4 pull-up resistors ensure that the input port will read highs (1's) if no key is pressed. When a key is pressed, the horizontal and vertical lines at that switch position are shorted together. If the output line (the vertical line) is high, then the input port will still read a 1 at that bit position. If the output port is low, however, then the input pin will also be low because the shorted switch allows the low coming from the output pin to pull the input pin low.

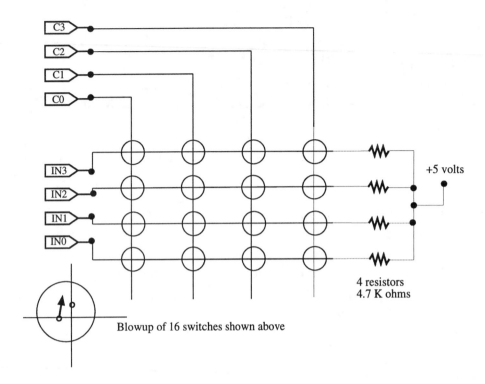

Figure 6.1: Sixteen switches arranged as a 4-by-4 matrix keypad.

We can quickly determine if *any* key is pressed by sending 4 0's to the output port. If the input port is read when no key is pressed, the data received will be all 1's or decimal 15. If one of the keys is pressed, then the input port will receive some number other than 15, such as 7 (0111_2), 11 (1011_2), 13 (1101_2), or 14 (1110_2). The position of the 0 in the data obtained will indicate in which row the key was pressed. Of course, if two or more keys are pressed, the data obtained from the input port may have more than 1 0 in it.

Figure 6.2 shows a module that can be used to determine if one or more keys is pressed using the algorithm discussed above. The module returns a 1 (TRUE) if a key is pressed and a 0 if no key is pressed. The variable **temp** is created and initially set to 0 to assume that no key is pressed. Zero is sent to the output port before the input port is read. If the lower 4 bits of the data obtained from the input port is not 15, then **temp** is set to 1 to indicate some key was pressed.

```
int   is_key_pressed(void)
      {
      int temp = 0;
      out4data(0);
      if(inputdata()&15 != 15);
           temp = 1;
      return (temp);
      }
```

Figure 6.2: This function can determine if a key is pressed.

```
int  is_key_pressed(void)
    {
    out4data(0);
    return (inputdata()&15 != 15);
    }
```

Figure 6.3: This efficient code performs the same task as the code in Figure 6.2.

The function **is_key_pressed**() in Figure 6.2 is easy to follow because it shows each of the steps involved. Since most readers of this text are not expected to be advanced C programmers, I will generally try to make the programs as readable as possible. However, I would not be doing my job if I failed to point out possible ways to write C code more efficiently. For example, Figure 6.3 shows an alternative method for implementing an **is_key_pressed**() function.

The code in Figure 6.3 may not be as easy to read for the novice C programmer, but it is very efficient. Not only does it require fewer programming statements, it also does not require any variable space. Eliminating the need to access data in memory greatly increases the speed of this routine. In Figure 6.2, we tested to see if a key was pressed and if this was TRUE, we set **temp** to TRUE and returned it. In this case, we just return the logic of the decision. (Throughout this text, I will try to make the programs as readable as possible. As we proceed though, I will also try to present more efficient methods when they are appropriate.)

The **is_key_pressed**() module cannot determine which key is pressed because the **is_key_pressed**() module cannot determine which column the pressed key is in. To create a module that can determine which key has been pressed, we first need to develop an algorithm for determining the column of the pressed key. Assume for a moment that the number sent to the output port was not all 0's. For example, let's assume that we sent the number 7 (0111_2) to the output port. Since only the first bit is low, only keys in the right-hand column will be able to short their input to 0. We can select a column to test by using a number with a 0 in the appropriate position.

As mentioned earlier, if a key is pressed in the selected column, then the number read by the input port will not be 15. Instead, it will be 7 (0111_2), 11 (1011_2), 13 (1101_2), or 14 (1110_2), depending on which row contains the pressed switch. The position of the 0 in the number read from the port can be used to indicate which row the pressed key was in.

Once you understand the above idea, the complete algorithm is easy. All that we have to do is to output a 0 to each column (one at a time) of the matrix keypad. After each output, the input port needs to be tested to see if all 4 lines are high. If they are, then we must test the next column. If all 4 input lines are not high, we know we have found the right column. By examining the number obtained from the input port, we can tell which row contained the pressed key. Once values have been established for **row** and **column**, we can create a unique code for each key with a formula such as:

```
                    code = 4 * row + column

int keycode(void)
    {
    int row, column, data;
    int mask = 0xF7;
    for(column=0; column<4; column++, mask = mask>>1)
        {
        out4data(mask);
        data = inputdata() & 15;
        if(data != 15)
            break;
        }
    // column now is correct and data can tell us which row
    for(row=0; row<4; row++, data = data>>1)
        if(! data & 1)
            break;
    return (4*column + row);
    }
```

Figure 6.4: This module returns a unique code for any key pressed.

The module in Figure 6.4 implements the algorithm just discussed. A variable called **mask** is used to generate the proper codes for sending 0's to each column. As **mask** is shifted, the 0 moves to the next column. Since the upper half of **mask** originally contains 1's, the bottom half will fill with 1's as the single 0 is shifted to the right. Outputting the mask to the port forces a 0 to be applied to each of the columns in succession until the **if**() determines that a pressed key was found. To keep track of which column is being tested, the variable **column** is incremented every time through the loop.

The second **for** loop in Figure 6.4 looks at each bit in the variable **data** (obtained from the input port when a pressed key was found) to see which row contained the pressed key. Rather than examine each bit *position*, the bits in data are shifted to the right so that only the LSB must be tested.

If no key is pressed when **keycode**() is called, then the column and row counts will both be 4, producing an illegal key code of 20. We can use this property of **keycode**() to check for key presses, but it would be far slower than our **is_key_pressed**(). Furthermore, we need some method for making sure that we don't read the same keypress twice. What we need is a way of waiting for keys to be pressed and waiting for them to be released.

Figure 6.5 shows how to build wait-till-key-released and wait-till-key-pressed functions. They will be called **wtkr**() and **wtkp**(). A **while**() loop in each function actually performs the desired wait by using **is_key_pressed**() to check the present status. Each function also waits for 10 ms after the key change is detected. All mechanical switches have contact bounce. The small delay provides enough time for any *noise* to die out before proceeding.

```
void wtkr(void)  // wait till key released
    {
    while(is_key_pressed() )
        ;     // empty loop
    delay1ms(10);
    }

void wtkp(void)  // wait till key pressed
    {
    while( ! is_key_pressed() )
        ;     // empty loop
    delay1ms(10);
    }
```

Figure 6.5: Waiting for a key to change its state is easy if you have an **is_key_pressed**().

For most applications, it is so unlikely that we would want to use **keycode**() without **wtkr**() and **wtkp**() we probably should just put them together. Figure 6.6 shows an improved **keycode**().

We might want to add one more feature to **keycode**( ) before we see how to use it in an application. The present code and hardware configuration will cause the codes for the keys on the keypad (arranged physically as in Figure 6.1) to be as shown in Figure 6.7. This is true because our hardware and software configurations dictate that column 0 is on the right side and row 0 is at the bottom.

```
int keycode(void)
    {
    int row, column, data;
    int mask = 0xF7;
    wtkr();  // these two lines wait for keys to be released and pressed
    wtkp();  // plus they ignore contact bounce
    for(column=0; column<4; column++, mask = mask>>1)
        {
        out4data(mask);
        data = inputdata() & 15;
        if(data != 15)
            break;
        }
    // column now is correct and data can tell us which row
    for(row=0; row<4; row++)
        if(! data & 1)
            break;
    return (4*column + row);
    }
```

Figure 6.6: This keycode checks for keys to be released and pressed.

15	14	13	12
11	10	9	8
7	6	5	4
3	2	1	0

Figure 6.7: The hardware and software discussed in Exercise 6 will result in these keycodes.

It is likely that any application you work with will expect the keys to be in a different configuration. You can rewire your keypad so that the keys appear in a different order, but making the transformation in software is easier. Rather than just returning the keycode with:

```
return 4*row+column;
```

we can return the code with

```
if(4*row+column <= 15)
        return newcodes[4*row+column];
else
        return ERRORCODE;
```

This change allows you to create an array **newcodes**[16] that can hold the codes you wish to use for each key. For example, the first element in the array should hold the code to be used for the key in the lower right-hand corner of the keypad. This method provides a lot more versatility than just being able to rearrange the keycodes. You can just as easily make the keys return ASCII codes or something more exciting. For example, assume the keypad is being used for the cash register for a local fast-food establishment that has pictures of the food on the keys to make it easy to train their employees. The **newcodes**[ ] array can contain the prices for each of the food items associated with each key.

This improved code also provides a way of detecting errors. If a noise spike should cause the system to think a key has been pressed, then the loops in Figure 6.6 will terminate without finding a valid key. In such a case, the column and row counters will both be set to 5 making the calculated keycode greater than 15. You should define **ERRORCODE** to be some number greater than 15 or less than 0 so that routines that call **keycode**( ) can determine if a valid keycode was detected.

To see how to use these routines in a program, let's examine a simple application involving a 4-by-4 keypad and a 2-digit 7-segment display. Let's assume that we want to write a program that will allow you to enter 2 numbers (maximum of 2 digits each) and display the sum of the 2 numbers (assuming the sum can be displayed with 2 digits). I will assume that the hardware has been connected as described in Exercises 5 and 6.

Imagine how easily this program could be written if we made only a few assumptions, such as those listed below.

- We have a module called **getnum**() that not only gets a number from the keypad, but displays it during the entry as well.
- The **keycode**() routine returns 0–9 for the keys of the same name and 10 for a key labeled ENTER.
- The **wtkr**() and **wtkp**() routines display the number in the global variable **displaynum** while waiting for a change in the key status.

Given these assumptions, Figure 6.8 shows a program that can implement the application.

```
int displaynum;
main()
    {
    int a, b;
    initialize_ports( );
    a = getnum();
    b = getnum();
    displaynum = a+b;
    keycode();   // displays the answer until a key is pressed to terminate the program
    }
```

Figure 6.8: This program displays the sum of 2 numbers entered from the keypad.

Of course, the program in Figure 6.8 works only if we create tools that validate our assumptions. Creating these tools is actually far easier than you might think. Let's look at the assumptions in reverse order. The last one stated that **wtkr**() and **wtkp**() displayed the number **displaynum** while waiting. Figure 6.9 shows how this can be done. Instead of just waiting for a key to be pressed or released, the routines now display the value of **displaynum** while they are waiting. The duration of 16 ms was used to allow each LED to illuminate for 8 ms. If the duration period is too long, 500 ms, for example, someone can press a key and release it before it can be detected.

```
void wtkr(void)  // wait till key released
    {
    while(is_key_pressed() )
        display_dec(displaynum,16);
    delay1ms(10);
    }

void wtkp(void)  // wait till key pressed
    {
    while( ! is_key_pressed() )
        display_dec(displaynum,16);
    delay1ms(10);
    }
```

Figure 6.9: These routines keep the display lit until a key transition is made.

The second assumption requires only that you implement the keypad as described in this exercise, so that will be left for the reader to do.

The first assumption takes for granted that a **getnum**() module can do all the work associated with obtaining numbers and displaying them. Figure 6.10 shows how easily this can be done. Actually, I embellished the code a little because this module will not just enter a 2-digit number. It can handle any number up to the size of an integer. Because of our display limitations, however, only 2-digit numbers should be used with this example.

The algorithm for converting the incoming codes to binary is easy to follow. The variable **displaynum** will hold the answer as it is being created. Each time a new key is pressed, the previous answer is multiplied by 10 and incremented by the value of the new key. Step through this code with a few sample numbers and you will see how it operates.

After examining Figure 6.10, you might wonder where the display routine is called. Remember, the **wtkr**() and **wtkp**() functions handle the display for us and they are called automatically every time **getnum**() calls **keycode**().

The **getnum**() module does a tremendous amount of work with a small amount of code. This is possible because it makes use of tools that have been previously discussed. Examine this example carefully, for this methodology is exactly what this text is about. Make sure you understand the hierarchy of all the routines involved. Investigate how the modules interact with each other to accomplish a larger goal. Draw a hierarchy-based organizational chart, as described in Exercise 1, if you think it would help you visualize the subordinate relationships.

```
int getnum(void)
    {
    int x;
    displaynum = 0;
    while( (x = keycode())<10)  // any key other than 0–9  terminates the entry
        displaynum = displaynum*10 +x;
    return displaynum;
    }
```

Figure 6.10: This module does a lot of work with a small amount of code.

Enter the modules discussed in this exercise and verify that they work properly. You might want to use the debugger to follow the actions performed by the modules. Proper use of the debugger will aid your understanding of the algorithms. The actual commands used for debuggers will vary by compiler, but any debugger should allow you to trace through your program and examine the value of variables at appropriate places. For example, if your program just read data from a port and stored it in a variable, then you can examine the value of that variable to see if the data matches the logic levels at the port pins.

ASSIGNMENT: After studying the examples in this exercise, write the following programs.
1. Write a program that will allow you to add or subtract 2 numbers and display the answer on 7-segment LEDs.
2. Modify the program in Assignment 1 so that a tone will provide audible feedback each time a key is pressed. Think about the structure of the program and where the code should be modified. You should be able to include your tone tools from Exercise 3. Since all the port pins (printer interface) are being used for the keypad and LEDs, you will need to modify your tone tools. One possible solution is to use a 4-input AND gate to drive the speaker. If the inputs to the AND gate are connected to the outputs from the 4-bit output port, the speaker will not energize unless all 4 bits are high. Since all 4 bits are never made high by the keypad routine, there will be no conflicts between the routines. Of course, if your computer has more ports or free pins, you can use them instead.

REVIEW QUESTIONS
1. Based on the code in this exercise, explain how the codes in Figure 6.7 are generated.
2. How would the codes in Figure 6.7 change if the formula used was 4*ROW+COLUMN?
3. Describe an application that can benefit from the ability to redefine the keycodes for the keypad.
4. What code would be returned by the **keycode**() in Figure 6.4 if it were called when no key was pressed? How did you arrive at your answer?
5. How can you modify **keycode**() so that it would return a negative 1 if no keypress is detected?

6. If you complete Assignment 2 in this exercise, you will see that the LEDs go out while the tone is being generated. Why is this true? You can solve the problem by lighting the LEDs during the delays for the tone routine or by creating tones while the LEDs are being multiplexed by toggling the speaker between each digit. What are the advantages and disadvantages of each method?

Exercise 7
Liquid Crystal Displays

PURPOSE: The purpose of this exercise is to understand how to interface a typical LCD (liquid crystal display) to a computer and to create a set of C functions for controlling and manipulating the display.

OBJECTIVES: After the completion of this exercise, the reader should be able to:
- Describe the hardware interface required to connect a liquid crystal display to a computer system.
- Describe the low-level software tools needed to control an LCD.
- Utilize low-level LCD software tools to build more complex tools that handle routine display functions.
- Create a simple application that utilizes an LCD.

THEORY: In previous exercises, we have learned how to interface and control 7-segment displays. As long as we are dealing with numbers, 7-segment displays are adequate, but when we need full text output from our programs, we need other alternatives. Liquid crystal displays have become so inexpensive that they are a viable alternative in almost any situation. Small 1- or 2-line displays are readily available through either standard channels or surplus stores.

A raw LCD is relatively complex to control. Each column of pixels has to be multiplexed in much the same manner that we handled multiple digits in a 7-segment display. The patterns that represent each character have to be stored and retrieved as needed for translation. The need to control a display is so universal, however, that custom chips have been created for the purposes of interfacing with and controlling LCDs. Nearly all small LCDs presently available are controlled by an HD44780 or equivalent, which has become the industry-standard interface. This means that nearly all 1- and 2-line displays use the same software commands and often have identical pin-outs for their hardware interface. Even so, check the specifications carefully for any display you intend to use.

The standard interface is defined by 14 I/O pins. Figure 7.1 shows the function for each of these pins. Because the HD44780 is an embedded controller, it is relatively sophisticated. Not only can we transfer ASCII codes to have them displayed, we can even send simple commands such as "clear the display" or "home the cursor."

PIN	SYMBOL	FUNCTION
1	Vss	Power supply ground
2	Vcc	Power supply +5 volts
3	Vee	Contrast adjustment (connecting to ground is usually okay)
4	RS	0 applied indicates **instruction** mode, 1 applied indicates **data** mode.
5	R/W	0 applied indicates **write** mode, 1 applied indicates **read** mode.
6	E	A high-to-low transition transfers data. Chip is disabled while E is high.
7	DB0	Data bus line 0
8	DB1	Data bus line 1
9	DB1	Data bus line 2
10	DB1	Data bus line 3
11	DB1	Data bus line 4
12	DB1	Data bus line 5
13	DB1	Data bus line 6
14	DB1	Data bus line 7

Figure 7.1: These pin assignments are standard for nearly all 1- and 2-line displays.

The actual timing for data transfers is relatively simple. If we want to send data to the display, for example, we place the data to be transferred on the data lines, a 0 on the write line (because we want to write to the LCD), a 1 on the RS line (because we want to send data, not an instruction), and then bring the E line low to initiate the transfer. If we perform the same steps with the RS line low, we can send instructions to the LCD. Instructions will be discussed in more detail later.

Since the LCD itself must process the data or instructions that we send to it, we must take care not to send the data faster than it can handle. One solution is to place a small delay in our programs immediately after transferring data to the LCD. Doing so, however, would not provide us with optimum performance. The minimum time required for the delay varies based on what was sent to the display. For example, the time needed to add a new ASCII code to the display buffer is dramatically different from processing a "clear display" command. Fortunately, the designers of the HD44780 gave us another option.

If we enable the LCD (by sending a low to E) with the R/W line high, we can read information from the display. (Actually, this capability has many interesting features that are not needed for this exercise. After we learn the basics of how to control the LCD, however, you may wish to study the data sheets on your LCD and enrich the tools we will discuss in this exercise.) For now, it is sufficient to know that when we read from the LCD, the status of DB7 tells us if the LCD is still busy processing the information we last sent to it. If the bit is high, the LCD is busy. If it is low, the LCD is ready to be sent instructions or data. If we monitor this bit instead of delaying for a preset period, we can be sure that we are sending data to the LCD as fast as possible.

Before we can write any software, we need to decide on the connections between our port pins and the LCD. Figure 7.2 shows the connections used for this exercise.

8-bit output port

Bits 0–6 connect to DB0 through DB6 (bit 0 to DB0, etc.).

Bit 7 connects to the enable pin E.

4-bit output port

Bit 0 connects to R/W.

Bit 1 connects to RS.

5-bit input port

Bit 4 connects to DB4.

Figure 7.2: Connect the LCD to the ports with these connections.

One of the questions you might be asking yourself, especially after we start writing software, is, Why is the enable pin connected to the 8-bit port rather than the 4-bit port with the other control lines? If you find yourself asking this question, I congratulate you because the software would probably be slightly simpler with all the control lines on the same port. In a later exercise, however, I want to use the LCD and the keypad in the same program. At that time, we will discuss how the connections used in this exercise will allow the operation of both devices without conflicts. For now, just accept the pin connections as given.

Since we cannot really send anything to the LCD unless we can determine if it is busy, let's start by building a routine that can read the MSB to determine the present status of the display. Figure 7.3 shows the code for this function.

To read the busy status of the LCD, the display must be in the command mode, so RS must be low. Since we are reading, the R/W line must be high. The LCD is enabled by sending a 0 to the MSB of the 8-bit port. We are, of course, assuming the MSB stays high in its normal state. As we proceed, we will see how to ensure that this assumption is always true. In this routine, for example, after we read the data, we return the enable line to its *normal* state. The **return**() statement ignores all the bits except bit 4 and returns TRUE only if bit 4 is high.

```
int is_busy(void)
    {
    int status;
    out4data(1);            // make RS low and R/W high
    out8data(0);            // enable the LCD by forcing the MSB low
    status  = inputdata( );  // read the information
    out8data(0x80);         // return LCD to disabled state
    return status&0x10;     // return TRUE if busy, otherwise zero
    }
```

Figure 7.3: This function determines if the LCD is still processing.

```
void wait_till_ready(void)
    {
    while(is_busy( ) )
        ;
    }
```

Figure 7.4: This function does not return until it is safe to send data to the LCD.

```
void print_character(int c)
    {
    wait_till_ready( ); // don't proceed if the LCD is busy
    out8data(c | 0x80);    // set the data lines while leaving E high
    out4data(0);           // make RS and R/W both low
    out8data(c & 0x7F);    // keep data stable and enable the LCD
    out8data(c | 0x80);    // return the enable line high and keep data stable
    }
```

Figure 7.5: Printing characters is easy because we have a **wait_till_ready**( ).

We can use this function to build another function that will wait until the LCD is ready to receive data. Figure 7.4 shows the code. A **while**( ) calls the **is_busy**( ) function and waits until the LCD is available before exiting the loop and returning from the function.

Now we are ready to send data to the LCD. Figure 7.5 shows how to build a function that can print a single character on the LCD. The character information must be placed on the data lines while the LCD is still in the disabled state. This gives the data lines time to stabilize before trying to write the data to the LCD. RS must be low because we are writing data, not a command, and the R/W line must be low to indicate we are writing, not reading.

Writing commands to the LCD requires almost the same actions as writing data (printing characters). In fact, as you can see from Figure 7.6, we can build a module that can send commands to the LCD by altering the code in Figure 7.5 so that it leaves RS high. Sending the number 1 as a command will clear the display and home the cursor. Sending a 2 will only home the cursor. There are many other commands, but they aren't needed at this time.

```
void LCD_ command(int c)
    {
    wait_till_ready( ); // don't proceed if the LCD is busy
    out8data(c | 0x80);    // set the data lines while leaving E high
    out4data(0);           // make RS and R/W both low
    out8data(c & 0x7F);    // keep data stable and enable the LCD
    out8data(c | 0x80);    // return the enable line high and keep data stable
    }
```

Figure 7.6: Sending commands to the LCD is almost the same as sending data.

```
void LCD_init(void)
    {
    LCD_command(0x30);      // sets 8-bit mode, 1-line display
    LCD_command(0x0C);      // display ON, cursor OFF, blink OFF
                            // bit 3 must be high for this command
                            // bit 2 display on/off
                            // bit 1 cursor on/off
                            // bit 0 blink on/off
    LCD_command(0x06);      // shift cursor right when printing characters
    LCD_command(0x01);      // clears the display and homes the cursor
    }
```

Figure 7.7: Initializing the LCD to a known state is a good idea.

Now is a good time to mention that the LCD will not operate properly unless it is initialized immediately after power is applied. Typically, this happens automatically. If the proper voltage transitions are adhered to when power is applied, an initialization sequence is handled internally.

If we wish to set our own initial state, we can set up the system as we wish. We might want to build an **LCD_init**( ) module that handles this task for us. An example initialization module is shown in Figure 7.7. Since our **LCD_**command( ) tool checks to see if the LCD is ready to accept characters, we should not have to worry about how long these commands take to process. If the reset power-up does not meet specifications, the internal reset sequence may not execute and then the busy-flag bit is not valid until a proper initialization is performed. If your system happens to have such startup problems, you will need to place delays (of about 10 ms) between each line of code in Figure 7.7.

We now have enough tools to begin using the LCD. For example, the code in Figure 7.8 will print HELLO on the LCD.

If you have worked with C or C++ using a standard computer (as opposed to a simple controller), you no doubt have used functions such as **printf**( ) and **cout** to display not only characters but strings and numbers. In most applications that use an LCD, we will find that memory is limited. Since a typical **printf**( ) function requires at least several thousand bytes of code, most control

```
void main(void)
    {
    LCD_init( );
    print_character('H');
    print_character('E');
    print_character('L');
    print_character('L');
    print_character('O');
    }
```

Figure 7.8: This simple program prints HELLO on the LCD.

```
void print_string(char * address)
    {
    while( * address)
        {
        print_character(* address);
        address++;
        }
    }
```

Figure 7.9: Printing a string is easy because we already have **print_character**( ).

applications will not have the luxury of using standard library functions such as **printf**( ). For example, let's assume that you are responsible for writing the code that controls a microwave oven with an LCD. It would make your job easier if you could use a standard **printf**( ), but the extra code could mean a larger ROM is required, maybe even a processor with more address lines. The extra cost for the ROM (and the extra circuit board traces, not to mention distributor markups, etc.) could easily add $1 to the cost of the microwave. If your company manufactures 100,000 microwaves a year, that really adds up.

What do we do? The answer is to create tool routines that perform only what we need for the product at hand. The microwave control program, for example, might need to display strings for prompting the user and numbers in a time format. Functions that can perform these tasks might require less than 100 bytes of code, making them a much better choice for the product. Let's see how these can be created.

Figure 7.9 shows how a string can be printed. The function expects to be passed the address of a string. As long as the character in the string at the present address is not a null (which tests FALSE) the character is printed and then the address is advanced to point at the next character.

Printing the time (up to 99 hours and 59 minutes) is also relatively easy if only we had a routine that can print numbers from 0 to 99. Figure 7.10 shows how we can construct such a function. We send it the number to be printed and a second argument, **how**, of 1 if we want leading 0's to be printed and 0 if we don't. By setting **how** to 0, the function defaults to not printing leading 0's if not told to do so.

The left and right digits are obtained as we did with the 7-segment LEDs. Since the ASCII code for 0 is 0x30 and for 1 is 0x31, etc., we can convert each of the digits to ASCII by ORing the original data with 0x30. Each of the digits can be printed with **print_character**( ). If the leading digit is a 0, we can use the variable **how** to decide how to handle it. The number will always stay in the same relative place on the display if we replace the leading 0 with a space instead of just skipping it. Notice that the value of **how** defaults to 0. This means that **print_number**() will not print leading 0's unless asked to do so. Only C++ compilers support default arguments, so don't try this in C.

```
void print_number(int num, int how = 0)
    {
    int left, right; // for storing the left and right digits
    left = num/10;      // integer divide truncates the fraction
    right = num%10; // the modulo operation provides the remainder
    left = left | 0x30;  // convert the digits to ASCII codes
    right = right | 0x30;
    if(left !=0x30)        // if the first digit is not a zero
        print_character(left);  // print it normally
    else            // but if it is a zero
        {
        if(how)        // decide what to do
            print_character('0');    // either print the leading zero
        else
            print_character(' ');    // or just a space (to keep spacing)
        }
    }
```

Figure 7.10: Printing numbers from 0–99 can be done with or without leading 0's.

Now that we have a **print_number**( ) function, printing *time* is easy. Let's assume that our microwave oven program keeps track of all times in seconds. This is not an unreasonable assumption because it will be much easier to handle time comparisons if everything is in seconds rather than minutes and seconds. We also save memory because we need only 1 variable instead of 2 to hold the time. We need the *time* in minutes and seconds only when we need to print it. Figure 7.11 shows the **print_time**( ) routine.


```
#define CLEAR 1

void print_time(int t)
    {
    int min, sec;
    min = t / 60;
    sec = t % 60;
    LCD_command(CLEAR); // clear screen
    print_string("Time = ");
    print_number(min);     // no leading zero
    print_character(':');     // a colon between minutes and seconds
    print_number(sec,1); // with leading zero
    }
```

Figure 7.11: It takes all the previous LCD tools to make this function.

```
void main(void)
    {
    int tm = 0;
    initialize_ports( );
    while(tm < 3*60)
        {
        print_time(tm);
        tm++;
        delay1ms(1000);
        }
    }
```

Figure 7.12: This program displays the elapsed time.

My version of the **print_time**( ) function adds the phrase "Time = ", but it could be customized to whatever was needed for the intended application. All these tools together are still orders of magnitude smaller than a **printf**( ) function.

It is worth restating that properly organized programs are composed of tools that are composed of smaller tools, and so on. The **print_time**( ) function is a good example. Because of the tools it uses, the flow of the code is easy to follow and the chance of making a logical error is reduced. The code is simple, however, only because we call functions like **print_number**( ) and **print_string**( ) to do the work for us. Even these functions call **print_character**( ), which in turn has to call **wait_till_ready**( ), which relies on **is_busy**( ). Learning to think this way is what creates your ability to handle large programming tasks. There are many side benefits too, not the least of which is improved problem-solving skills.

Figure 7.12 shows how we can write a program that will display the elapsed time in minutes and seconds on the LCD. The program terminates after 3 minutes.

Of course, the program in Figure 7.12 will operate only if you include all the tools that we have constructed in this exercise. Test each of the tools as you create them. After they are working, place them in an include file.

ASSIGNMENT: Prepare and test all of the examples in this exercise. Refer to the data sheet on the LCD you have chosen to work with because there may be some differences. The principles discussed in this exercise should enable you to make any necessary alterations. When you have the program in Figure 7.12 working, make the appropriate changes so that it will display the time with hours, minutes, and seconds instead of just minutes and seconds. To test your code without waiting around for hours, you might want to decrease the delay temporarily.

REVIEW QUESTIONS

1. Explain the timing for writing data and commands to an LCD. Draw waveform-timing diagrams to illustrate your explanation.

2. How does using the *busy* signal enable your program to print at optimum speed?

3. When is it unwise to use standard library functions? Why?

4. The HD44780 LCD controller has the capability of interfacing with only 4 data bits rather than all 8. The advantage, of course, is that fewer I/O pins are needed. This can really cut costs and can make a big difference in the profit margin of an inexpensive product. The data sheet for the HD44780 discusses how to multiplex 8 bits of data to the 4-bit interface. To answer this question, you *don't* have to interface the LCD using the 4-bit mode, but discuss how many of the modules in this exercise you would have to modify *if* you wanted to make such a modification. The answer may surprise you. Relate your findings to the advantages of creating modular tools in a hierarchy-based structure.

Exercise 8
Digital to Analog Conversion

PURPOSE: The purpose of this exercise is to introduce methods for generating analog signals using a digital computer.

OBJECTIVES: After the completion of this exercise, the reader should be able to:
- Discuss various methods for converting a digital word into an equivalent analog voltage.
- Describe the software needed to convert an array of digital data into an analog signal.
- Create an application that allows the computer to generate one of several analog waveforms as requested by the user.

THEORY: Although digital computers are generally the best choice when it comes to processing data and interacting intelligently with the environment, the external environment is primarily composed of analog entities. In this exercise and the next, we will discuss how to convert information in analog form to digital and from digital form to analog. In this exercise, we will learn how to convert from digital to analog (D/A).

The binary words used in a digital system are weighted such that each successive bit is valued at twice that of the one before it. To create an analog voltage with the same characteristics, we need only to arrange resistors so that they will create a voltage divider network that mimics the weight of the data applied to it. Figure 8.1 shows one method for accomplishing this.

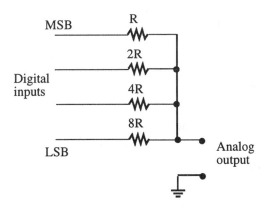

Figure 8.1: A binary ladder transforms digital data into analog form.

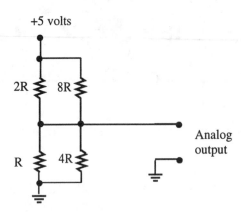

Figure 8.2: This voltage divider circuit results from applying the number 5 to Figure 8.1.

The resistors at each bit position correspond to the digital weight assigned to that position. The most significant bit is attached to the smallest resistor, enabling it to generate the most current. Each lower bit is attached to a resistor that is twice the size of the one before it, cutting the effect of that bit to half of the one before it. Resistors arranged in this manner are referred to as a binary ladder. This circuit is also referred to as a current summer, but I think its operation is easier to see as a voltage divider (more on this in a moment.).

To see how this network of resistors can translate a binary number into an analog voltage proportional to that number, let's look at an example. Let's assume that the number 5 (0101 base 2) is applied to a binary ladder. If we assume that a TTL 1 is 5 volts, then 8**R** and the 2**R** resistors in Figure 8.1 should connect to 5 volts. Similarly, the logic 0 applied to 4**R** and **R** will make those resistors connect to ground. The resulting circuit is shown in Figure 8.2.

The output voltage for Figure 8.2 is dictated by the voltage divider rule, which states that when voltage is applied to two resistors in series the voltage across **B** can be expressed as follows:

$$\text{Voltage}_{\mathbf{B}} = \frac{\mathbf{B}}{\mathbf{A} + \mathbf{B}} * \text{Total Voltage}$$

In Figure 8.2, the value of **B** is the parallel resistance of 8**R** and 2**R** and the value of **A** would be the parallel of 4**R** and **R**. Since parallel resistance is calculated as the product of the two resistors divided by the sum of the two resistors, the output voltage from Figure 8.2 can be expressed as follows:

$$Vout = \cfrac{\cfrac{R*4R}{R+4R}}{\cfrac{2R*8R}{2R+8R} + \cfrac{R*4R}{R+4R}} *5 \text{ volts}$$

This reduces as follows:

$$Vout = \cfrac{\cfrac{4R^2}{10R}*5}{\cfrac{16R^2}{10R} + \cfrac{4R^2}{5R}} = \cfrac{\cfrac{4R^2}{10R}*5}{\cfrac{24R^2}{10R}} = \cfrac{16R^2*5}{24R^2} = \cfrac{1}{3}*5 = \cfrac{5}{15}*5 \text{ volts}$$

As you can see, if we apply the number 5 to the binary ladder, the output voltage will be 5/15 of the voltage used to represent a logical 1. If we went through a similar reduction for the number 6, we would see that the output voltage would equal 6/15 of the possible total. The point is, for any value **n** applied to a 4-bit binary ladder, the output voltage will be **n**/15 of the possible maximum. The value of 15 equates to the largest number we can count with 4 bits. A number **n** applied to a 5-bit binary ladder would provide **n**/31 of the possible maximum.

The resistors in a binary ladder theoretically can be any value as long as the values double from one resistor to the next. Practically speaking, however, the smallest resistor must be large enough to ensure that the source voltage does not fluctuate significantly due to the load. This is true because a low load resistance would alter the voltage division equations discussed above. If we are driving the ladder from a TTL port, the minimum resistance that we might want to use in the ladder would be 10 K ohms. If we are driving with an 8-bit port, the resistor attached to the MSB would have to be 256R, or 2.56 million ohms. This relatively large value for one of the resistors is cause for concern.

To ensure the accuracy of the voltage division of the ladder network, it is imperative that the impedance of the load we drive with this circuit is very large compared to any resistors in the divider itself. A load with an input impedance of 50 megohms (20 times) would be required for an accuracy of 5%, and this assumes that all the resistors are exactly the right value. Where will we get all the nonstandard values required, especially since we prefer 1% tolerance or better? The difficulty in obtaining precision resistors in many different values plus the need for a very high impedance load makes the binary ladder unsuitable for applications that require more than a few bits of resolution.

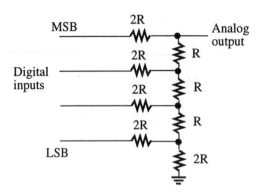

Figure 8.3: The R-2R ladder has many advantages over the binary ladder.

The R-2R ladder shown in Figure 8.3 solves both of the problems associated with the binary ladder and, from a user point of view, it acts almost exactly the same.

You can construct the circuit of Figure 8.3 easily using 12 10-K resistors (or any other reasonable value), making it easy to get precision parts. We still have to avoid loading the outputs of this circuit, but the requirements are not as imposing as those of the binary ladder. If a buffer is required for either the binary ladder or the R-2R ladder, a simple operational amplifier circuit, as shown in Figure 8.4, should work fine.

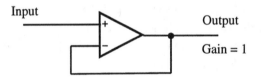

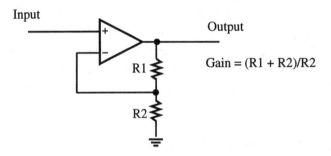

Figure 8.4: Operational amplifiers can provide gain as well as buffering.

```
while(!is_pressed( ))      // or just while(1) if the keypad is not connected
  for(i=0; i<=15; i++)     // change 15 based on the number of bits implemented
    out8data( i );         // assumes the D/A is connected to the 8-bit port
```

Figure 8.5: This small code fragment will generate a ramp waveform.

Since the input impedance for the operational amplifier circuits in Figure 8.4 is very large, it will have little effect on the voltages obtained from a resistive ladder. The top configuration in Figure 8.4 provides a unity gain. If you need to increase or decrease the total range of the output voltage, you can use the lower configuration.

Although the basic operation of the two resistive networks described above is very similar, the actual formula for the analog voltage obtained from these circuits is slightly different. If the binary number 0001 were applied to both circuits (with a 1 being 5 volts), then the voltage at the output of the binary ladder would be 1/15 of 5 volts, as we have seen. For the same situation, the voltage from the R-2R ladder would be 1/16 of 5 volts. Similarly, if we apply the binary number 12 (1100) we would get 12/15 and 12/16 of the voltage representing a 1 from each of the ladders. The proportional effect is the same for both ladders. The only difference is that the maximum voltage on the R-2R ladders is slightly reduced when compared with the binary ladder.

Since the voltage used to represent a 1 directly affects the analog output from these circuits, the accuracy will depend on the consistency of that voltage. Unfortunately, that is a problem if we drive the networks with standard TTL signals, which can easily vary from 3 to 4.5 volts for a logical high. Even so, for demonstration purposes such as this exercise, you can obtain reasonable results by connecting the ladder of your choice directly to the output port. Adding a tristate buffer or even 2 K pull-up resistors to each bit position will improve the accuracy by forcing the voltage level for a logic high to be closer to 5 volts than we would normally expect for a standard TTL gate.

If we apply some appropriate data to a ladder network, the inaccuracies can be seen on an oscilloscope attached to the output. Look at the code fragment in Figure 8.5. It assumes that a 4-bit D/A converter is connected to the lower 4 bits of the 8-bit port. The **for**( ) sends the numbers 0–15 to the port. Since the numbers increase in succession, so will the voltage generated by the resistive network. This increasing voltage is called a ramp.

The **while**( ) in Figure 8.5 repeats the ramp waveform continually, so you can observe the voltage output from the D/A converter on an oscilloscope. It should look something like Figure 8.6. Since the input impedance of the oscilloscope is very high, you should not need buffers.

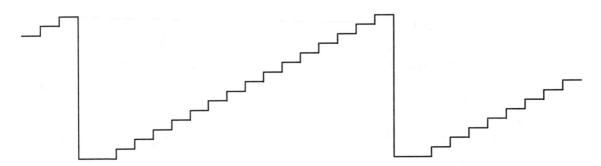

Figure 8.6: A ramp output should look similar to this on an oscilloscope.

The ramp should be made up of 16 equal size steps if all the bits are working properly. Each step should be the same vertical size if the actual voltage representing a logic 1 at each bit position is the same. The relative vertical size of each step will also be affected by the tolerance of the ladder resistors. Try changing the value of each of the resistors slightly (one at a time) and note how the output changes. As you perform these changes, relate what is happening to the binary numbers that are being applied. For example, if you change the resistor (use a potentiometer) connected to the bit just below the MSB in a binary ladder, you will see that the output steps will change in size in 8 places corresponding to the values where that bit is high. In this case, you will see a variance in steps 4, 5, 6, 7, 12, 13, 14, and 15. If you vary the other resistors in the ladder, you will see that each bit affects 8 steps in the waveform, but not the same 8 steps.

Depending on your computer and compiler, you might also be able to see a slightly longer period between the individual ramps when compared to the step times, especially if you are using the **is_pressed**( ) decision. The time taken by the **while**( ) to restart the loop will make this period longer than the loop times for normal passes through the loop. Notice also that this code is generating the highest frequency possible for a ramp with this resolution. We can lower the frequency by inserting delays into the loop, but without resorting to external hardware, the maximum frequency is limited by the speed of the computer and by the number of bits of resolution desired.

Another experiment that can provide some insight into the operation of a D/A converter is disconnecting each bit from the port (one at a time) and seeing the effect of connecting that resistor to either ground or 5 volts. For example, if you connect the LSB to ground, then the numbers 0 and 1 (as well as 2 and 3, 4 and 5, etc.) produce the same step voltage.

If we increase the number of bits of our D/A converter to 8, the number of steps will increase to 256, making the ramp appear to be nearly a straight line on an oscilloscope. (Don't forget to change the 15 in the **for**( ) of Figure 8.5 to 255.) If you wish to try this enhancement, you should consider using an integrated circuit with an internal resistive ladder. Many D/A chips are available and are interfaced easily with the output port. Many manufacturers supply data sheets and application notes on the Internet, so information on any chip you choose should be readily available.

```
#include <math.h>          // required for the sin function
void main(void)
    {
    int i, angle, x[16];
    initialize_ports( );
    // first calculate the values needed
    for(i=0, angle=0; i <= 15; i++, angle+=6.28/16)
        x[i] = 7*(sin(angle)+1);
    while(!is_pressed( ))
        for(i=0; i <= 15; i++)
            out8data(x[i]);
    }
```

Figure 8.7: The values for a sine wave should be calculated in advance because they are so time-consuming.

If the **for**( ) in Figure 8.5 is stepped backward, as shown below, the analog output decreases over time and is called a sawtooth waveform.

```
for(i=15; i >= 0; i--)
```

If we want to generate multiple waveforms from a D/A converter, a square wave can be produced by sending 15 and 0 alternately to the port. If you want the frequency to remain the same as the ramp and sawtooth waveforms, you must send both the 15 and 0 8 times each (or insert proper delays).

You can create a sine wave if your compiler handles floating point numbers and has the proper library available. Figure 8.7 shows how easily this can be accomplished. Since trigonometry is a time-consuming operation for the computer, the values are calculated first and stored in an array and then transferred to the D/A converter. The **for**( ) in this example works with 2 variables. It increments **i** to use as an index for the array and **angle** to use as an argument for the sine function.

The **sin**( ) function in C requires its argument to be in radians, so **angle** is incremented by a value that will fill the array with values of 1 period (2π) of the waveform. Adding 1 to the value obtained from **sin**( ) makes it vary from 0 to 2 (instead of -1 to $+1$), and multiplying that value by 7.5 gives us a full-scale answer for the D/A converter. If you are using an 8-bit converter, you would use 127.5 as the multiplier. If you are implementing this example on a controller using a C without floating point capability, use a PC or even a calculator to find the values needed for the array. Since all the values are integers, a simple controller using an integer-based C will be able to display a sine wave.

ASSIGNMENT: After testing all the examples in this exercise to verify that your D/A hardware is operating properly, design and implement an application program that will generate one of several waveforms (ramp, sawtooth, square, sine) based on keys pressed on a keypad as discussed in Exercise 6.

REVIEW QUESTIONS

1. How would the waveform of Figure 8.6 change if each of the bits were disconnected one at a time from the port and connected to either ground or 5 volts? Draw each of the 8 resulting waveforms. Choose 2 of the waveforms and explain why the action taken caused the observed changes.

2. What are the advantages of using an integrated circuit D/A instead of a resistive ladder?

3. How could you use the waveform displayed on your oscilloscope to determine the time it takes your computer to execute the **is_pressed**( ) routine? How would the delay caused by **is_pressed**( ) affect the waveform generated by Figure 8.7?

4. If you used an 8-bit converter to display the sine wave generated by Figure 8.7, it would obviously look much better than one with only 16 levels of resolution. The waveform generated with 256 levels of resolution, however, would have a maximum frequency considerably lower than the 16-level version. Why is this true? What is the relationship between the 2 maximum frequencies?

Exercise 9
Analog to Digital Conversion

PURPOSE: The purpose of this exercise is to demonstrate how to convert the analog quantities of the real world into digital numbers that the computer can read, store, and analyze. This gathering of information is often referred to as data acquisition.

OBJECTIVES: After the completion of this exercise, the reader should be able to:
- Discuss the need for analog to digital conversion and situations where it can be used.
- Describe several methods for performing analog to digital conversion and compare and contrast the advantages and disadvantages of each.
- Utilize an appropriate interface to allow the computer to collect analog information.
- Create a tool function for collecting analog information so that the tool can be used in later applications.

THEORY: The real world is composed of many analog quantities, such as the volume of a sound, the brightness of a light, the angle of a robot arm, or the speed of a motor. For the computer to control an environment with any intelligence, it must be able to obtain information about that environment. Until now, this text has viewed the external world as digital events. For example, the elevator in Exercise 1 was at a particular floor or it wasn't. The elevator moved at a single speed until it reached its destination. Using analog techniques, though, we can provide new features for the elevator. For example, instead of stopping the elevator motor when the floor is reached, it might be nice for the passengers if the elevator slowed down when it approached its destination.

If the computer is to slow the elevator as it approaches the correct floor, it must be able to determine the remaining distance to the floor, not just when the floor has been reached. As you can see from this simple example, a computer with the ability to deal with analog information has tremendous advantages over a computer that must view its environment as digital events.

Real-world analog quantities may take on many forms such as light, heat, or sound. In most cases, it is easy to convert these quantities to an electrical voltage that varies proportionally with the quantity being observed. Appropriate devices for this conversion might be phototransistors, thermistors, microphones, or even potentiometers.

Converting the real-world activity to an electrical voltage, though, is only the beginning. The voltage must be converted into a digital number that can be obtained, stored, and manipulated by the computer. As you would expect, if you deal with computers regularly, methods for such a conversion range from slow and cheap to fast and expensive. For the first example in this exercise, let's look at a method that is somewhere between the two.

Successive approximation is a method of analog to digital (A/D) conversion that is modestly fast and relatively inexpensive. Another advantage of this method is the fact that it is easy to implement in software so that we can understand better the inner workings of the methodology.

The basic idea is simple. Imagine telling a young child that you have thought of a number from 1 to 100 and that you want them to guess the number. In many cases, the child might ask, "Is it a 1?", "Is it a 2?", "Is it a 3?", and continue until the correct number was found.

Obviously, a better solution would be to ask the question, Is it larger than 50? and, based on the answer, rule out half the numbers from further consideration. The next question should guess a number (either 25 or 75) centered in the remaining numbers. This process should continue until the answer is found. This method of successive approximation will find the solution in far fewer guesses than the linear approach mentioned first.

To allow the computer to deal with such a situation, we must provide a means for it to offer a guess and a way for it to know if the guess was too high (or not). The hardware needed to provide such capabilities is shown in Figure 9.1.

The D/A box in Figure 9.1 represents any of the D/A circuits from Exercise 8. A simple resistive ladder will work, but it will not provide the accuracy of an integrated circuit version. The purpose of the D/A is to allow the computer to make a *guess* at the correct answer by sending a digital number (0–255) to an output port. Since this number is converted to an analog signal by the D/A, the output of the D/A represents the guess made by the computer. Naturally, if the voltage output from the D/A ranges from 0–5 volts, then the signal being sampled should have the same range.

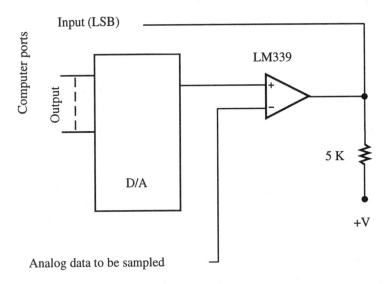

Figure 9.1: Successive approximation A/D requires a D/A converter.

Guess (dec)	Hex	Binary
128	80	10000000
64	40	01000000
32	20	00100000
16	10	00010000
8	08	00001000
4	04	00000100
2	02	00000010
1	01	00000001

Table 9.1: The guesses can be created by shifting.

The LM339 is a 5-volt operational amplifier circuit configured as a voltage comparator. Both analog signals (the guess and the signal being sampled) are sent to the comparator. If the signal applied to the plus input (the guess in this case) is larger than the data signal, then the comparator's output is high. When the minus input is higher, the output is low. This high/low indication of *too large* or *okay* can be read by a single input pin on a computer port. The 5 K pull-up resistor is required because the LM339 has an open collector output, making it easy to interface with various logic levels. Nearly any 5 volt, single supply op-amp can be substituted if an LM339 is not available.

Since the numbers in our possible guesses are all 8-bit, they may range from 00 to FF hex or 0 to 255 decimal. Our first guess should be in the middle (128). If we find that the number is smaller than 128, the next guess might be 64. If that guess is still too large, we might try 32, etc. The fact that each guess is half the last guess is very nice if we are working with binary numbers. The guesses above, and their hex and binary equivalents, are shown in Table 9.1.

Notice that each subsequent guess in Table 9.1 is the previous guess shifted right (see the binary column). Remember, these guesses were made with the assumption that the previous guesses were too large. Suppose we guessed 128 and were told that the guess was not large enough. The next guess would be halfway between 128 and 255, or 192. Notice that 192 is 128 + 64, which means that the binary column in Table 9.1 can be used to form the next guess. Once we see this basic relationship, it is easy to create an algorithm for solving our problem.

Imagine that we have a number called a **mask** and it starts at 128. Let's also assume that we have an **answer** that starts at 0. Remember, for an efficient algorithm, the task must be accomplished by repeating the same set of steps over and over. Let's start by ORing together the **mask** and the **answer**. I realize that the **answer** is 0, so the OR does nothing in this case, but as we will see, we will need it in later repetitions. If we send the OR of the **answer** and the **mask** to the output port (and to the D/A converter), the analog output of our *guess* will be compared with the signal being sampled. This means that the LSB of the input port will be high or low, indicating whether our guess is too large (high) or not (low). If it is not too high, we need to *keep* the *guess* and shift the **mask** one bit to the right. We can then repeat and OR the **mask** and the **answer** again to get our next *guess* (192_{10}).

If the input port indicates that the guess is too high, we should not keep the last change to our guess (the last OR of the mask with the answer). Instead we shift the mask and continue the repetition. The above discussion may seem a little complicated at first. If you pick a random binary number and follow the above steps, however, I think it will become clear. Figure 9.2 shows how to implement the algorithm as a C tool function called AtoD. When called, the tool will return the numeric value representing the value of the signal being sampled.

```c
int AtoD(void)
    {
    int mask, ans;
    for( mask = 0x80, ans = 0 ; mask ; mask = mask>>1)
        {
        out8data(mask | ans);       // send the present guess to the port
        if(!(inputdata( ) & 1))     // is the LSB low (not too large)
            ans = ans | mask;       // keep the present guess (it's OK)
        }
    return ans;
    }
```

Figure 9.2: This tool performs successive approximation A/D.

The **for**() initializes the previously mentioned values for **mask** and **ans** and executes the body of the loop as long as any 1's are left in the **mask**. On each pass through the loop, the present guess is made by ORing the **mask** and **ans** together and sending it to the port. If the guess is not too large, the ORing is made permanent by storing the guess back into **ans**. After each pass through the loop, the value of **mask** is shifted 1 position to the right. After the mask is empty of 1's (8 passes in this case) the answer is valid and is returned.

Assume that we had a potentiometer connected across a 5-volt supply with the wiper output connected so that it can be sampled by our A/D converter system. Figure 9.3 is a code fragment that shows how to use the **AtoD**() tool and two tools from Exercise 7 to display a number from 10 to 255 on an LCD. Turning the potentiometer to a number less than 10 terminates the program.

We have to be very careful with our code because the 8-bit port drives both the LCD and our D/A converter. When we send data to the LCD, the D/A converter will react by changing its output. This won't affect us, however, because we will send new data to the D/A before we read the output of the comparator. When we perform an A/D conversion, however, the shifting data that is sent to the 8-bit port will certainly enable the LCD. If the LCD is in the WRITE mode, any garbage that may be on the 8-bit port at the time the LCD is enabled will be transferred to the LCD. To prevent this from causing problems, the program in Figure 9.3 uses the 4-bit port to place the LCD into a READ state before calling the **AtoD**( ) routine.

Make sure you understand how this simple action lets us use the same port pins to control different devices. It is important to realize, however, that this is not *the* solution, rather it is only

```
void main(void)
    {
    int x;
    initialize_ports();
    initialize_LCD();
    do {
        out4data(1); // puts LCD in the READ mode so enabling it
                     // will not cause a garbage WRITE
        x = AtoD();    // while this conversion enables the LCD
        LCDcommand(CLEAR);
        printNumber(x);
        } while(x);
    }
```

Figure 9.3: This code fragment shows how to use the **AtoD()** tool.

one of many alternatives that can avoid potential conflicts. For example, the successive approximation algorithm could have been limited to 7 bits instead of 8. This would have allowed the LCD enable bit to remain high during conversions. Another possibility would have been to control the enable pin from the 4-bit port. Such a solution would have worked well here but would have caused conflicts when using the LCD with the keypad routines.

Understanding these conflicts and analyzing various alternative solutions is a very valuable exercise that should not be overlooked. Too many texts provide answers so that the reader sees them as the only solutions. Once that happens, it is easy for the reader to perform the exercise to see that the solution works rather than to see how and why it works. If you want to be able to apply the specific solutions in this text to general problems in the future, it is imperative that you understand both how and why these solutions work.

Figure 9.4 shows how we can sample a signal and then display it on an oscilloscope using the D/A converter in our A/D system. The samples are first stored in an array and then played back in the while loop section. A total of 256 samples are taken at a sample rate of 1000 samples per second (1 sample every millisecond). The program assumes that a switch is connected to the next available bit (B1) on the input port. Using the switch to enter a 0 on that pin will terminate the program.

The input signal could be any waveform (sine wave, for example) that has been offset to vary between 0 and 5 volts. Most signal generators can provide this offset easily. Due to the sample rate used here, the waveform being sampled should be at a relatively low frequency. A frequency of 100 Hz, for example, will be displayed with 10 samples for each waveform, with about 2½ waveforms being displayed on a scope connected to the output of the D/A converter.

```
void main()
    {
    int data[256];
    initialize_ports();
    for(i=0;i<256;i++)            // store samples
        {
        data[i]=AtoD();
        delay1ms(1);
        }
    while(inputdata() & 2)  // wait for switch press
        {
        for(i=0;i<256;i++)  // send data out
            {
            out8data(data[i]);
            delay1ms(1);
            }
        }
    }
```

Figure 9.4: This code captures data and displays it on an oscilloscope.

The waveform displayed by Figure 9.4 will be fairly smooth due to the resolution of the A/D system of 256 steps. If we changed the **for( )** in our **AtoD( )** tool from

```
for( mask = 0x80, ans = 0 ; mask ; mask = mask>>1)
```

to

```
for( mask = 0x80, ans = 0 ; mask>0x08 ; mask = mask>>1)
```

then **AtoD( )** will have a resolution of only 16 steps. If you use such a tool with the code in Figure 9.4, it will be easy to see the steps in the waveforms being displayed.

We can make our **AtoD( )** tool more useful if we can change the resolution by passing a parameter. If we simply pass an integer value named **resolution** and make the following change to the **for( )** statement, the module will change the resolution accordingly.

```
for( mask = 0x80, ans = 0 ; mask>((resolution*2)-1)/2 ; mask = mask>>1)
```

Of course, the actual resolution must always be an even power of 2 (256, 128, 64, 32, etc.), but the above formula will make the module use the smallest possible value greater than or equal to the resolution requested.

The major disadvantage to our **AtoD()** tool is that it is slow because software must handle shifting and comparing of the numbers. It is easy to see how shift registers and comparators can be used to implement our algorithm in hardware. The ADC0804 is a successive approximation A/D converter chip that provides relatively fast conversion times. Figure 9.5 shows the basic interface for the ADC0804 and many similar chips.

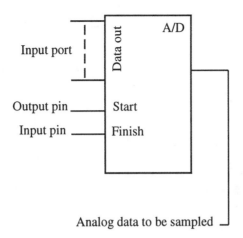

Figure 9.5: A/D chips can implement the successive approximation algorithm.

The general format for this type of circuit is that the analog signal is applied to one of the pins and the digital equivalent is read by a port (or bus) connected to the data pins. An additional output port pin can pulse a start line that initiates the conversion process. Another line can be read through an input pin to find out when the conversion is complete. This line is sometimes called the *intr* line because it can be used to trigger a hardware interrupt line on a controller chip. In many cases, the start can be connected to the finish so that each completion triggers a new conversion, creating a free-running mode. The ADC0804 can complete a conversion generally within 100 microseconds.

More features are available on other chips. The MAX161, for example, multiplexes 8 analog channels to a single converter. It even has on-board memory that stores the digital data automatically so that each channel can be read at any time (without delay). The MAX161 can perform conversions in 20 microseconds. Don't feel that these are the only 2 chips you should consider. Many A/D converters are available. Check manufacturers' data books and the Internet. Learning how to find the information you need from a data sheet is very important. After all, any chip presented here can easily be obsolete in the near future.

Flash A/D converters use many comparators to provide nearly instantaneous conversion times, but at a higher cost. When sampling video or other high-speed signals, such chips can be indispensable.

At the other extreme, there is a need for very inexpensive conversion systems. For example, some computer games need to read the position of a joystick potentiometer. Let's examine a totally different method for determining the position of the potentiometer. Figure 9.6 shows a 555 timer chip. This versatile chip can be configured in the monostable (one-shot) or astable (oscillator) mode. For this example, assume that the oscillator mode is being used.

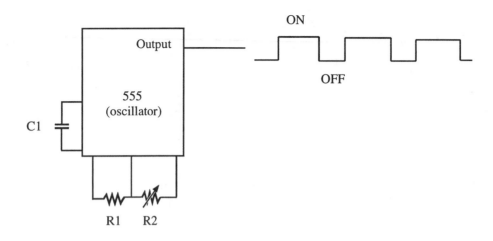

Figure 9.6: A 555 timer can be used as a cheap A/D.

Basically, two resistors (one of which can be a potentiometer) and a capacitor determine the time constants that control the ON and OFF times of the output waveform. Depending on which of the two resistors is variable, the ON time or the OFF time (or both) will change as the resistance is varied. This means that the resistance (and thus the position of the potentiometer) can be determined by measuring the ON (or OFF) time of the waveform. For this example, let's see how to measure the ON time. You should refer to the data sheet for a 555 (or other chip that you might select) and perform your own experiments to determine a configuration that will give you the maximum time variation as the potentiometer position is varied.

The basic principle we will use is simple. The output from the 555 will be connected to an input port pin; let's assume the LSB. The program will set the variable **ans** to 0 and then increment that variable during the period where the port pin is high. The longer the pin is high, the larger **ans** will get, thus making it proportional to the position of the potentiometer.

What makes this principle difficult at all is that we must make sure the computer does not start counting in the middle of a high pulse. Therefore, we must wait for the input pin to go low and then wait for it to go high. At that point, we can count until it goes low again and we have our answer. Figure 9.7 shows the code for accomplishing this task.

If the **readPOT()** routine is entered when the signal is already low, it will immediately fall through to the second loop. In any case, the second loop will prevent progressing to the third loop until a rising edge occurs at the port pin. The third loop will count as long as the port pin remains high. If the value of **ans** is too large we have several options. A small delay can be inserted inside the loop or the value of **ans** can be divided by an appropriate scale factor.

Another alternative is to adjust the values of the components associated with the 555 timer so that the ON time is shortened. In fact, to maximize our performance, we should try to keep the conversion times as short as possible. The frequency of the 555 should be fast, but not so fast

```
int readPOT(void)
    {
    int ans=0;
    while(inputdata()&1)
        ;      // loop as long as the LSB is high
    while(!(inputdata()&1))
        ;      // loop as long as the LSB is low
    while(inputdata()&1)
        ans++;   // increment until low again
    return ans;
    }
```

Figure 9.7: This **readPOT**() routine can determine the position of a potentiometer.

that the computer cannot count to the desired resolution. Finally, you should probably place a small resistor in series with the potentiometer to prevent killing the oscillation when the potentiometer has a 0 resistance reading.

Calculate proper values for your components after referring to a data sheet. Determining the appropriate component values for acceptable operation on your computer might take a little effort, but the low cost of this converter can make it very worthwhile. Notice that the low cost is not just the price of the 555. The fact that this method requires only 1 I/O pin makes it a viable solution even in minimal system configurations.

A major drawback to this method is the long conversion time required compared with other methods. Even so, many applications do not require high speed sampling. Assume that we are using a thermistor to measure the temperature of an automobile engine block. Even reading the temperature only once per second is probably adequate, and this method can do far better than that.

If we need more accuracy but still want to use a single I/O pin, we can use an A/D chip with a serial interface. This solution will be explored later in the text.

A/D converters provide a means for the computer to sample many external processes. For example, thermistors change their resistance based on their temperature. Photoresistors are affected by light and strain gauges by force. A voltage divider made up of one of these devices and a fixed resistance can provide an appropriate signal to be read using an A/D converter. Another alternative is to use one of the above devices as one of the resistors controlling the oscillation behavior of a 555 timer.

As a final note, many embedded controllers, such as the Motorola 68HC11, have internal successive approximation A/D converters that can be used with no additional external components. Refer to the manuals of any embedded controller that you might be using to determine how to initiate the conversion process and/or read the digital values created by its converters.

ASSIGNMENT: After studying the examples in this exercise, create appropriate tools for reading analog voltages and/or potentiometer positions. Ensure that the tools work with small demonstration programs and then write programs that perform as indicated below. In some cases, there may be conflicts because 2 devices are connected to a single I/O pin. Resolve any conflicts that you may have by using a different method of A/D, changing the hardware/software interface for one or both of the devices, or by other methods that you find appropriate.

1. Display the value read from an A/D converter on an LCD.
2. Display the value read from an A/D converter on 2 multiplexed 7-segment LEDs. Allow the user to choose if the display is in hex or decimal.
3. Capture several different waveforms (sine, triangle, and ramp, for example) and store them in different arrays. Use switches or the keypad to allow the user to select which waveform will be displayed on an oscilloscope.
4. Create a bar graph on the LCD using X's or some other character and control the amplitude displayed with a potentiometer.
5. Connect a variable voltage source to the input of an A/D converter. Scale the reading so that it reflects the actual voltage being sampled and display that value in some appropriate manner.
6. Use a photoresistor, thermistor, or other appropriate device and demonstrate that the readings obtained vary as expected as some external condition is varied. For example, you can move a soldering iron close to a thermistor.

REVIEW QUESTIONS
1. Why are A/D converters necessary? How are they used?
2. Explain how the successive approximation algorithm accomplishes its goal. Compare the time required to make a reading with a 256-step resolution to one with only 16 steps.
3. How can a program detect a rising or falling edge of a waveform connected to an input pin?
4. Why would hardware-based successive approximation chips be faster than a software implementation?
5. Why is the 555 method of A/D conversion not appropriate for all situations? Give some examples of when it might be an appropriate solution.

Exercise 10
DC Motor Speed Control

PURPOSE: The purpose of this exercise is to introduce the interface hardware and programming concepts needed to control the speed and direction of a dc motor. As in previous chapters, the programming modules developed for controlling the motor will be implemented as tools so that they may be used in later exercises to develop system-oriented projects.

OBJECTIVES: After the completion of this exercise, the reader should be able to:
- Describe the hardware and software requirements for interfacing a dc motor to a computer.
- Identify the potential problems associated with controlling a dc motor and describe some solutions to those problems.
- Construct the necessary hardware to interface a dc motor to a computer.
- Implement the software tools necessary to control a dc motor from a computer.
- Utilize software tools to control a dc motor that has been interfaced to a computer.

THEORY: Although many items have been interfaced to the computer in previous exercises, none of these items has required any significant amount of power. This allowed us to connect to the external devices with little or no buffering of the port lines. A dc motor, however, will draw substantially more current than the port (or even the inverting buffers used in previous exercises) can supply. As such, we will need to use transistors to buffer the port. This exercise will utilize standard bipolar transistors, but *Darlington* transistors can be substituted if higher currents are needed. FETs or JFETs are also viable options and should be explored in very high-current situations.

Let's begin by examining how a transistor can be used as a buffer. Look at Figure 10.1.

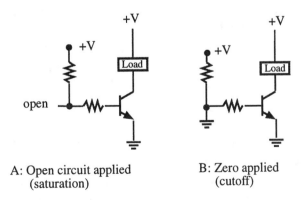

A: Open circuit applied
(saturation)

B: Zero applied
(cutoff)

Figure 10.1: An NPN transistor allows a port pin to control a device needing more current.

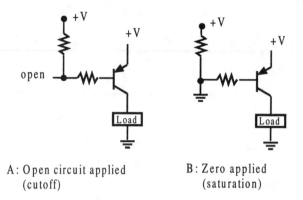

A: Open circuit applied   B: Zero applied
       (cutoff)   (saturation)

Figure 10.2: A PNP transistor can also be used, but a low from the port activates the motor.

The load shown in Figure 10.1 represents the motor. To turn the motor on, we need to force the transistor towards *saturation* by making the base voltage more positive than the emitter. Figure 10.1A uses two resistors to do this, thus creating current flow through the base of the transistor. This causes the emitter-collector junction to reduce its resistance and conduct current to the load. If enough base current is supplied, the transistor will reduce the emitter-collector resistance to near 0. The amount of base current required depends, of course, on the gain of the transistor and the current requirements of the load.

Figure 10.1B shows how to divert the current from the base to ground. This places the transistor in *cutoff* and shuts down the motor. Thus, we can control the ON-OFF state of the motor by supplying a 1 or a 0 from the port to the junction between the two resistors. A 1 from the port would turn the motor ON and a 0 would turn it OFF. We can also use a PNP transistor to control the motor, as shown in Figure 10.2.

In the case of Figure 10.2, base current is provided by grounding the base to create the proper bias on the base junction. Notice that this is the opposite of the NPN circuit. In this example, a 1 from the port turns the motor OFF and a 0 turns the motor ON. Although we can easily use NPN or PNP transistors to control our motor, let's stick with NPN transistors, at least for the moment.

Figure 10.3 shows a complete circuit for turning a dc motor ON or OFF with a signal from a port pin. Notice that an inverter has been added to act as a buffer. Buffering is optional, of course, but as mentioned in earlier exercises, some form of buffering is wise because it lessens the chance of port damage if you make a mistake wiring your circuit. Another advantage of the buffer, especially if it is of an open-collector type, is that it allows the voltage for the transistor (and thus the motor) to be higher than the 5 volts used for standard TTL gates and computer ports.

Another addition to Figure 10.3 is the diode between the transistor's collector and emitter. Since a motor is composed of a relatively large inductor, it has the capacity to generate a large back EMF voltage when the magnetic fields collapse. This voltage can damage the transistor if it is not handled correctly. The diode is oriented so that a reverse voltage (the back EMF) will forward bias the diode and prevent damage to the transistor. The circuit will work without the diode, but the life span of the transistor will be greatly reduced.

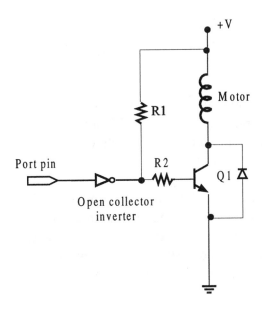

Figure 10.3: The full circuit for turning a motor ON and OFF.

Now that we see how transistors are used, let's examine them more closely. Notice that the load resides in the collector leg of both the NPN and PNP circuits. Also, note that since the NPN and PNP transistors are reversed in their emitter-collector orientations, the load appears in the ground lead of the PNP circuit and the supply lead of the NPN circuit. This was not an accident. Figure 10.4 shows a NPN circuit, but with the load in the emitter leg.

At first, it might appear that the circuit of Figure 10.2 will work as well as the circuit of Figure 10.1. Unfortunately, this is not the case. Since a standard TTL signal will supply about 4 volts for a logic 1, the base of the transistor will be at that voltage. For the base-emitter junction to remain forward biased (to turn the motor ON), the emitter must be no higher than 3.3 volts. This is true because a forward-biased PN junction drops 0.7 volts. The 3.3 volts supplied to the motor is a result of the 4 volts applied to the base minus the 0.7-volt junction drop.

This simply means that, with the load in the emitter lead of an NPN transistor driven by a TTL port, the voltage supplied to the load can be no higher than about 3.3 volts. Notice that

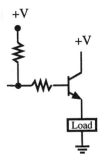

Figure 10.4: The load should ***not*** be placed as shown here.

increasing the voltage supplied to the collector does no good. In fact, since the increased voltage will be dropped across the transistor itself, all increasing the supply voltage will only heat up the transistor.

There are many solutions for problems such as this. For example, if an open-collector inverter is used, then the voltage applied to the base is not the 4 volts from the port but the higher transistor supply voltage. Rather than worry about all the possible problems and their respective solutions, however, I simply suggest that you place loads in the collector circuits.

Although we are not finished discussing the hardware portion of the interface, it is time to shift our attention to software. If we need only to turn the motor on and off using the circuit of Figure 10.3, then the actions needed are almost trivial. We simply send a logic 0 to the proper pin when we want the motor turned on and a logic 1 when we want it turned off. (If a PNP transistor is used instead of an NPN, a logic 1 will turn on the transistor.) If we want to control the speed of the motor, though, the problem is a little more complicated.

One solution that might come to mind is using a D/A converter to control the base current of a transistor. Changing the base current affect the collector current and thus controls the speed of a motor placed in the collector circuit. This method causes the transistor to get very hot, however, especially if the motor drew even a modest amount of current. Let's see why. Assume for a moment that the motor is a 12-volt motor that draws 500 ma for a given load situation. Assume further that we control the base current to lower the speed so that the motor is being supplied 6 volts at 250 ma. If the motor is getting 6 volts, the transistor must be dropping the remaining 6 volts (12–6). Since both the motor and the transistor must conduct the 250 ma of current, the transistor must dissipate 1.5 watts ($.250 \times 6$).

Many small transistors are capable of handling 500 ma, but it is harder to find one that can handle the heat generated from dissipating 1.5 watts—at least not without a hefty heat sink. From another point of view, why should we spend money on energy to heat the transistor? Our goal is to get that energy to the motor where it can be converted into motion rather than heat. Because of these problems, we generally don't want to control a motor's speed this way.

On the other hand, the ON/OFF control discussed earlier in this exercise is very effective and efficient. When the motor is ON, the transistor is in saturation, providing a high current but dropping zero voltage (because the collector-emitter resistance is near 0). In the OFF state, the current through the transistor is 0. Since the power dissipated by a transistor is the voltage across the transistor times the current through it we can see why the ON/OFF method is efficient. When the motor is ON, the voltage across the transistor is near 0, and when the motor is OFF, the current is 0. This means that nearly all the power is transferred to the load and the transistor stays cool.

What we need is a way of controlling the motor's speed without abandoning the ON/OFF principles. Fortunately, this is easy. All we have to do is *pulse* the motor at different duty cycles. Figure 10.5 shows the waveforms for different duty cycles.

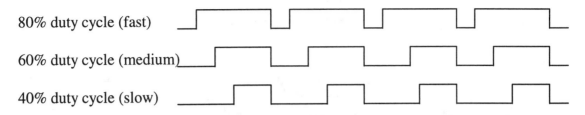

80% duty cycle (fast)

60% duty cycle (medium)

40% duty cycle (slow)

Figure 10.5: Controlling motor speed with the duty cycle is very efficient.

The principle is simple. The greater the ratio of ON time to OFF time, the faster the motor turns. The waveforms of Figure 10.5 assume that the motor is ON when they are HIGH and the motor is OFF when they are LOW. You might expect a 50% duty cycle to cause the motor to run at half speed. Generally, this is not true. Depending on the load connected to the motor, it might take a 30% duty cycle just to get the motor to begin to turn, which would mean that half speed can be achieved with something near a 65% duty cycle.

Notice also that all the waveforms in Figure 10.5 has the same frequency. The question is, What frequency should be used. It should be obvious that too low a frequency will cause the motor to surge. Take this case to the extreme, for example. Assume the motor is ON for 1 second and OFF for 1 second. Unless the motor's load is acting as a tremendous flywheel, you won't get a motor running at medium speed. It will simply be fast for 1 second and then slow for 1 second, etc.

As we increase the frequency, the motor will eventually appear to be running smoothly at a constant reduced speed. If the frequency becomes too high, however, the inductive reactance (which increases with frequency) of the motor will reduce the motor current to the point where the motor's torque is reduced, if it is not lost altogether. The exact frequency will depend on the motor's inductance and the flywheel effect of the load. I have found that frequencies between 50 and 100 Hertz seem to work fine for most applications involving small to medium motors.

Figure 10.6 shows a small code fragment for controlling the motor. It assumes that the motor circuit is connected to the LSB of the 8-bit port. This example lets the motor run at the specified speed until a key is pressed on the keypad (Exercise 6). Of course, you can use a forever loop such as **while**(1), or a **for**( ) loop that specifies how many cycles to provide.

```
// the variable speed (value 0–15) controls the speed
while( ! is_key_pressed() )
    {
    out8data(1);      // turn motor on
    delay1ms(speed);
    out8data(0);      // turn motor off
    delay1ms(15-speed);
    }
```

Figure 10.6: This code fragment controls the speed of the motor.

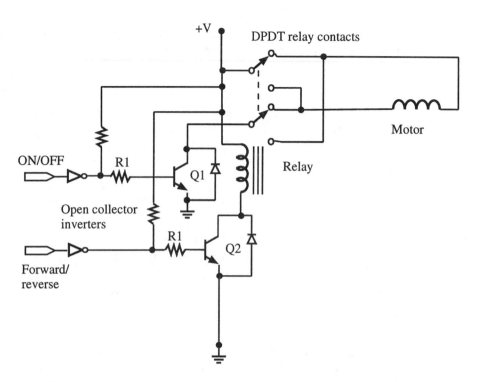

Figure 10.7: A relay can provide a simple means of reversing a dc motor.

Notice how the code creates the proper duty cycle while maintaining the same frequency. The total period for the waveform will always be 15 ms as long as the value of the variable speed is between 0 and 15, inclusive. A value of 15 will make the motor run at full speed, while a value of 0 will stop the motor. If you are using a transistor circuit where a port value of 0 turns on the motor, just reverse the **out8data(1)** and **out8data(0)** statements.

Now that we can control the speed of a motor, we need to consider the ability to control its direction as well. Figure 10.7 shows how a relay can be used to reverse the leads to the motor itself to make it run in reverse.

Two port pins are now used. One provides the ON/OFF or speed control that we just discussed. The other controls whether or not a DPDT relay is energized. When the relay is active, it reverses the power connections to the motor. Since the relay is also an inductive load, transistor Q2 also requires a protecting diode. The software needs only to hold the F/R pin at the proper state while the ON/OFF line is being pulsed. We will discuss this software more in a moment, but for now let's examine some of the shortcomings of this circuit.

The fact that it uses a mechanical relay means that the circuit will have a relatively short life, at least when compared to a full solid-state circuit. Another disadvantage of a relay is its slow reaction time, again compared to solid-state devices. Look at Figure 10.8 to see a better method for controlling speed and direction.

If only transistors Q1 and Q4 are turned on, then the current flows down through Q1 and from left to right through the motor to Q4. To reverse the motor, turn transistors Q2 and Q3 on. Notice

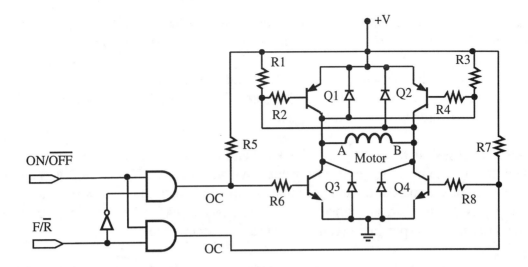

Figure 10.8: Four transistors provide a fast, trouble-free method for controlling speed and direction.

that this causes the current to flow from right to left through the motor. If all 4 transistors are turned ON (or even just Q1 and Q3 or just Q2 and Q4), there will be a direct short across the power supply and the conducting transistors will go up in smoke.

Another item worth mentioning is that the bottom 2 transistors are NPN and the top 2 are PNP. This conforms with our desire to keep the motor in the collector legs of each transistor. Notice also that a logic 1 (applied at the base of the transistor) is needed to turn on the bottom transistors and a logic 0 is needed for the top transistors. The AND gates on the left of the figure are used to turn the NPN transistors ON and OFF. The gates also make sure that only one of the NPN transistors can be turned on at a time, thus preventing the disaster mentioned in the previous paragraph.

When the ON/OFF line from the port is low, both AND gates send a logic 0 to the NPN transistors, placing them in cutoff. When the ON/OFF line is high, the F/R line decides which gate will send a 0 and which will send a 1. This explains how the NPN transistors are controlled. But what about the PNP transistors?

Remember, the PNP transistors require a low on their base to activate them. Examine Figure 10.8 and you will see that the base of Q1 is connected to the collector of Q4 (through R2). When Q4 is turned on (by the AND gate) its shorting action (collector-emitter) will turn on Q1. Similarly, when Q3 is turned on it turns on Q2. The actual resistors needed depend on the transistors and motors used, but 1 K for R2, R4, R6, and R8 and 10 K for R1, R3, R5, and R7 will work in most situations. As previously mentioned, open collector gates are better if the motor supply is significantly greater than 5 volts. If your motor draws more than a few hundred milliamps, you should probably use Darlington transistors throughout the circuit.

Now that we have a fast, reliable interface for the motor and a general algorithm for the controlling software, let's develop a tool module for controlling the motor. At the very least, we should be able to specify a speed and a direction. It will make our tool more flexible, however, if we can also specify how long, in milliseconds, the duration of the specified speed should last. This addition will allow us to run the motor for a short period and then regain control so that we may check the keypad or other devices for activity. Figure 10.9 shows a listing for such a tool. The algorithm is basically the same as the one in Figure 10.6 but with a few improvements. It assumes that the motor is connected to the 8-bit port, with the speed governed by the LSB (B0) and the direction governed by the next bit (B1).

FORWARD and REVERSE have been defined so that the calling program can specify the direction without remembering the specific values. We will see why FORWARD was defined as 2 in a moment. The first part of the program makes sure that the calling routine asks for a speed within range. The **for** loop creates **duration**/15 cycles, each of which is 15 ms long (67 Hz). This allows the duration to be specified in milliseconds and is accurate to 15 ms.

The motor is turned on only if the speed is greater than 0. This prevents short spikes of current from being sent to the motor when a speed of 0 is requested (as would happen with the code in Figure 10.6). This isn't really necessary, because the short spike would not be enough to energize the motor. Even so, it makes sense to prevent any motor current when the motor is off.

When the motor is turned ON, the data sent to the port should be a 1 (to turn the motor ON) bitwise ORed with the direction data. If the direction is 2, then the F/R bit is set. If the direction is 0, then the F/R bit is clear. If a different bit is used to control the F/R line, the appropriate changes will have to be made. For example, if the MSB were used to control the F/R line, then FORWARD would have to be defined as 128 or hex 80. Similarly, the number that controls the ON/OFF state should be changed to reflect the port pin used for that purpose.

```
#define FORWARD 2
#define REVERSE  0
void DCmotor(int speed, int direction, int duration)
    {
    int i;
    if(speed>15)
        speed=15;
    if(speed<0)
        speed=0;
    for(i=0; i<duration/15; i++)
        {
        if(speed>0)
            out8data(direction | 1);
        delay1ms(speed);
        out8data(0);
        delay1ms(15-speed);
        }
    }
```

Figure 10.9: Tool module for controlling a dc motor.

Let's see how we can use the tool module in an application program. Figure 10.10 shows how to use the keypad (Exercise 6) to control the speed of the motor. Remember, the keypad generated keycodes from 0–15. The motor runs at the selected speed (1–14) as long as a key is not pressed. When a key is pressed, the code is obtained and used to set the speed. Each time the motor is stopped (by entering a speed of 0) the direction is modified so that when a new speed is selected, the motor will reverse its motion. It is assumed that the motor tool has been saved as a library tool and included prior to this main(). In this example, selecting a speed of 15 will terminate the program.

The motor is turned ON at the present speed and direction for approximately 100 milliseconds. The keypad is checked and if a key has not been pressed, the motor will run again for 100 milliseconds. This sequence continues unless a key is pressed.

```
void main(void)
    {
    int speed = 0, dir = FORWARD;
    initialize_ports( );
    while(speed!=15)
        {
        DCmotor(speed, dir, 100);
        if(is_key_pressed( ) )
            {
            speed = keycode( );
            if(speed = = 0)
                dir = dir ^ FORWARD;
            while(is_key_pressed( ) )   // keep motor running until key released
                DCmotor(speed,dir,100);
            }
        }
    }
```

Figure 10.10: The dc motor tool makes controlling the motor easy.

When a keypress is detected, the code for the key is obtained and used to set the speed. If it is 0, the state of the direction is toggled by EXCLUSIVE-ORing it with the value FORWARD. The main loop continues until the value of the speed is set to 15.

Although the previous hardware designs are adequate for many motors, problems can arise if current surges exist because the motor draws very large amounts of power or if the motor brushes are particularly noisy. Either condition can generate enough noise through the common ground between the motor power supply and the computer power supply to cause a computer failure. In such cases, it is not enough to have separate supplies for the computer and the motor; the 2 supplies must not even have a ground connection in common. One method for providing such isolation is through optoisolators, as shown in Figure 10.11.

An optoisolator is basically an LED and a phototransistor enclosed in a plastic case. When the LED is turned ON, the light emitted forces the transistor to conduct. Since we have been using

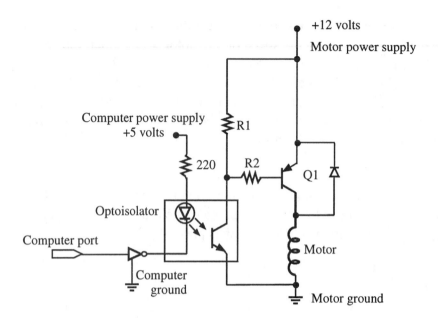

Figure 10.11: Optical isolation can prevent noise generated by the motor from interfering with the computer's operation.

NPN transistors in most of the previous examples, I chose to use a PNP here. When the computer port pin goes high, the output of the inverter goes low, causing the LED to light. This forces the junction of R1 and R2 to ground potential, which forward biases the base-emitter junction of Q1. The resulting base current turns Q1 ON, which delivers power to the motor.

Optical isolation is not often needed, but when it is, it is a far easier solution than trying to filter the noise. Although the drive circuits and software tools in this exercise were used primarily to control motors, they can be used anytime you need the computer to control the power to an external device.

ASSIGNMENT: After constructing an appropriate hardware interface for a dc motor and testing the motor interface routines described in this exercise, write application programs to perform as indicated below.
1. Utilize 1 of the analog to digital functions from Exercise 9 so that the speed of a motor can be controlled with the value obtained from a potentiometer. The ports and pins used to control the motor may need to vary based on which A/D functions you use.
2. Expand on Problem 1 above so that the potentiometer can control the speed and direction. The motor should be OFF when the potentiometer is in the center position, and it should increase in speed as the potentiometer is turned away from the center. The motor should reach its maximum forward speed when the potentiometer is turned all the way to the right. Likewise, turning the potentiometer all the way to the left will cause the motor to reach maximum speed in reverse. Hint: If x is the value obtained from the A/D and it varies from 0–255, then we can convert it to a proper speed and direction with the following code.

```
        if(x<128)
            {
            x = (127–x)/8;
            dir = REVERSE;
            }
        else
            {
            x = (x–128)/8;
            dir = FORWARD;
            }
```

3. Use 2 keys on the keypad as increment and decrement keys. Each press of the keys will cause the motor to increase or decrease in speed. A third key should be used to toggle the direction of the motor. Finally, a fourth key should be used to terminate the program.

REVIEW QUESTIONS

1. How does a transistor act as a buffer?
2. Why should the load generally go in the collector leg when controlling a transistor with a TTL signal?
3. What is back EMF and how do we prevent it from causing problems?
4. Why is varying the duty cycle a better method of speed control than varying the amount of base current?
5. When using the duty cycle method of control, why is the frequency of the speed control waveform important?
6. What are 2 disadvantages of using a relay to control the direction of a motor?
7. Why are both NPN and PNP transistors used in Figure 10.8?
8. Why do we need a duration parameter in the dcmotor() function in Figure 10.9?
9. What are optoisolators and why are they needed?
10. Explain how the hint provided for Assignment 2 works. What are the ranges for the value of x when the code has completed its transformation? How does the value of x change as the potentiometer is varied? How many numbers in the original potentiometer reading will provide a speed of 0 to turn off the motor? List these numbers.

Exercise 11
Controlling Stepper Motors

PURPOSE: The purpose of this exercise is to introduce the hardware and software needed to control the speed, direction, and position of a stepper motor.

OBJECTIVES: After the completion of this exercise, the reader should be able to:
- Describe the hardware needed for interfacing a stepper motor to a port.
- Describe a basic software algorithm for controlling stepper motors.
- Compare and contrast normal-step, half-step, and full-torque drive.
- Utilize stepper motor tool routines to create a set of specified motor actions.
- Understand how stepper motor control functions can be converted to a class system.

THEORY: In Exercise 10, we saw how to control a dc motor's speed and direction. In later exercises we will also see how to control the position of a dc motor. While it is possible to control the position of a dc motor, often a stepper motor is a better choice when precise positioning is required.

Stepper motors generally have less torque than dc motors and nearly always have very low speeds when compared to dc motors. They have a big advantage, however, when it comes to moving their shaft to a particular position.

Stepper motors come in several varieties. This exercise assumes a unipolar motor (single supply voltage) with a 4-coil, 5- or 6-wire interface. Electrically, the motor appears as shown in Figure 11.1.

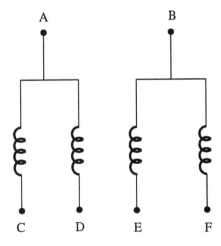

Figure 11.1: A unipolar stepper motor consists of 4 coils.

As you can see in Figure 11.1, the 4 coils are arranged with a 6-wire connection. In a 5-wire motor, points A and B are connected together internally. In a typical situation, points A and B are both connected to +V of the motor supply. Any of the coils (motor windings) can be energized by grounding the appropriate wire (C, D, E, or F).

When energized, each of the motor windings becomes a magnetic source that attracts the motor rotor to the next stator position. If the windings are energized in the proper sequence, the rotor is *pulled* around its axis, causing rotation. The step size depends on internal construction and can range from 90 degrees to less than 1 degree, with 3.75 and 7.5-degree steps being very typical.

Interfacing a stepper motor to a port can, and often should be accomplished with integrated circuits designed specifically for that purpose. For now though, let's examine a brute force approach so that we can acquire as much knowledge as possible. Figure 11.2 shows how to interface a stepper motor to a port. Naturally, other methods (PNP transistors, optoisolators, etc.) also apply.

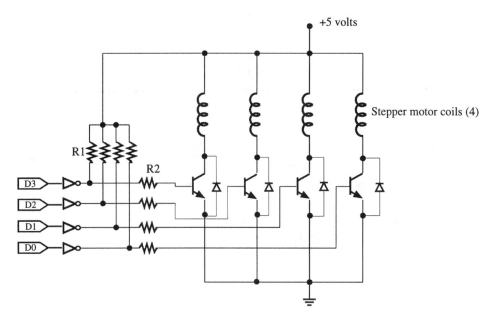

Figure 11.2: Interfacing a stepper motor with transistors requires 4 port pins.

In Figure 11.2 4 port pins are used to control the ON/OFF state of 4 transistors that supply current to the individual windings of the stepper motor. If the windings are in the proper order and if they are turned on in sequence, the motor will rotate. If we assume that the LSB is at the bottom of the figure, then the port must put out the following 4-bit binary numbers in sequence:

1000   0100   0010   0001

This means that the code fragment in Figure 11.3 will step the motor continuously. It assumes that the motor is connected to the 8-bit port on the lower nibble. Each pass through the loop steps the motor 4 times. The 100-ms delay establishes a speed of 10 steps per second. The RPM rate will depend on the step angle of the motor being used. If the interface is working correctly and the motor does not step, then the order of the windings needs to be rearranged.

```
while (1)
    {
    out8data(8);
    delay1ms(100);
    out8data(4);
    delay1ms(100);
    out8data(2);
    delay1ms(100);
    out8data(1);
    delay1ms(100);
    }
```

Figure 11.3: This code fragment will drive a stepper motor.

Let's see how we can make the program of Figure 11.3 more efficient. Notice that we are doing the same actions 4 times and the only difference is that different data is being sent to the port. Typically, if we want a loop to operate on different data as the loop progresses, then the data should be stored in an array. Look at the code fragment in Figure 11.4.

The code in Figure 11.4 is much more efficient than that of Figure 11.3. The data items needed to step the array are stored in an array. The index variable **n** is used to access the array. By incrementing **n**, each element is sent to the port in proper order. When **n** exceeds 3, it is set back to 0. If we want to run the motor in reverse, all that we need to do in Figure 11.4 is decrement **n** each time through the loop. Of course, we also need to check to see if **n** becomes negative. If it does, set **n** back to 3.

In addition to the 1, 2, 4, 8 sequence used in Figure 11.4, we have 2 other alternatives. First, instead of having only 1 winding ON at a time, we can have 2. With 1 winding ON, it is easy to imagine the rotor pointing toward the magnet. If 2 adjacent magnets are ON, imagine the rotor being between the 2 poles. If we send the binary numbers 1100 0110 0011 1001 to the port, then the motor will behave as before, except that its step points will be between 2 poles rather than at each pole. Since two windings will be pulling the rotor to the next position, the motor will have much greater torque.

```
int data[4]={8,4,2,1};
int n=0;
while(1)
    {
    out8data(data[n]);
    delay1ms(100);
    n++;
    if(n>3)
        n=0;
    }
```

Figure 11.4: Using an array makes the code for stepping a motor more efficient.

The third way of controlling the motor combines the first 2 methods. The idea is to point the rotor at a step position by turning ON 1 coil, then moving it halfway between the present position and the next by turning ON 2 coils, then moving it the remaining halfway by turning ON 1 coil, etc. This method doubles the resolution of the motor by moving it in half-step increments. The half-step method requires 8 elements in the array, because it takes 8 half-steps to complete a full sequence. Figure 11.5 shows how all 3 methods can be combined and implemented as a tool to make controlling a stepper motor easy.

```
#define NORMAL          0
#define FULLTORQUE      1
#define HALFSTEP        2

void step(int steps, int speed, int style)
  {
  // place all 3 methods in a table
  static int table[3][8] =    {1,2,4,8,1,2,4,8,
                               3,6,12,9,3,6,12,9,
                               1,3,2,6,4,12,8,9};
  static int ptr = 0;
  int i,num,dir=1;
  if(steps<0)
      dir=-1;
  num = abs(steps);    // absolute value function
  for(i=0; i<num; i++)
      {
      ptr+=dir;           // increment or decrement ptr as needed
      if(ptr>7)
          ptr=0;
      if(ptr<0)
          ptr=7;
      out8data(table[style][ptr]);
      delay1ms(speed);
      }
  }

void main(void)    // example use of the above tool
  {
  int st;
  int sequence[5] = {100,-50,50,-100,0};
  initialize_ports( );
  for(st = 0; sequence[st]; st++)
      step(sequence[st],200,FULLTORQUE);
  }
```

Figure 11.5: A step tool makes controlling a stepper motor a snap.

The two-dimensional array allows the data words for all 3 movement methods to be stored at once. To simplify the program, the numbers for both normal and full torque are repeated so that all data sets are each composed of 8 numbers. The variable **style** that is passed to the function is used to control which step data to use. The variable **ptr** keeps track of which array element is presently being used. Notice that **ptr** is a *static* variable, so it is not destroyed when the function terminates. This allows the motor to continue stepping where it left off the last time the function was used.

No direction is passed to this function. Instead, the number of steps to take is assumed to be positive or negative to represent forward and reverse. In the sample **main()**, a step sequence is stored in an array and processed until a step number of 0 is encountered.

If you are programming using a controller such as the 8051 or 68HC11, you might be using the C language rather than C++ because of the limited memory available on a controller. If you are using a PC, however, you are probably using a full-featured C++ compiler, which would allow you the option of dealing with objects. Figure 11.6 shows a straightforward translation of the code in Figure 11.5 to a class-oriented structure. If you are not familiar with classes and objects, you can skip this section.

```
class Stepper
    {
    private:
        int style;
    public:
        Stepper::Stepper(int how = 0)
            {
            style = how;  // default: normal steps
            }
        void step(int,int);
        void setstyle(int);

    };

void Stepper::setstyle(int st)
    {
    if(st>=0 && st<=2)
        style=st;
    }

void Stepper::step(int steps, int speed)
    {
    static int ptr = 0;
    static table[3][8] =  {1,2,4,8,1,2,4,8,
                           3,6,12,9,3,6,12,9,
                           1,3,2,6,4,12,8,9};
    int i,num,dir=1;
```

Figure 11.6: A class implementation of the step tool.

```
      if(steps<0)
          dir=-1;
      num = abs(steps);
      for(i=0; i<num; i++)
          {
          ptr+=dir;
          if(ptr>7)
              ptr=0;
          if(ptr<0)
              ptr=7;
          out8data(table[style][ptr]);
          delay1ms(speed);
          }
      }

  void main(void)
      {
      int st;
      Stepper motor(HALFSTEP);   // create instance of type Stepper
      int sequence[5] = {100,-50,50,-100,0};
      initialize_ports( );
      for(st = 0; sequence[st]; st++)
          motor.step(sequence[st],200);
      }
```

Figure 11.6: (continued)

If you are familiar with classes, the transformation to Figure 11.7 should be easy to follow. It gives us a default value for style that is encapsulated into the object, but little else is gained. It is a starting point, however, and it is valid to see it as a bridge between functional tools and objects. If we really want to take advantage of objects, the class should allow us to create *instances* for each motor we want to use. This would be possible if we had more ports available. Each time a **Stepper** variable is created, our code should assign a port and motor for it to use. Without this idea, the reuse of the code is limited at best.

The final portion of this exercise will examine how to redesign Figure 11.6 so that up to 4 motors can be controlled, each as an instance of the class. We don't have enough port pins to control 4 motors using the previous techniques, so this final program will also demonstrate how to use an integrated circuit designed to ease the interfacing problems associated with stepper motors.

If we examine the step algorithm described in this exercise, it should be plain that it can be implemented in hardware with a shift register organized as a ring counter that can be shifted forward or backward. The method of stepping can be controlled by parallel loading the register with the appropriate initial value.

```
class Stepper
  {
  private:
      int motor_num;
  public:
      Stepper::Stepper(int mot=0)
          {

              style = how;  // default: normal steps
              motor_num = mot;  // default motor # 0
              }
      void step(int,int);
};

void Stepper::step(int steps, int speed)
  {
  // establish masks for each motor for selecting the proper bits
  static motorONdata[4] = {0x80,0x20,0x08,0x02};
  static motorDIRdata[4] = {0x40,0x10,0x04,0x01};
  int i,num,dir;
  dir = motorDIRdata[motor_num];
  if(steps<0)
      dir=dir^motorDIRdata[motor_num];
  num = abs(steps);
  out8data(dir); // estabish the direction before stepping
  delay1ms(1);
  for(i=0; i<num; i++)
      {
      out8data(motorONdata[motor_num] | dir); // step line high
      delay1ms(speed/2);
      out8data(dir);  // step line low, direction kept constant
      delay1ms(speed/2);
      }
  }

void main(void)
  {
  // create 4 motors, each with a different motor number
  Stepper m0(0), m1(1), m2(2), m3(3);
  // step each motor, pass steps and delay
  initialize_ports( );
  m0.step(15,200);
  m1.step(-50,100);
  m2.step(-35,150);
  m3.step(100,50);
}
```

Figure 11.7: This class implementation controls 4 motors.

Integrated circuits such as the UNC5804 place the shift register and the transistor drivers along with the necessary control logic on a single chip. The interface to the computer consists of only 2 signals. The high/low level applied to one of the inputs controls the direction of the rotation. The other pin steps the motor in the selected direction each time it is pulsed. The controlling software has little to do but decide how fast to pulse the step pin.

For this example, we will assume that 4 stepper motors are interfaced to the 8-bit output port using 4 integrated circuits such as the UNC5804. The 2 least significant bits control the first motor. The next 2 bits control the next motor, etc. The LSB of each 2-bit pair controls the direction. The upper bit must be pulsed to step the motor. Obviously, the LSB must remain stable (either high or low) while the other bit is being pulsed.

A motor number has been added to the private section of the class. This controls which bits will be used when a motor is accessed. The constructor for the class allows the motor number to be specified and assumes a motor number of 0 if none is specified. Once a motor object has been initialized, the member function **step**() can move the motor any number of steps, forward or backward, and at any speed acceptable to the physical limitations of the motor.

No style has been implemented in this example. Stepper motor driver chips have options for selecting a style, but it is assumed here that the style is selected by the hardware, perhaps with DIP switches. If we had enough port pins available, we could certainly add this function to our software system.

The program assumes that all the port lines remain low when they are not in use and are pulsed high as needed, meaning they return to the low state when the pulse is completed. The direction line is set to its proper state and given 1 millisecond to settle before the actual stepping begins. The proper direction is ORed with the step signal when the step line is sent high. The direction is sent alone when the pulse line is returned to ground. This keeps the direction line stable while the step line is being pulsed.

In Exercise 17, we will address the need to control the stepping action of several motors simultaneously; that is, we might want to move several motors at different speeds, with each requiring a different number of steps so that all the motors arrive at their destinations at the same time. For now, however, you will have to be content with controlling a single motor.

ASSIGNMENT: Implement a hardware interface for a stepper motor and test the examples in this exercise to verify that they work properly. Create a stepper motor tool file so that it may be used to create your own applications associated with stepper motors. Once you have finished the file, create the following programs.
1. Use a potentiometer and the **AtoD**() or **readPOT**() function so that the potentiometer can be used to control the speed of a stepper motor.
2. Modify Assignment 1 so that when the potentiometer is in its center position, the motor stops. As the potentiometer is turned left or right, the motor should turn (forward or backward) with increasing speed the further the potentiometer is turned.

3. Use a potentiometer and the **AtoD()** or **readPOT()** function so that the stepper motor tracks the position of the potentiometer. Connect some type of pointer to the shafts of the motor and the potentiometer so that it is easy to see that the shafts always form the same angle.
4. Use the keypad to control the speed and direction of a stepper motor. Define your own interface.
5. Use the keypad to control the position of the motor. Have at least 10 stops (use a pointer connected to the shaft again) and allow different keys on the keypad to move the motor to the selected positions.

Note: In the above assignments, the pins used for the stepper motor may have to be changed based on what pins you use for the A/D and keypad routines.

REVIEW QUESTIONS
1. Compare a stepper motor and a dc motor in several ways, including torque, ease of interfacing, and methods of software control.
2. Discuss normal, full-torque, and half-step methods of controlling a stepper motor.
3. What advantages does a UNC5804 or similar chip have for interfacing a stepper motor to a computer port?
4. Explain how the **table**[ ] array simplifies the programming needs for Figure 11.5.

Part III
Introduction to Systems

This section utilizes the software tools and principles developed in Part II to develop simple systems that not only demonstrate valuable concepts but perform some interesting, exciting tasks. Although these exercises are reasonably complete, they occasionally force the reader to synthesize the information that has been provided to implement the suggested solutions fully. This approach has been adopted to enhance the critical thinking skills of the students to the point that they are prepared to design and implement interface projects on their own.

Exercise 12
DC Motor Positional Control

PURPOSE: The purpose of this exercise is to demonstrate how the position of a dc motor can be controlled.

OBJECTIVES: After the completion of this exercise, the reader should be able to:
- Identify at least two ways for determining the position of a dc motor.
- Describe a simple algorithm for controlling a dc motor so that it can be moved to a specified position.
- Describe how the simple algorithm can be improved to increase performance.
- Create a C library function that can move a dc motor to a specified position.
- Utilize a C tool for controlling a dc motor to demonstrate the principles discussed in this exercise.

THEORY: In previous exercises, we have seen how to control the speed of a dc motor and the position of a stepper motor. While precise positioning is easier to accomplish with a stepper motor, if the application requires more torque or greater speed than can be obtained from a stepper, a dc motor might be necessary. This situation brings us to the point of this exercise: How can we control the position of a dc motor?

Obviously, if we are to control the position of a motor, we must be able to determine its position. For example, we can connect a thin disk to the motor's shaft. The disk can have holes around the edges so that when the disk rotates with the shaft, the holes make and break a light beam that falls on a phototransistor. If the on/off state of the transistor is read with an input pin, the computer can count the number of pulses that occur and thus determine how far the shaft has rotated.

This principle would be very effective if the motor has a gear train for connection to the load (probably necessary anyway if the application required any significant amount of torque), and the perforated disk is connected on the motor side of the gear train. Even if the disk has only a few holes, the load can be positioned with a high degree of resolution if the gear ratio is high enough. This is true because a large gear ratio will force the motor shaft to make many revolutions, and thus generate many pulses, to get a small movement of the load.

Another possible solution is to connect the output shaft that rotates the load to a potentiometer. The position of the potentiometer (and thus the position of the load) can be determined with any of the A/D techniques discussed in Exercise 9.

When comparing the above two methods, one difference stands out. With the disk, the computer must constantly monitor the input pin while the motor is running so that the pulses can be counted. This is necessary because the sensor system is supplying only *incremental* information. The potentiometer method, on the other hand, provides a number representing an *absolute* position. When the potentiometer is read, that value alone tells us where the shaft is positioned.

There are many ways to make the incremental information easier to handle. For example, instead of sending the pulses to an input pin, they can be used to trigger a hardware interrupt. The interrupt routine can count the pulses by incrementing or decrementing (depending on the present direction of the motor) a memory location. Programs needing the absolute position information can simply read the value of that memory location. This method is relatively easy and it is certainly inexpensive, but since this text attempts to be general, and since interrupt control methods vary from computer to computer, any further study in this area is left to the reader. If you have a computer or controller with interrupt capability, I urge you to explore the above method.

Let's turn our attention then to the potentiometer solution. Let's assume that the number obtained from our A/D system is between 0 and 255. For the purpose of explanation, let's refer to that number as **pot_value**. This value, remember, tells us where the motor is presently positioned. Let's also assume that we have another variable, **desired_pos**, that indicates the destination position to which we want the motor to move.

If the above 2 numbers are not equal, then we need to turn the motor ON. The motor direction should be set based on which of the 2 numbers is larger. If we assume for now that the motor is turned ON at full speed (15), the code in Figure 12.1 controls the motor.

Each time through the loop, the potentiometer is read and the motor is turned ON, in the proper direction, for 100 ms. The loop continues until the motor reaches the desired destination. The major problem with this example is that the motor, if it is moving at any reasonable rate of speed, will continue to coast even after the motor is turned OFF. If the motor should pass its intended destination, it will reverse and move back toward its goal. The resulting oscillation is very undesirable. One solution is to lower the speed from 15, but that makes the performance of our system less than optimal.

```
//    assume pot_value = the present position
//    assume desired_pos = the desired position
//    assume range of speed is 0–15
while(pot_value ! = desired_pos)
    {
    if(pot_value > desired_pos)
        DCmotor(15, FORWARD, 100);          // 100ms duration
    else
        DCmotor(15, REVERSE, 100);
    }
```

Figure 12.1: This code fragment provides very simple positional control.

```
//    assume pot_value = the present position
//    assume desired_pos = the desired position
//    assume range of speed is 0–15
while(pot_value ! = desired_pos)
    {
    int factor = 1;// increase to increase sensitivity
    distance = abs(pot_value – desired_pos;
    speed = factor*(distance/16);
    if(speed>15)      // set maximum speed
        speed = 15;
    if(speed<3)       // assumes a speed of at least 3 is needed to move the motor
        speed = 3;
    if(pot_value > desired_pos)
        DCmotor(speed, FORWARD, 100);      // 100ms duration
    else
        DCmotor(speed, REVERSE, 100);
    }
```

Figure 12.2: This code fragment provides proportional control of a dc motor.

A more elegant solution is to control the speed of the motor based on the distance the motor has to move. If the present and the desired positions are far apart, then the motor can be turned on at a high speed. As the distance left to travel is reduced, the motor can be slowed down so that when the destination is reached, there will be little if any overshoot. The code in Figure 12.2 offers a method for implementing such a solution.

The code in Figure 12.2 is far better than that of Figure 12.1. The speed chosen is based on the amount of movement that is necessary. The further the motor is from the desired destination, the faster it will move. As it gets closer, the motor will continue to slow down until it reaches some predetermined minimum speed (3 in this case). The only way to get the motor to run at maximum speed in this example is to have the motor at one end of the potentiometer's possible travel and the desired destination at the other end. Unfortunately, this means that the motor will seldom run at the maximum speed. Increasing the value of **factor** to 2, 3, or even more will make the motor more sensitive so that it will not start decreasing its speed until it is closer to the destination.

This control system is referred to as *proportional control* because the speed is proportional to the distance left to travel. The proper value for **factor** can be determined mathematically if you know information such as the motor's specifications, the inertia of the load, and the level of overshoot that is acceptable. For our purposes, however, choose a value by experimenting until you get an acceptable performance. While you are experimenting, try different values for the motor duration.

You might want to make one change to the code in Figure 12.2. The way it is written, the motor will continue until it is exactly at the desired destination. Depending on the quality of your motor, gears, potentiometer, and A/D system, you may have trouble getting the present and desired destinations to be exactly equal. We can allow for a little tolerance by changing the while loop to

```
while(abs(pot_value - desired_pos)<range)
```

where **range** should be around 2 or 3. Again, experiment to determine what works best for your system.

We can increase the performance of our simple system if we make the speed of our motor change based not only on the distance left to travel but on the accumulated error over time and also on how fast the gap is closing. If you are familiar with calculus, these concepts refer to the integral and the derivative of the error (the difference between the present and the desired position). A text on control systems can provide more detail on PID (proportional, integral, derivative) control systems.

ASSIGNMENT: Construct a physical system consisting of 2 potentiometers and a dc motor with a gear assembly. Each potentiometer should have a straw or other lightweight pointer connected to the shaft so that it is easy to see the orientation. Connect one of the potentiometers to the motor gear assembly. Since there is little torque required, this connection can often be made by forcing a short length of rubber tubing over the shafts of the potentiometer and the motor.

Implement an appropriate hardware and software interface to read the values of both potentiometers and control the speed and direction of the motor. Create a program that will continually read the value of the isolated potentiometer and activate the motor so that the motor will move the second potentiometer to the same position as the first. Adjust the algorithm and parameters of your program until it performs satisfactorily (reasonable speed with minimal overshoot).

REVIEW QUESTIONS
1. Discuss the differences between incremental and absolute positioning systems.
2. Discuss the limitations of the code in Figure 12.1 and explain why these limitations create problems.
3. What is proportional speed control and how does it improve the ability to position a dc motor?
4. Explain in detail how the variable **factor** controls the sensitivity of the positioning code in Figure 12.2.
5. If the value of **factor** is increased too much, what will be the effect on the positional system of Figure 12.2 if it has a fast motor?
6. What effect would a heavy load (with a lot of inertia) have on a positional system? How can the program be modified to correct the problem?

Exercise 13
Intercomputer Communications

PURPOSE: The purpose of this exercise is to introduce the principles of inexpensive RS-232 communication by means of a software UART.

OBJECTIVES: After the completion of this exercise, the reader should be able to:
- Discuss the need for inexpensive communication for today's microcontrollers.
- Describe the basic principles of RS232 communications.
- Analyze C modules that mimic many of the hardware capabilities of a UART.
- Utilize a software UART to communicate with another computer or other RS-232 device.

THEORY: As mentioned in earlier exercises, microcontrollers are embedded in many of the products on the market today. In some cases, the internal processors need to communicate with external computers or devices.

Let's look at some examples. The processor in your automobile needs to transfer data to the diagnostic computer when you take your car for repairs. A modern hi-tech heating system might have computer-controlled vents in each room that receive their instructions about how much to open or close from a computerized thermostat. An embedded processor in your computer mouse or trackball must send data to the main system. These types of communication are often handled with serial rather than parallel transmissions because they don't require high-speed transfers. Besides, the hardware for serial communications is typically much cheaper than a parallel port version. A serial cable has fewer wires than a parallel cable does, so it is even cheaper. Even so, it is often not cheap enough.

The standard hardware implementation for serial communication is centered around a chip called a UART (universal asynchronous receiver transmitter). The serial port on the standard PC is made from a UART, which may be on a serial card added to one of the expansion slots or perhaps built into the motherboard.

Although a UART is not terribly expensive, it is too expensive to provide the communication link for a $20 mouse. The processors inside devices such as mouse pointers are often single-chip controllers that contain RAM, ROM, and I/O ports in addition to the CPU. PIC processors and the 68HC05 are examples of such devices. These controller chips are very limited in the amount of memory they have, but for simple applications, their low cost makes them ideal.

Simple controllers are also limited when it comes to the number of I/O pins available, making it impractical, in most cases, to attach a device such as a UART because of the number of I/O lines required.

The solution explored in this exercise is to create a software version of a UART that communicates using only 1 input pin and 1 output pin. Such a solution can be very cost effective, especially if the product is produced in large quantities, because the labor cost involved in writing the code can be spread across many units.

Before we proceed, we need to review the basics of RS-232 communication for readers who are not familiar with it. Instead of using 8 wires to send an 8-bit word to another device, a serial port sends the bits 1 bit at a time over a single wire. The inside of the transmission portion of a UART is basically a shift register with the appropriate control logic. Data to be transmitted is stored into the shift register and then shifted to the right with the output taken from the LSB. With each shift, the next bit is moved to the LSB. If you were watching the output pin (the LSB), you would see each bit in turn, starting with the LSB. The speed that the data would be sent would be based on how fast the register is shifting.

The number of bits transferred per second can be loosely referred to as the baud rate. The inverse of the rate would be the bit time (the time each bit is present on the output pin).

At the receiver end, the data is clocked into another shift register. When all the data bits have been received, they are gated in parallel to an output register so that they can be used. If you have been following this discussion closely, the main question you should be asking is, How does the receiver know when to clock its shift register? This is the tricky part because the data is arriving asynchronously (remember the A in UART). *Asynchronously*, in this case, means that the data can arrive at any time, completely unannounced.

The UART solves this problem by having an internal clock that (typically) runs at 16 times the shift rate of the registers. The transmitting device is required to send a 0 for 1 bit time immediately prior to the data bits. This initial 0 is referred to as a *start bit*. The leading edge of the start bit can trigger a counter so that the UART can determine when to clock the shift register. Since the internal oscillator is only 16 times the baud rate, the accuracy of shifting is limited to 1/16 of a bit time, but that is acceptable for short 8-bit transmissions.

To ensure that the leading edge of the start bit can be seen, we must make sure that the data line returns to a normal high position when the transmission is complete. If the data is sent continuously and the last bit sent in a word (the MSB) is 0, then the leading edge of the start bit ceases to exist. To prevent this from happening, the transmitting device must bring the data line high for at least 1 bit time. This is referred to as a *stop bit*. Older systems, particularly teletypes, required 2 stop bits because they were so slow at processing the information they had just received. Without the little extra delay, they missed the start bit.

In a hardware UART that transfers 8 bits of data, we can implement the start and stop bits by using a 10-bit shift register. When the 8 bits of data are loaded, we can simply load a 0 on one end for the start bit and a 1 on the other for the stop bit. When the register is shifted, the start and stop bits are sent just as if they were part of the data stream.

```
void serial_out(int data)
    {
    int i;
    // send the start bit
    send(0);
    wait_one_bit_time( );
    for(i=0; i<8; i++)        // send 8 data bits
        {
        send(data & 1);   // send the LSB of data
        data = data>>1;  // shift data right to get the next bit into the LSB
        wait_one_bit_time( );
        }
    send(1);    // send the stop bit
    wait_one_bit_time( );
    }
```

Figure 13.1: This routine will transmit the data passed to it, including start and stop bits, in serial form.

A UART chip has additional features, but this description is sufficient for our purposes. If we were to construct a UART as described above using discrete gates, it would be relatively complex. As we will soon see, however, we can perform all these operations in only a few lines of C code. Based on the description above, all we need to build a UART are operations like shift, count, and copy. Those operations are easily performed in software.

Our goal will be to construct two modules, one called **serial_in( )** and one called **serial_out( )**. Let's look first at the **serial_out( )** module because it is the easiest. Figure 13.1 shows the basic code needed. It assumes that we have a **send( )** tool that can send 1's and 0's to the output line. It also assumes we have a function **wait_one_bit_time( )** that can provide the delay we need.

If we assume the data is transmitted on the LSB of the 8-bit port, the **send( )** function is very simple, as shown in Figure 13.2.

```
// assumes the data is transmitted on the LSB of the 8-bit port
// assumes the data is either a 1 or a 0
void send(int d)
    {
    out8data(d);
    {
```

Figure 13.2: The **send( )** routine places the bit to be transmitted on the output line.

```
int serial_in(void)
    {
    int i, data=0;
    while(!bit_in( ))   // waits until the input is high – just in case
        ;
    while(bit_in( ))     // waits until the input bit goes low
        ;                // note: bit_in( ) returns 0 or 128
    wait_half_bit_time( );
    // now we are in the center of the start bit
    for(i=0; i<8; i++)   // bring in the 8 data bits
        {
        wait_one_bit_time( );
        // now we are in the middle of the next bit
        data = data>>1;  // shift the bits to the right
        data = data I bit_in( );  // and add place the new bit in the MSB
                            // works because bit_in( ) returns 128 for a high
        }
    wait_one_bit_time( );  // get us out of the last bit so there is no chance
                            // of seeing it twice

    }
```

Figure 13.3: This module collects the data in serial form and converts it to an 8-bit word.

For example, if you wish to use bit 6 (next to the MSB) on the 8-bit port for the output pin, you would have to change the line in **send( )** to:

```
out8data( d>>6);
```

This action would move the provided 1 or 0 to the proper bit position. You should construct a **send( )** for your programs that is appropriate for the pin and port that you choose to use for the output.

The receive module is a little more complicated because it has to watch for the start bit. This module is shown in Figure 13.3. It assumes we have a **bit_in( )** function that can return 128 or 0 based on the status of the input line. It also assumes that we have a delay that can pause for one-half a bit-time.

The one-half bit-time delay is necessary because it allows us to read the data when it is the most stable, in the center of the pulse. Since we need to add each bit to the data word at the MSB, we simply make it the responsibility of the **bit_in( )** routine to return 128 to represent a high and 0 to represent a low. This may seem unconventional, but this is our tool so why not make it meet our needs? Let's see how to create **bit_in( )**, which is shown in Figure 13.4.

```
// assumes the input line is the MSB (bit 4) of the 5-bit input port
int bit_in(void)
    {
    if(input_data( ) & 0x10)  // checks only bit 4
        return 128;
    else
        return 0;
    }
```

Figure 13.4: This routine determines if the input line is high or low.

If you are using our **serial_in**( ) to communicate with another computer that is using our **serial_out**( ), then selecting the delays we need is easy because they only have to match each other. You could, for example, delay 2 ms for a bit time and 1 ms for one-half a bit-time. If you need to communicate with a PC or other system that is using a hardware UART, however, you need to match the bit times of the hardware UART to within about 2% to ensure accuracy.

If the PC serial port is operating at 1200 baud, for example, the bit time is 1/1200 second, or 833 microseconds. We can easily approximate this by creating a delay, just as we did for the **delay1ms**( ) routine in Exercise 5, except that we should loop only about 83% as many times as was required for the millisecond delay. Similar methods could be used to create the one-half bit-time delay. This should get you operating pretty close to the correct frequency. We'll examine a method to calibrate the serial tools more accurately shortly. Now I have to give you a little more information.

A standard serial port (either RS232 or RS232C) does not use standard TTL signals to represent its logic levels. Instead, a 1 can be represented by a voltage between –12 and –5 volts and a 0 can be represented by a voltage between +5 and +12. Such levels can damage a TTL-compatible parallel port, so something must be done to convert the voltages. The circuit in Figure 13.5 shows one possible solution.

If the voltage from the serial port is over 5 volts, the zener action of the diode will prevent the output voltage from exceeding the 5-volt TTL level. If the input voltage is negative, the diode will forward bias and force the output voltage to 0. The only problem is that a 1 will be represented by

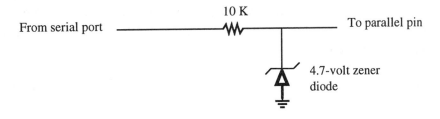

Figure 13.5: The serial port voltage swings can be reduced to TTL levels.

```
void main(void)
    {
    int code;
    initialize_port( );
    do  {
        code = keycode( );
        if(code>=0 and code<=9)
            serial_out(code | 0x30);   // convert to ASCII before sending
        } while(code !=15);
    }
```

Figure 13.6: You can test your **serial_out**( ) by sending data to a terminal program running on a PC.

0 volts and a low will be represented by 5 volts. This problem can be solved by inverting the output using a 7404 inverter or by altering the software.

Figure 13.4 can be reversed by simply switching the code for the true and false sections of the **if**( ) statement. The logic in Figure 13.2 can be reversed by replacing the statement **out8data**(d) with **out8data**(d^1). This code change will invert the value of the LSB by using the XOR operator. If your hardware uses a different bit, perform the XOR operation using a constant with a binary 1 in the proper bit position.

It is also reasonable to assume that we need to convert the TTL signals from our software UART to RS232 levels. The easiest way to do this is with an integrated circuit such as the MAX232, which handles the conversion (and the inversion) for you. Its internal voltage pump allows it to generate ± 12 volts from a 5-volt supply. In practice, however, I have found PC serial ports to have tolerant voltage requirements. As long as the TTL signal is inverted properly, I have not had any trouble connecting it directly to the input pin on the serial port. (I wouldn't necessarily recommend releasing a commercial product using such a shortcut, but for experimental purposes, it seems to work fine.)

The program fragment in Figure 13.6 will transfer numeric data from the keypad to the serial port. Let's assume that a terminal program is running on a PC to display the incoming data.

If the program in Figure 13.6 cannot send data reliably to the terminal, observe the waveform on a storage scope and measure the bit times to make sure they are correct. If they are close, change the time delay in 2% increments (up and down) until you get reliable transmission. When the system begins to work reliably, determine what the high and low limits are for the bit times and set your delays halfway between the extremes.

Once you have the **serial_out**( ) working, you should be able to set the delays easily in **serial_in**( ). You can test both routines by connecting your system to a PC running a terminal program and letting your program return a lowercase letter when it receives an uppercase and an uppercase when it receives a lowercase. Figure 13.7 shows how easily this can be done. The program will ignore all keystrokes except for the ESC key (which terminates the program) and the upper- and lowercase letters.

```
void main(void)
    {
    initialize_ports( );
    do  {
         code = serial_in( );
         if(isupper(code))
              serial_out(tolower(code));
         if(islower(code))
              serial_out(toupper(code));
         }while (code!=27);  // receiving the ESC code terminates the loop
    }
```

Figure 13.7: This code tests both the **serial_in**( ) and **serial_out**( ) routines simultaneously.

You should turn off the echo in the terminal program. You should also turn off hardware handshaking because our software system ignores it.

Once you get the serial routines working, you have many new options. You can get very low-cost A/D converters that have a serial interface. PIC microcontrollers or even BASIC Stamps from Parallax can act easily as intelligent peripherals that can off-load time-consuming tasks from the main system or add extra I/O capabilities. For example, you can program one computer to act as an intelligent display system and have it display items on an LCD that are sent to it over a serial port. With a few tool routines, you can have a complete display system using only a single I/O pin.

Entire systems can be designed using multiple processors networked together with serial connections. For example, separate processors can be responsible for controlling the speed and position of each joint in a robot arm. Other processors can collect data and relay it to other processors that need it. The main computer would not have to do any of the low-level work. As a supervisor, it would be responsible only for *what* has to be done—not *how* to do it. Before you decide that such a system is too expensive, do some research on 68HC05 and PIC processors. These simple controllers contain not only a CPU but RAM, ROM, and even I/O ports, and can cost less than $2 in reasonable quantities.

If you really want to see the advantage of our software UART, check out a new serial LCD interface chip from E-Lab Digital Engineering, Inc. With the **serial_out**( ) function discussed in this exercise, the EDE702 can provide full control over a standard LCD (see Exercise 7) using a single port pin. You might consider substituting an LCD for the PC terminal program in the assignment for this exercise.

In conclusion, a software UART is a simple and inexpensive means of adding serial communication capability to nearly any system. The C language can also be used to control standard hardware-based serial ports, but the methods will vary greatly depending on the hardware platform and the compiler you are using. Since a goal of this text is to provide exercises that apply to different types of computers and controllers, the details of using hardware-based serial ports are left for the reader to research.

ASSIGNMENT: Test all the examples in this exercise and verify that they work properly. When you have a working serial port system, locate an A/D converter with a serial port (such as the ADC0834CCN) and read the serial data from the chip using **serial_in( )**. Have your program act as a digital voltmeter by using **serial_out( )** to display the value of the voltage on a terminal program running on a PC.

Use a voltage divider on the input to the A/D to allow a full-scale reading of 10 volts. Calibrate your software so that it provides reasonably accurate voltage readings when compared with a multimeter. Once the meter works correctly at the 10-volt scale, design a relay system so that the voltage divider can be altered by your program. You might, for example, have three scales, such as 0–1, 0–10, and 0–50 volts. Design your program so that it automatically ranges by reading the voltage at the 50-volt scale first. If the voltage is lower than 10 volts, it switches to that scale and takes another reading. If the voltage is less than 1 volt, then it switches to the lowest scale. The program should take advantage of the scaling to provide the most accurate answer possible at each range, given the resolution of the A/D used.

REVIEW QUESTIONS
1. What does UART stand for?
2. What are the advantages and disadvantages of software UART over hardware UART?
3. What is the purpose of the start and stop bits in a serial transmission?
4. When data is sent over a standard serial connection, which bit is sent first, the LSB or the MSB?
5. Why is a half-bit delay needed for **serial_in( )** but not for **serial_out( )**?
6. Explain the design you used to complete the assignment for this exercise. Show schematics and give details of both how and why you made the choices you did. Explain how your program works and include any tools that you created to make the program easier to write.

Exercise 14
An LCD Numeric Line Editor

PURPOSE: The purpose of this exercise is to introduce the principles involved in a line editor and to demonstrate how those principles can be implemented using the LCD tools developed in Exercise 7 and the keypad functions from Exercise 6.

OBJECTIVES: After the completion of this exercise, the reader should be able to:
- Discuss the basic principles of a line editor and how it can be organized as an edit section and a display section.
- Describe the problems associated with using the same I/O pins to drive 2 different devices and discuss how conflicts can be eliminated.
- Analyze the operation of a C function that will allow numeric data to be entered and edited from a keypad while being displayed on an LCD.
- Describe an algorithm for converting a string of numeric characters into a binary number.
- Create an **editNum( )** tool that will allow numeric data to be entered and edited on an LCD using a keypad and, when the editing is terminated, return the equivalent binary value of the string being edited.

THEORY: In Exercise 7 we created some basic tools for displaying information on an LCD. Our first goal in this exercise is to integrate the keypad routines from Exercise 6 so that the LCD and the keypad can be used together.

If you review Exercises 6 and 7, you will see that we have very little I/O pin conflict between the keypad and the LCD. The keypad used the lower 4 bits of the input port and the LCD used the fifth bit. As long as the functions for each device mask the bits they do not wish to use, then no conflicts exist.

The LCD used the 8-bit output port. This presents no conflict because the 8-bit port is not used at all by the keypad routines. However, the 4-bit output port is a different situation. The **keycode()** function used all 4 bits to scan the keypad while the LCD routines used the 2 least significant bits. On the surface, there is a conflict between the 2 devices because, when data is written to 1 device, it will also be sent to the other. Luckily, no real conflict exists, especially if we are careful.

It is true that, when the LCD routines write to the 4-bit port, the data being written is also sent to the keypad matrix. Unless the keypad tries to read the input port at that time, however, the data being written will have no effect. The keypad always sends the data that it wants on the 4-bit output port before reading the input port, so no problems exist here. Let's look at the situation in reverse. When the keypad is scanning, it will be changing the state of the RS and R/W lines of the LCD. These lines certainly affect the operation of the LCD, but only when the LCD is enabled. Look at the code for the LCD routines. They make sure the LCD is disabled whenever a routine is terminated. This means that, unless you were to call the keypad routines from *within* the LCD routines, there should be no conflict. Notice that if the enable line of the LCD had been connected to the 4-bit rather than the 8-bit I/O port, a conflict would have been unavoidable.

Now that we have ascertained that the keypad routines of Exercise 6 and the LCD routines of Exercise 7 can work together without conflict, we can turn our attention to the basic principles of a line editor. As with most algorithms in this text, I want to simplify the task at hand by subdividing it whenever possible. To this end, I want to divide the editing task into a section that edits a string of characters (but does not worry about how to display them) and another section that displays a line of text and positions the cursor (but does not worry about how the text got there).

Let's begin by deciding on what editing functions we want to implement. We have only 16 keys in our keypad. Since 10 of the keys (0–9) are used to enter data, that leaves us with only 6 keys for other functions. Figure 14.1 shows the key codes and the desired functions for the remaining keys. Two key codes have been left unused for now. They will be used in Exercise 16.

The basic form for our function is shown in Figure 14.2. To simplify this listing, there is no code for accessing the LCD. A single comment shows where the string being edited should be displayed on the LCD. This code edits the string, which is the character array **linedata**[ ], that was passed to the function. The function itself never changes the length of the string, so the string must be initialized by the calling function. If you want the user to be able to enter a maximum of 8 characters, for example, you should fill the string with 8 spaces before passing it to **editNum**( ).

Key Code	Key Name	Action Performed
0–9	Keys 0–9	Insert the character at the cursor position and move the cursor one position to the right.
10	Enter	Terminate the edit function.
11	Left arrow	Move the cursor one position to the left.
12	Right arrow	Move the cursor one position to the right.
13	Backspace	Delete the character to the left of the cursor and move all the characters to the right of the cursor one position to the left.
14	(Unused for now)	
15	(Unused for now)	

Figure 14.1: Four of the 16 keys will be used for edit control.

```
int editNum(char * linedata)
    {
    // string being edited is in the char array linedata[ ]
    // the cursor is at character position cp
    // make the code more readable with #defines
    #define ENTER          10
    #define LEFTARROW      11
    #define RIGHTARROW     12
    #define BACKSPACE      13
    int cp, len, done, i, k;
    cp = 0;   // start editing with the cursor at the beginning of the line
    done = 0; // assume not done editing
    len = strlen(linedata);  // find initial length of string (no change during edit)
    do  {
        //  **** display to LCD will go here ****
        k = keycode( );    // wait for a keystroke
        switch(k)
            {
            case ENTER:
                    done=1; // cause loop to terminate
                    break;
            case LEFTARROW:
                    if(cp>0)
                        cp--;
                    break;
            case RIGHTARROW:
                    if(cp<len-1)
                        cp++
                    break;
            case BACKSPACE:
                    if(cp>0) // don't backspace if at the beginning of line
                        {
                        // don't backspace if at the end with no space
                        if((cp<len-1) || linedata[len-1] == ' ')
                            {
                            for(i=cp; i<=len; i++)   // move the characters left
                                linedata[i-1]=linedata[i];
                            cp--;   // then move cursor left one position
                            }
                        linedata[len-1]=' ';  // erase last character in the line
                        }                     // by replacing it with a space
                    break;
```

Figure 14.2: This portion of **editNum**( ) handles the editing of the string itself.

```
default:  if(k>=0 && k<=9)
              {
              k += 0x30;    // convert to ASCII
              if(cp! = len-1)
                  {
                  for(i=len-2; i >= cp; i++)
                          linedata[i+1] = linedata[i];
                  linedata[cp++] = k;
                  }
              else
                  {
                  linedata[cp] = k;
                  }
              }
          }
       } while(!done );
// **** editing is done—now return the value of the string ****
}
```

Figure 14.2: (continued)

The variable **cp** keeps track of the current cursor position, which starts at the beginning of the line. After displaying the string on the LCD, the module waits for the user to press a key on the keypad. A **switch-case** control structure decides what to do based on which key is pressed. If the enter key is pressed, the editing loop is terminated. If either the left or right arrow keys are pressed, then the cursor position (**cp**) is incremented or decremented (unless the cursor is already at either end of the line).

The **default** portion of the **switch-case** must insert the character into the line, which generally means that the characters to the right of the cursor must be moved right one position (to make room to insert the new character). The only time the characters are not moved right is if the cursor is at the last position in the string. In that case, the new character just replaces the last character in the line.

If the backspace key is pressed, the characters to the right of the cursor are moved one position to the left. This leaves two copies of the last letter in the string, one at the next to the last position and one at the last position. The module completes the backspace operation by replacing the last character in the string with a space.

One special case must be handled in the backspace code. When the cursor is at the last position in the string and the last character in the line is not a space, then instead of deleting to the left (as is normally done), the character immediately under the cursor is replaced with a space. When the last character is a space, then the normal delete is performed, even if the cursor is in the last position of the line. This may seem complicated, but if you try the operations while editing, I think you will see that they seem quite natural. If your code is intended for general use, you should make the interface intuitive and uncomplicated for the user.

Before we proceed, let's try to get an overview of what is happening in **editNum**( ). The code that we have examined so far changes the string itself as the keys are pressed. The new string may have some of the characters shifted to the right (if we have inserted a character) or shifted to the left (if we have deleted a character). In either case, however, the string will be exactly the same length as it was before a key was pressed. Let's assume we have the code that can display the string on the LCD and that we have inserted this code at the position specified in Figure 14.2.

Look at the loop and you will see that three basic actions take place. The string is displayed, it waits for a key to be pressed, and (depending on which key is pressed) the string is altered. This process continues until the enter key is pressed. If the display is updated every time a key is pressed, then the LCD will always show the updated line. It will appear as if the keystrokes are deleting, moving, and inserting the characters on the screen. The same thing is true when you edit C code or type a report on a word processor. It appears that your keystrokes are altering the screen when, in fact, you are only changing the character data and then the data is displayed. In some cases, the entire computer screen is redisplayed every time a key is pressed.

One of the tasks we need to do for finishing our **editNum**( ) module is to create code that can display the string on the LCD. The modules we created in Exercise 7 can be a big help. Using them, the code below will display the string:

```
LCD_command(2);   // moves the cursor to the first position on the display
print_string(linedata);
```

By positioning the cursor at the beginning of the display, the new string will be printed on top of the original string. The new string will be printed so fast that the characters will seem to be shifting rather than being reprinted. The only problem we have now is that the user cannot tell where the cursor is. Even if we have the LCD cursor turned on, it will appear at the end of the string that was just displayed. There are more sophisticated ways of moving the cursor on an LCD, but since this text will be used by people using different types of hardware, let's use a generic method that can work on nearly any display. Look at the code below.

```
LCD_command(2);     // move the cursor to the first position on the display
for(i=0; i<cp; i++)      // move cursor cp positions to the right
    LCD_command(0x14);
```

It moves the cursor to the beginning of the line and then moves it right until it gets to the proper position. Of course, we need to make sure that the cursor is active. We don't necessarily need the cursor to be on while the movements are being made, so we might as well turn it off. However, it has been my experience that LCD screens are so slow to react that you will not see the cursor moving even if you leave it on. The final code is shown in Figure 14.3. It uses commands that should be valid on most LCDs (see Exercise 7).

```
LCD_command(0x0C);      // turn the cursor off
LCD_command(2);         // moves the cursor to the first position on the display
print_string(linedata);
LCD_command(2);         // move the cursor to the first position on the display
for(i=0; i<cp; i++)     // move cursor cp positions to the right
    LCD_command(0x14);  // command for moving the cursor one position to the right
LCD_command(0x0D);      // turn the cursor on
```

Figure 14.3: This code displays the string on the LCD and positions the cursor.

Of course, you will want to study the data sheets for the LCD you are using to make sure that these commands are valid. I have kept the code as generic as possible and have assumed a one-line display, so everything should work on nearly any LCD that you might have. There are many other features, including user-defined characters, multiline displays, and direct screen memory access that can provide you with interesting displays. Examine your documentation and consider building the tools that you need to create custom characters, print to any position on the screen, and display or clear text by wiping on the screen (left to right, right to left, etc.).

The last task our **editNum( )** module must do is convert the ASCII data in the string **linedata[ ]** into a binary value that can be returned to the calling program. Let's examine a simple algorithm for making this conversion. Imagine that we have the number 382 stored as ASCII codes 0x33, 0x38, and 0x32. First, assume that we have a variable **answer** that is initialized to 0. If we start at the left side of the number, get the digit 3, add its *value* to **answer**, check the next digit, multiply the **answer** by 10 if it is a numeric item, add the value of the digit, and continue this process until we get to a nonnumeric digit, then **answer** will contain the value of the string. Figure 14.4 shows the calculations as the processing of "382" takes place.

```
answer equals 0 initially
answer = answer + 3
answer  equals 3
since the next character is a digit
    multiply answer by 10
    answer equals 30
    add the value of the next digit
    answer = answer + 8
    answer equals 38
since the next character is a digit
    multiply answer by 10
    answer equals 380
    add the value of the next digit
    answer = answer + 2
    answer equals 382
since the next character is not a digit, we are done
```

Figure 14.4: Demonstration of the ASCII to decimal conversion algorithm.

```
answer = 0;
for(i=0; isdigit(linedata[i]); i++)
    {
    if(isdigit(linedata[i])  // or use if(linedata[i]>='0' && linedata[i]<='9')
        {
        answer *=10;   // multiply answer by 10
        answer+=(linedata[i]&0xF);   // add value of digit to answer
        }
    else
        break;   // end of number, exit loop
    }
return answer;     // editNum should return the value of the string
```

Figure 14.5: This code finds the value expressed by the ASCII string **linedata[ ]**.

After you see the principles of the algorithm, it is easy to create a C module that can implement it. Figure 14.5 shows a method for accomplishing this task. You should insert this code into Figure 14.2 where the comment indicates.

ASSIGNMENT: Connect an LCD to your system as described in this exercise. Study the data sheets for your LCD and verify that the code shown in this exercise will work as described. Type in all the modules and confirm that they perform correctly. Once you have a working editor and understand how it operates, try one or more of the following problems:

1. Modify the **editNum( )** code so that the numbers are entered starting at the right side of the display and shift left as entered (like a calculator display), instead of being entered at the left side and shifting right. Maintain the ability to edit with the arrow and backspace keys.

2. Use the routines in this exercise to create an application program that functions as a simple calculator. The 2 unused keys on the keypad can be used for the plus and minus keys and the enter key can be the equals key. You will have to modify the **editNum( )** module so that it will exit if any of these 3 keys are pressed: +, –, or =. Expand the **print_number( )** algorithm discussed in Exercise 7 so that it will work for numbers as large as your application will allow.

3. Modify the **editNum( )** module so that the line being edited is enclosed in brackets [ ]. With the brackets, the user will see how many characters can be entered and will know when they are at the end of the line. Don't forget to position the cursor at **cp**+1 to account for the beginning bracket.

REVIEW QUESTIONS

1. Explain how the R/W line on the LCD can be pulsed by the keypad routines without causing information to be written to the LCD.
2. Explain how the backspace code operates. Be specific.
3. Explain how characters are inserted into the line. Be specific.
4. Normally when characters are entered into the line, the cursor is moved 1 space to the right. When the cursor is at the last position in the line, however, the module will allow you to enter a character, but the cursor is not advanced. How is this accomplished by the code?
5. If you entered the **editNum**( ) code as directed by this exercise (and by Exercise 7), you will see that the cursor does not appear until you have pressed at least one key. Explain why this happens and how you can fix the problem.
6. How large a number can be handled by the algorithm implemented by Figure 14.5? How did you arrive at your answer?

Exercise 15
Displaying Text on an Oscilloscope

PURPOSE: The purpose of this exercise is two-fold. First, it shows how text and graphics are generated and displayed on a computer monitor. Second, it provides a relatively complex problem on which we can sharpen our software skills. This problem differs dramatically from previous exercises in this text because it requires all the speed available from the computer. Because of this new perspective, Exercise 15 should give you a much better appreciation of the tremendous power and versatility of computer-based control.

OBJECTIVES: After the completion of this exercise, the reader should be able to:
- Describe the principles of displaying information on a CRT system.
- Identify the problems and solutions associated with synchronizing the beam control to provide a stable picture and prevent flicker.
- Utilize the principles discussed in this exercise to create a tool for displaying characters on an oscilloscope.
- Utilize the tool described above by combining it with the **edit_num**() tool from Exercise 14 to create an edit system that can display the line being edited on the scope.

THEORY: I've often discovered that most skilled programmers and even many engineers and technicians take the technology of their computer's display system for granted. They seldom have an in-depth understanding of how characters are actually displayed when a **cout** or **printf**( ) statement is executed. One of the objectives of this exercise is to remove some of the mystery associated with a computer display. We shall see that once the mystery is explained, the underlying principles are really quite simple.

We need to start by examining the fundamentals of the computer monitor itself. Like a standard television, a computer monitor is usually built around a CRT, or cathode ray tube (at least until LCDs get just a little more economical). Figure 15.1 shows the basics of a CRT system. When

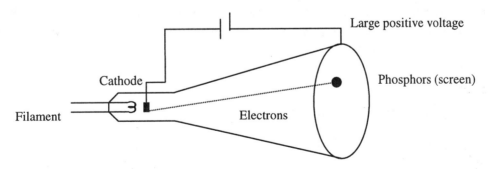

Figure 15.1: A cathode ray tube is the basis for a computer monitor.

voltage is applied to the filament (just like a light bulb), it heats a cathode, which causes the electrons in it to increase their energy. When they have enough energy, the electrons are ejected from the surface of the cathode, making them easy to move. A large positive voltage (15,000 volts is a reasonable amount) is applied to the face of the tube so that it will attract the free electrons. The electrons accelerate as they approach the face of the tube and strike it with tremendous speed and energy. The face of the tube is coated with phosphors so that it will glow when energized by the striking electrons.

To create text or graphics on the face of the tube, we need *only* to make the electron beam strike the appropriate positions on the end of the tube. Of course, when we move the beam to a new position, the light being emitted at the old position will die out. This simply means that our system must continually redraw the image being displayed. This process is referred to as *refresh*.

The question that you should be asking yourself is, How do I move the beam? Electrons can be attracted or repelled with either electrostatic or electromagnetic forces. Televisions and computer monitors typically use magnetic coils surrounding the neck of the tube to focus and control the electron beam. Oscilloscopes must operate on a much wider range of frequencies, so they use electrostatic plates along the neck of the tube. In either case, one set of coils or plates controls the vertical position of the beam, while a second set controls the horizontal.

The beam can be directed to any place on the face of the tube by applying an appropriate voltage to the deflecting coils or plates. It certainly would be possible to move the beam only to the points that we want illuminated, but there is a more efficient method. In a standard television, the beam is forced to scan systematically over the entire screen.

Figure 15.2 shows two waveforms. Imagine that a voltage ramp is applied to the horizontal control plates or coils. As the voltage increases, the beam is pulled across the screen (let's assume from left to right). When the ramp voltage falls back to its original value, the beam returns to the left side of the screen. If the ramp repeats continuously, the beam moves relatively slowly across the screen and then quickly returns to the left side, only to start across the screen again.

If a second voltage ramp (of a lower frequency) is applied to the vertical coils or plates, then the beam moves slowly down the screen while continuing its horizontal motion. This action traces a

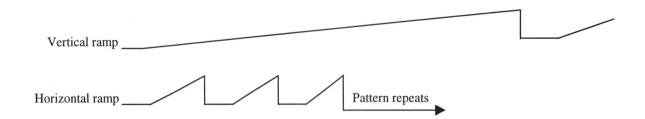

Figure 15.2: Voltage ramps move the beam to form a raster.

rectangular area on the surface of the face of the tube. This area is called a *raster* and appears as a white rectangle on a black-and-white television. To prevent flicker, this raster must be redrawn about 60 times per second. If we want to control the image being displayed on the tube, we need only to turn the beam on and off at the appropriate times as it sweeps across the screen. In a computer video system, the video RAM (memory) holds the pattern to be displayed. Hardware counters manipulate the address lines to the memory, forcing the data to be accessed in the correct order. The value of the data at any given bit position is then used to control the on/off state of the beam. This means that each bit in the memory can control the on/off state of 1 pixel on the screen. Of course, an entire byte or word of memory can be connected to one or more D/A converters so that the intensity (gray or color) can be controlled. For our examples, however, we will retain simplicity by sticking with on/off control.

Since our system will be implemented primarily in software, our video RAM can be an array. If we want to control the display in a graphic mode, each bit in the array would have to control 1 dot on the screen. In our case (and in text-based computer displays), we have a more efficient alternative. Our video RAM array need only hold the ASCII codes for the letters that we want displayed because we can use a look-up table (like we did in earlier exercises with 7-segment codes) to obtain the desired patterns. The position in the array where an ASCII code is placed should correlate with the position on the screen where the character should appear. If we want to clear the screen display, we would fill the array with the ASCII codes for spaces.

To make this exercise easier to implement, we will make use of the **edit_num**() module from previous exercises. We have to make some modifications, but they will be relatively minor. Recall that the **edit_num**() function allowed the user to enter and edit ASCII codes (for numbers) in a string and to return the value of the number when the editing was terminated. The string (and the display) was updated every time a key was pressed on the keypad.

For this exercise, we can remove the code that sent data to the LCD because we want the data to be displayed on the oscilloscope. We had to update the LCD display only when a key was pressed. In the case of the oscilloscope, however, we need to update the display continually (60 times per second). The easiest way to handle this is to update the oscilloscope display from within the **wtkr**() and **wtkp**() (wait-till-key-released and wait-till-key-pressed) subroutines discussed in Exercise 6. This means that an application program will spend most of its time updating the screen and will pause from that action only when a key is pressed. The processing of the key data should require minimal time (perhaps milliseconds in a worst case scenario), so the display should remain stable and jitter-free.

Let's turn our attention to the process required to create a character display on the screen. The overall goal is to translate the ASCII data in an array into a bit stream that can turn the oscilloscope beam on and off. Naturally, if our routine is to be effective, it must synchronize the beam control so that the dots appear at the proper place on the screen and the display must be free of vertical roll and horizontal tear. This need should become clearer as we continue.

Let's turn our attention for a moment to the oscilloscope itself and see what is required to control it. The normal input terminal for an oscilloscope allows an external voltage to position the beam vertically on the display screen. A ramp (similar to those in Figure 15.2) is generated internally to the scope so that it scans the beam horizontally. The horizontal sweep control allows us to change the frequency of the ramp waveform, but that is not enough. We also need a way of starting the sweep at a specific time so that we can position each pixel properly (relative to the starting time). If we set up the oscilloscope controls properly (the details of your particular equipment can be obtained from your reference manual), we can initiate a beam scan by pulsing the *trigger* input on the scope. While the beam is scanning, we can control the on/off state of the beam by applying a TTL-level signal to the z-input (usually found on the back of most scopes). Examine the routines in Figure 15.3. They assume that the z-input of the scope is connected to bit 6 on the 8-bit I/O port.

```c
// assumes bit 6 of the 8-bit port is connected to the z-input
// assumes bit 7 is connected to the scope trigger
void pixelON(void)
    {
    int i;
    out8data(0x40);
    for(i=0;i<10;i++)
        ; // empty for() to create delay if needed
    }

void pixelOFF(void)
    {
    out8data(0);
    // add delay as above, if needed
    }
```

Figure 15.3: These simple routines turn the beam that creates the pixels on and off.

Once we have the routines to turn the beam on and off, it is easy to create a line of pixels. The code fragment in Figure 15.4 creates a dotted line composed of 160 pixels. The even-numbered pixels are turned off and the odd-numbered pixels are turned on. The code fragment assumes that the scope trigger input is connected to bit 7 (the MSB) of the port.

```
while(1)
    {
    // pulse the trigger (connected to the MSB, bit 7, of the 8-bit port)
    out8data(0x80);   // pulse high
    out8data(0);  // return to 0
    // create a dotted line of 160 pixels
    for(i=0; i<80; i++)
        {
        pixelON();
        pixelOFF();
        }
    // delay just a little to allow the beam to finish its trace across the screen
    delay1ms(1);
    // start over
    }
```

Figure 15.4: This code fragment demonstrates how to draw a dotted line across the screen.

The actual setting for your oscilloscope will vary based on the speed of your computer because the time duration of the pixels displayed will be based on how long it takes your computer to execute the **pixelON()** and **pixelOFF()** functions. You should set the horizontal sweep control so that the dotted line extends nearly all the way across the screen. You may have to add a slight delay to the on/off routines, as shown in Figure 15.3. If you examine the line drawn on your scope carefully, you should see that the off-time is slightly longer than the on-time. This is true because the **for()** takes time at the end of the loop to decide whether to continue or not. This extra time, while small, may be apparent in the screen display, especially if you did not add any extra delay time to the on/off routines.

Adjust the focus on the scope until you get clear dots on the screen. There is little need to continue until you get the dotted line working. If you have trouble, verify that the z-input and the trigger are working as expected. The delays in the code should not be critical because the horizontal sweep adjustment should provide ample control—especially if you use the fine adjustment. The delays may be necessary, however, depending on the speed of your computer. I have not performed this experiment on computers of every speed variation, but I have achieved acceptable results on slower machines by eliminating the delays, fine-tuning the oscilloscope, and reducing the size of the line being displayed. Once you get the line displayed, play with the code and attempt to make the dots into dashes or some other alteration to the visual display. For example, you can get a line made of alternate dots and dashes by changing the **for()** in Figure 15.4 to that shown in Figure 15.5.

```
for(i=0; i<20; i++)
    {
    pixelON();      // turn 3 pixels on
    pixelON();
    pixelON();
    pixelOFF();         // turn 2 pixels off
    pixelOFF();
    pixelON();          // turn 1 pixel on
    pixelOFF();         // turn 2 pixels off
    pixelOFF()
    }
```

Figure 15.5: Different styles of lines are easy to create.

If you have followed everything so far, the rest should be easy. If you are confused, study the above material until it makes sense.

Now that we can draw a line and control the state of the pixels, we have two new areas to confront. First, we need to be able to draw 8 lines—each at a different vertical position—across the screen. Second, we must be able to control the on/off state of the pixels in each line so that they will form the characters whose ASCII codes are stored in an array. This may sound difficult, but we will see that it takes only a small amount of code to implement.

First, let's see how we can control the vertical position of the beam. Assume that the lower 3 bits of the 8-bit port are connected to a D/A converter as shown in Figure 15.6. If you use a single chip D/A, ground the unused inputs. Depending on the full-scale output from your D/A, you may need a potentiometer to reduce the voltage applied to the input of the oscilloscope. As long as the voltage is small enough, we can use the gain controls on the scope to control the relative position of the lines on the display. Make sure the scope is in the dc mode and use the vertical position controls to center the lines on the screen.

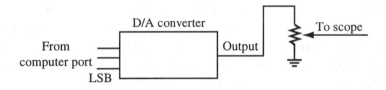

Figure 15.6: A D/A converter controls the vertical position of each line on the display.

Test the circuit in Figure 15.6 by applying various inputs to the D/A. You can use switches if you wish. Set the scope to auto-trigger mode temporarily so that a steady line can be seen on the screen. As the binary value of the input changes, you should see the line move up or down. Adjust the scope controls so that the movement of the line is only about $^1/_{16}$ inch each time the numeric input is incremented.

Figure 15.7 shows how to combine the principles discussed so far. The code shown produces a screen display consisting of 8 lines of 160 pixels each. In this example, every line is a dotted line produced as we did in Figure 15.4.

As you look at the code in Figure 15.7, notice that the pixel ON and OFF routines were altered. Since we are using the same port to control both the D/A and the on/off state of the pixels, we must make sure that we don't change the beam's vertical position when we change the state of a pixel. By adding (or ORing) the beam position (line_num) with the pixel control code, we ensure that the inputs to the A/D do not change while we are controlling the pixels. The same situation applies when we trigger the beam.

The first **for**( ) inside **main**( ) generates values of **line_num** ranging from 0 to 7. These values are used to dictate which of the 8 lines is presently active. Notice that this loop generates the raster on the screen. If we used a 4-bit D/A and made this loop operate from 0–15, then we would display 16 lines of 160 pixels on the screen. Remember, to prevent flicker, we must produce this raster at least 60 times per second. This 60-Hz frequency is not timed directly by our program. Rather it is a by-product of the time it takes to draw a pixel and the number of lines we scan. The maximum amount of lines and pixels that you can display depends primarily on the speed of your computer. With today's high-speed microprocessors, even relatively slow computers can handle 8 lines of 160 pixels. For our code, the only thing you should need to do is select the proper delay (see Figure 15.4) to make sure that the beam has time to finish its scan before you trigger the next pass.

```
// assumes lowest 3 bits of the 8-bit port connect to the D/A converter
// assumes bit 6 of the 8-bit port is connected to the z-input
// by adding line_num we can turn the pixels ON and OFF without
//      changing the vertical position of the beam

void pixelON(int line_num)
    {
    int i;
    out8data(0x40 + line_num);
    for(i=0;i<10;i++)
        ; // empty for() to create delay if needed
    }

void pixelOFF(int line_num)
    {
    out8data(line_num);
    // add delay as above, if needed
    }
```

Figure 15.7: This code fragment creates a raster composed of dotted lines.

```
main( )
    {
    initialize_ports( );
    int i, line_num
    while (1)
      {
      for(line_num=0; line_num<8; line_num++)
        {
        // pulse the trigger  (connected to the MSB, bit 7, of the 8-bit port)
        out8data(0x80+line_num);// pulse high and set vertical position
        out8data(line_num);  // return to 0 and maintain vertical position
        // create a dotted line of 160 pixels
        for(i=0; i<80; i++)
            {
            pixelON();     // ON and OFF have been modified (above) to maintain
            pixelOFF();   // the present beam position
            }
        // delay just a little to allow the beam to finish its trace across the screen
        delay1ms(1);        // may have to shorten for slow machines or long lines
        // start over
        }
      }
    }
```

Figure 15.7: (continued)

Now that we have a raster being displayed, the final step is to control the dot pattern being displayed. We can use an array with each element corresponding to one of the 1280 (160*8) pixels, but that would be necessary only if we wanted to display graphics. For this example, let's assume that we want to display only the numbers 0 to 9. Furthermore, let's assume that each character cell of our display is made up of 8-by-8 pixels, as shown in Figure 15.8.

The diagram in Figure 15.8 shows how to create the character 3. Notice that I did not say "the number 3." The number 3 has a binary value of 00000011. Our character 3 will be identified by its ASCII code 0x33 (binary 00110011) and will be composed of 8 dot patterns of 8 bits each.

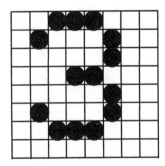

Figure 15.8: Characters for our oscilloscope display are composed of dot patterns.

Notice also that the actual matrix for the character is composed only of 5-by-7 dots. The extra space around the character pattern will automatically provide the spacing between the characters on the display.

We need a place to store the patterns for each of the characters in our desired character set. Since the patterns are 8 bits wide, an unsigned character array is ideal. Our 10 digits (0–9), at 8 bytes each, require 80 bytes. Since we are not using a complete ASCII character set and since we want to minimize the space required by our array, let's use the character colon (:) to represent a space. I chose it because it is the next ASCII code after nine (9). This means that our character patterns will require 88 bytes of space and can be initialized as shown below.

```
unsigned char display_code[80] = { ............ place codes here ............. }
```

You should determine the 8 numeric values for each of the rows of dots for each of the needed characters and initialize the array to those codes. The first 8 locations in the array should be the 8 codes for the character 0, the next 8 should describe the character 1, etc. The last 8 bytes in the array will be 0 because it represents our space, and a space has no pixels on. Since our raster generating code creates 8 lines, with line 0 at the bottom and line 7 at the top, we should place the character codes into the array starting at the bottom row of dots. We don't want the characters to be displayed upside down, do we? Of course, there are other choices. Many scopes have a switch for reversing the vertical polarity and we can always alter the code slightly so that the array can be accessed in the proper order.

For now, let's just assume that the codes are stored in the array starting at the bottom of the character. The code in Figure 15.9 should replace the inner **for( )** in Figure 15.7.

Of course, we also need to initialize a few variables at the beginning of Figure 15.7. The lines to insert are shown in Figure 15.10.

```
for(char_num = 0; char_num < 20; char_num++)
    {
    // get the proper piece of the character and store it in the int variable temp
    temp = display_code[ (line_data[ char_num]&0xf) * 8 + line_num];
    // use each subsequent bit in the word to control the next pixel state
    for(int k=0; k<8; k++, temp=temp<<1)
        if(temp&0x80)
            pixelON(line_num);
        else
            pixelOFF(line_num);
    }
```

Figure 15.9: This code controls the pixels displayed based on the ASCII codes in **line_data[ ]**.

```
int char_num, temp, k;
char line_data[21] = "100::200::0123456789"
```

Figure 15.10: These lines provide the proper variable initialization for
the additions of Figure 15.9.

The second line in Figure 15.10 contains the data that will be displayed on the oscilloscope. It
must be exactly 20 characters long, unless you have altered the **for**() in Figure 15.9 to handle a
different number of characters (due, perhaps, to the speed of your machine). Remember that the
colons in the line will be displayed as spaces unless you insert special codes into the
display_code[ ] array.

ASSIGNMENTS:

1. Implement all the examples discussed so far in this exercise and make sure you have the
    proper timing and hardware for them to work correctly. Create a tool function that will
    display one line of characters once on the oscilloscope. It should prototype as shown below:

        void scope_display(char line_data[ ]);

2. Create a new **scope_edit_num**() system that will allow numbers to be edited like they were
    in Exercise 14, but the characters will be displayed on an oscilloscope rather than on an LCD.
    Rather than positioning the cursor with the LCD commands, a flashing or nonflashing cursor
    can be created using the lower, presently unused row of pixels in the character display (see
    Figure 15.8). All modifications for creating a cursor can be made in the **scope_display**() tool,
    except that programs using the tool will have to pass a parameter to it to indicate where they
    want the cursor to be displayed. An **if**( ) statement can be used to determine when the cursor
    pixels need to be activated. If a counter is used to keep track of the number of passes through
    the loop, it is easy to decide when to activate the cursor if you want it to flash. Since keeping
    the oscilloscope display active is our responsibility, we must call the **scope_display**( ) tool
    continuously while we are waiting for keys to be pressed and released. The editing capability
    should be built around the **editNum**( ) function. Since we wrote the **edit_Num**() module
    using the **keycode**() module, which uses the **wtkp**() and **wtkr**() modules, the modifications
    can be made easily. We simply must call the **scope_display**() function from within the loops
    of the **wtkp**() and **wtkr**() modules. The address of **line_data**[ ] will have to be passed around
    a lot unless we defined it as a global variable.

REVIEW QUESTIONS
1. How are the pixels illuminated on a CRT screen?
2. Why are vertical and horizontal ramps (Figure 15.2) of different frequencies?
3. Why is the D/A converter necessary in this exercise?

4. Compare graphic and character displays with respect to both the amount of memory needed for the screen buffer and the translation tables.
5. Using a listing of your **scope_display**() tool, discuss in detail how it works.
6. Explain how you implemented a cursor for your system (Assignment 2).
7. After you have displayed characters on your oscilloscope, experiment with the scope adjustments to change the horizontal and vertical size of the characters. Explain what controls did what, and why.
8. What changes would have to be made to our hardware and software if we want to display 2 or more lines of characters on the oscilloscope?
9. Assume that we want the line of text to be displayed in reverse (black letters on a white background instead of white letters on a black background). How would you change the code of Figure 15.9 to do this?

Exercise 16
Understanding DRAM Operation

PURPOSE: The purpose of this exercise is to increase the readers' ability to understand complex hierarchical relationships by adding to the complexities of Exercise 15, which is itself based on previous exercises. As a by-product of this endeavor, we will explore the operation of a dynamic random access memory (DRAM) chip in detail and create a simple software-based DRAM controller. The software-based DRAM controller will then be used to implement a simple external storage system for programs such as the oscilloscope-based editor of Exercise 15. Because of the increased complexity of the interface, we will also examine how port pins can be assigned multiple functions. The real value of this exercise goes far beyond editing data and DRAM chips. The knowledge gained from understanding how multiple tasks can be integrated and controlled will enhance your ability to handle other problems.

OBJECTIVES: After the completion of this exercise, the reader should be able to:
- Describe the fundamental operation of a typical DRAM chip.
- Describe the software and hardware requirements for controlling and accessing a DRAM chip with a C program.
- Create tool modules for refreshing a DRAM, writing data to a DRAM, and reading data from a DRAM.
- Utilize the modules mentioned above in other application programs.
- Enhance the oscilloscope editor of Exercise 15 to allow the data being edited to be saved to and retrieved from a DRAM chip.

THEORY: The first thing that we need to do is to become familiar with the operation of a typical DRAM chip. Although today's memory chips are affordable and can store millions of bits of information, memory chips did not exist until about 1970. Even by 1977, enough memory chips to store 16 K (not meg) bytes cost over $500.

If you happen to have any of these older chips, you can certainly use them for this exercise because our application will require only a minimal amount of memory space. You should be aware, however, that many of the newer chips are easier to use. The ancient 4116-DRAM, for example, required three power supply voltages (–5, +5, and +12). Nearly all the DRAM chips that came after the 4116 operate on a single 5-volt supply. They are easy to recognize because they are 64 K or larger. This exercise assumes that you use a DRAM chip, not a memory module such as a SIMM or a SIP.

Before we get into the operation of a DRAM, we should compare it briefly to a static RAM (SRAM). SRAM chips are composed of standard F/F cells that hold each bit of information. A DRAM chip uses a very small capacitor for the storage cell, allowing DRAM chips to be less expensive and require less power than their SRAM counterparts. DRAM memory does have its drawbacks, however. It has slower access times than SRAM and, because the capacitors discharge, it must be refreshed continually to prevent memory loss. Often this refresh operation is handled by a hardware controller, but in this exercise, our program will perform the refresh operations.

Since DRAM chips consume less power, they can be produced in smaller packages (because there is less need to dissipate heat). In the past, when DIP packaging was prevalent for memory chips, the small size was difficult to achieve because of the large number of address pins that were needed for memory chips. The problem was solved by multiplexing the address and cutting the number of pins needed in half.

Refer to Figure 16.1 for a simple block diagram of a DRAM chip. Notice that the address for the chip is fed to 2 latches. In this example, each latch is 8 bits, which provides a total of 16 bits to be applied to the memory cells. In a typical computer system, hardware multiplexes the 16-bit address by first applying the top half to the address lines and then pulsing the RAS (row address select) line to latch it in an internal register. Next, the lower half of the address is applied to the chip and the CAS (column address select) is pulsed. This allows a 64 K memory chip (which normally needs 16 lines) to have only 8 address pins. Likewise, a 1-meg memory chip requires only 10 pins instead of 20.

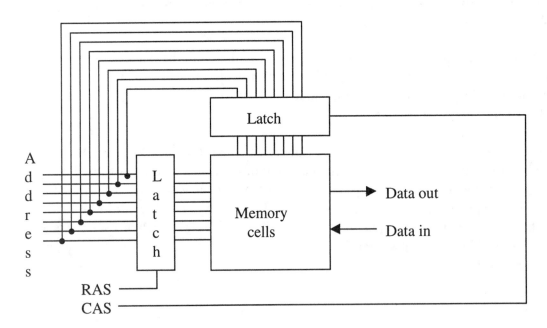

Figure 16.1: DRAM chips multiplex the address information using the RAS and CAS lines.

DRAM chips are often arranged as 1-bit words to give maximum flexibility. You can use 8 chips in parallel, for example, to get an 8-bit memory system or 16 in parallel for a 16-bit system. In the memory-hungry machines of today, memory is often implemented in SIMM or SIP packaging with surface-mount memory chips permanently soldered to the SIMM and SIP boards. This exercise assumes that you are using a standard DIP package DRAM composed of at least 64 K 1-bit words. If you are using other memory types, you should make appropriate modifications.

The 64 K 1-bit cells in the memory of Figure 16.1 is implemented as 256 rows of 256 cells in each row. Internally, DRAM chips are designed so that whenever any cell in a row is accessed, the capacitors for all the cells in that row are refreshed (that is, all the partially charged capacitors are recharged).

Most DRAM chips specify that each of the rows must be refreshed at least every 2 milliseconds to ensure memory integrity. While this is certainly true in a standard configuration where cells are written somewhat randomly, the nature of this exercise is that all the cells being used will be written in a single sequence of operations. I found that many memory chips used in this way maintain their data even if the refreshes were far out of tolerance with the published specifications; a refresh time period of nearly 1 second worked in some cases. Even so, we should try to make our designs conform to the specifications. (I mention this only because I have found many of my students are comforted by the knowledge that the timing for this exercise is not nearly as critical as they might have suspected after reading the data sheets for the DRAM chips they chose to use.)

The requirements for utilizing a DRAM chip from our C programs can be broken down into 3 distinct areas, so we should develop tool modules for providing each of the 3 functions for us. The 3 basic areas to be addressed are reading data from the chip, writing data to the chip, and refreshing the chip so that the present data will not be lost. Before we can get specific with our software design, we need to decide how to connect the port pins to the necessary DRAM pins. If we needed only to operate the DRAM or if we had plenty of ports available, such decisions would be easier. As mentioned at the beginning of this exercise, however, we want to utilize the DRAM chip with the oscilloscope editor discussed in Exercise 15.

Refer to Figure 16.2 to recall the suggested pin use for Exercise 15 and make a mental note of any changes that you might have made for your actual implementation. Since readers will be using a wide variety of hardware options, interface designs will vary from those suggested in the exercises. As long as you understand this discussion, you should be able to integrate the DRAM storage into your oscilloscope editor.

Eight-bit output port
Bit 7:   Scope trigger
Bit 6: z axis (turns the scope beam on and off)
Bits 3–5:   Unused
Bits 0–2:   Provides input for the D/A converter (vertical scope position)

Four-bit output port
Bits 0–3:   Used for matrix keypad scanning (driving)

Five-bit input port
Bits 0–3:   Used for matrix keypad scanning (reading)
Bit 4:   Unused

Figure 16.2: Suggested I/O pin assignments for the oscilloscope editor.

Next, let's examine the I/O requirements we will need for the DRAM interface. We will need 1 output pin for each of the following functions:

- Data in (data to be sent to the chip for storage)
- RAS (to latch address information for the ROW)
- CAS (to latch address information for the COLUMN)
- WRITE (to tell the chip if we are reading or writing)

We will also need some I/O pins to supply the address to the chip. The number of lines needed depends on the amount of memory we require. The oscilloscope editor in Exercise 15 suggested 20 characters, but some readers might have implemented more. Let's assume that we want enough memory to store at least 32 characters. If each character is represented by 8 bits, then we need 32 * 8, or 256, memory locations (1-bit words). That would require 8 address lines ($2^8 =$ 256). We can implement this as 4 bits of column data and 4 bits of row data, so we need only 4 I/O pins for address information. This means we need a total of 8 output pins. If you refer to Figure 16.2, you will see that we do not have that many pins available, at least not if you are using the standard parallel printer port on a PC. There are many ways to solve this dilemma and more complex solutions with more versatility will be discussed later in this text. For now, however, let's see how we can solve the problem by allowing some of the I/O pins to perform 2 functions. Figure 16.3 shows one possible solution for connecting the keypad, oscilloscope, and DRAM chip to the parallel printer port.

Eight-bit output port
Bit 7:   Scope trigger
Bit 6:   *z* axis (turns the scope beam on and off)
Bit 5:   *Sends data-out to the DRAM chip's data-in pin*
Bit 4:   *Connects to the DRAM chip enable pin*
Bits 0–3:   *Provides address to the DRAM chip*
Bits 0–2:   Provides input for the D/A converter (vertical scope position)

Four-bit output port
Bits 0–3:   Used for matrix keypad scanning (driving)
Bit 2:   *RAS line*
Bit 1:   *CAS line*
Bit 0:   *Write line*

Five-bit input port
Bits 0–3:   Used for matrix keypad scanning (reading)
Bit 4:   *Receives data-in from the DRAM chip's data-out pin*

Figure 16.3: Possible I/O pin assignments for the oscilloscope editor and the DRAM interface. (New assignments are in *italic*.)

Let's examine each of the additions to the pin assignments and see how we can ascertain or ensure that none of the devices interferes with the others. Let's start with the 5-bit input port because it is the easiest. We simply used bit 4 to read the data-out pin on the DRAM. We can easily mask the lower 4 bits when reading bit 4, but we must make sure that any data on bit 4 does not interfere with the operation of the keypad. If you refer to Figures 6.3 and 6.4, you will see that the keypad routines already mask all bits except those being used.

The 4 bits in the 4-bit output port were already used to drive the columns on the keypad. We are now using 3 of these lines to drive the RAS, CAS, and write lines of the DRAM chip. Pulsing the RAS, CAS, and write lines will not affect the operation of the keypad because these lines will be reset by the keypad routines before the row data is read. The reverse, however, is a potential problem. When the keypad scans the keys, it will pulse the RAS, CAS, and write lines on the DRAM. Pulses on the RAS and CAS do not cause any particular problems, but pulsing the write line can cause some random data to be written into some random address. My solution (not the only solution) is to use a bit on the 8-bit output port to control the chip enable of the DRAM chip. If the DRAM is not enabled, then pulsing any of the lines, including the write line, will have no effect.

As you can see from Figure 16.3, bit 4 connects to the DRAM chip enable. We must ensure that this bit is held high (the chip enable is active low) when other devices use the 8-bit port. The keypad does not use the 8-bit port, so we have no conflicts there. If you refer to Figures 15.3 and 15.4, you can see where the oscilloscope routines access the 8-bit port. In each case, we can ensure that bit 4 stays high by ORing the original data with 0x10. For example, in Figure 15.4, the oscilloscope trigger was pulsed with the following code:

```
out8data(0x80);
out8data(0);
```

We can replace these lines with:

```
out8data(0x80 | 0x10);  // or just use 0x90
out8data(0x10);
```

If we perform this type of action every time the oscilloscope routines access the 8-bit port, we will ensure that the DRAM chip is never enabled while the shared lines are being pulsed. Next, we need to ensure that, when the DRAM routines access the 8-bit port, there will be no interference with the oscilloscope routines. The DRAM routines must leave the most significant bit of the 8-bit port low at all times. Since the oscilloscope routines left the trigger pin low as a normal state, we can prevent any edges from occurring by simply keeping it low. If the sweep is never triggered, then we don't have to worry about what values may be on the other pins.

The above discussion is relatively complex, but it is worth the effort to review it until you understand it completely. Once you see what is happening you will find that the whole idea is pretty obvious.

Now that we have finalized the pin assignments and have a basic understanding of DRAM operation, we can start developing the DRAM functions. The first basic tool that we need is a routine called **refresh( )**, which pulses the RAS line (from high to low and back high again) for each of the 16 row addresses. Figure 16.4 shows how easily this can be accomplished.

If you've followed everything so far, the **refresh( )** routine should be easy to understand. If anything does not make sense, review the earlier material. You might wonder why we don't

```
void refresh(void)
    {
    int address;
    for(address=0; address<=15; address++)
        {
        out8data(0x10 | address);  // sends the address with the chip disabled
        out4data(7);  // makes sure the RAS, CAS, and write lines are high
        out8data(address);  // enables the chip while keeping the address stable
        out4data(3);   // pulses the RAS line low while the chip is enabled
        out4data(7);   // brings the RAS line back high
        out8data(0x10 | address);  // returns the chip to the disabled state
        }
    }
```

Figure 16.4: Refreshing the DRAM is simply a matter of pulsing the RAS line for the appropriate addresses.

```
void writeDRAM( int data, int address)
    {
    int addrlow, addrhigh;
    addrlow = address&0xF;
    addrhigh = (address&0xF0)>>4;
    data = (data<<5)&0x20; // places the data (0 or 1) at the correct bit position
    out8data(0x10 | addrhigh | data);   // sends the high address and data
                                        //  with the chip disabled
    out4data(7);  // makes sure the RAS, CAS, and write lines are high
    out8data(addrhigh | data);  // enables the chip while keeping the address
                                //  and data stable
    out4data(3);   // pulses the RAS line low to latch the high address
    out4data(7);   // brings the RAS line back high
    out8data(addrlow | data); // sends the low address
    out4data(5);                  // and latches it
    out4data(7);                  // with the CAS line
    out4data(6)                   // brings the write line low
    out4data(7);                  // completes the write
    out8data(0x10 | addrlow | data); // returns the chip to the disabled state
    }
```

Figure 16.5: Writing to the DRAM involves latching the address and then pulsing the write.

need any delays in the routine. If you examine the data sheet on a DRAM chip, you will see that the lines that we are manipulating must be stable, but only for periods measured in nanoseconds. Unless you have a very efficient compiler and a processor faster than anything available at the time this book was written, the pulses your code can generate will be measured at the microsecond level. Even so, it is worth remembering that delays must be inserted into code when the pulse width matters. We saw that as early as the sound routines presented in Exercise 3.

The next tool function we will need is a **writeDRAM( )** routine that will allow a data bit (1 or 0) to be written to a specified address in the DRAM chip. Figure 16.5 shows how this can be accomplished. The first 3 lines of the module in Figure 16.5 separate the address into the upper and lower nibbles and move the data bit to the proper position in the word. The code is well commented, so it should be easy to follow. Examine it carefully to see how events happen in the proper sequence. For example, notice that the address lines do not change at the same time that the RAS or CAS is pulsed. It is imperative that the address is stable when it is latched and that the data is stable when it is written.

Figure 16.6 shows how the **readDRAM( )** function can be created. If you understand the **writeDRAM( )** module, then Figure 16.6 should be easy to follow.

```
int readDRAM( int address)
    {
    int addrlow, addrhigh, data;
    addrlow = address&0xF;
    addrhigh = (address&0xF0)>>4;
    out8data(0x10 | addrhigh);    // sends the high address, chip disabled
    out4data(7); // makes sure the RAS, CAS, and write lines are high
    out8data(addrhigh); // enables the chip while keeping the address
                         // and data stable
    out4data(3);  // pulses the RAS line low to latch the high address
    out4data(7);  // brings the RAS line back high
    out8data(addrlow ); // sends the low address
    out4data(5);              // and latches it
    out4data(7);              // with the CAS line
    data = inputdata( );  // reads the input port
    data = (data>>4) &1; // moves the data bit to the LSB position
    out8data(0x10 | addrlow | data);  // returns the chip to the disabled state
    return data;
    }
```

Figure 16.6: Reading from the DRAM is easier than writing to it.

Now that we have the basic tool functions for dealing with the DRAM chip, it is easy to create higher level tools that can save and load data to and from the memory. Figure 16.7 shows the code for writing all the ASCII codes in a string (whose address is passed to the module) to the DRAM. The formula used to calculate the address in the call to **writeDRAM**( ) places the next bit written into the next sequential address.

```
void saveToDRAM(char array[ ] )
    {
    int charpos, bitpos, data;
    for(charpos=0; array[charpos]; charpos++)  // sequence through until the null
        {
        data = array[charpos];   // made data equal the next ASCII code
        for(bitpos=0; bitpos<8; bitpos++)  // sequence through all 8 bits in the code
            {
            writeDRAM(data&1, 8*charpos+bitpos);  // write the LSB  to the DRAM
            data = data>>1;  // move the next bit to the LSB
            }
        }
    }
```

Figure 16.7: The function to save data is simple because all the work is done by the lower-level tools.

```
void loadFromDRAM(char array[ ] )
   {
   // assumes array already contains the correct number of ASCII codes
   // this routine simply replaces each code with data from the DRAM
   int charpos, bitpos, data, newbit;
   for(charpos=0; array[charpos]; charpos++)  // sequence through until the null
      {
      data = 0;  // prepare to shift in new data bits
      for(bitpos=0; bitpos<8; bitpos++)  // sequence through all 8 bits in the code
         {
         newbit = readDRAM(8*charpos+bitpos);  // read the next bit
         newbit = newbit<<7;  // move the bit to the MSB
         data = data >> 1;  // move the data bits right to prepare for a new bit
         data = data I newbit;   // place the new bit into data at the MSB position
         }
      array[charpos] = data;  // place the new data word into the array
      }
   }
```

Figure 16.8: The function to retrieve data from the DRAM chip is very similar to the code in Figure 16.7 because the address sequences are identical.

A **loadFromDRAM( )** function is shown in Figure 16.8. It is similar to the **saveToDRAM( )** function except that the data is read from the chip and shifted into each word. Recall that the save routine sent the bits of each word to the chip, starting with the LSB. This means that the same address sequence reads the bits for each word, starting with the LSB. As you can see from Figure 16.8, the bits are added to the word at the MSB position and then are shifted right. When completed, the first bit obtained will arrive at the LSB position, where it belongs.

The routine in Figure 16.8 assumes that the array passed to it already has characters in it. This is necessary because the length of this array (string) determines how many bits to read from the DRAM. This is not really a restriction, because our **editNum( )** tool assumed that the string was a fixed length and was filled with spaces initially. As new data is read from the chip, the **loadFromDRAM( )** replaces the characters in the string with the data being read.

The final step in this exercise is to add these tool functions to the oscilloscope editor program so that the number being edited can be stored and retrieved from the DRAM chip. Let's review the keypad assignments used in the editor and add 2 new keys for interfacing with the DRAM. All the key codes are listed in Figure 16.9.

Key Code	Use
0–9	The numbers 0 through 9
10	Enter
11	Left arrow
12	Right arrow
13	Backspace
14	*SAVE to DRAM*
15	*LOAD from DRAM*

Figure 16.9: These codes are used to control the **editNum( )** function. (The new codes for interfacing with the DRAM are in *italic*.)

To keep the DRAM continually refreshed, we need to call the **refresh( )** routine (Figure 16.4) on a regular basis. To accomplish this goal, we need only to place the call inside the **while()** loops of the **wtkp( )** and **wtkr( )**, just as we did to refresh the oscilloscope display. This means that the DRAM and the oscilloscope display will be refreshed while we wait for a key to be pressed or released, which is most of the time. Technically, we are not refreshing the DRAM as fast as most specifications require, but I've had no problems with data loss. If the chip you use does require a faster refresh, call the **refresh()** routine from within the oscilloscope refresh code shown in Figure 15.7. An appropriate place to insert the call is immediately before the trigger is pulsed.

Recall that when a key is detected in **editNum()**, a **switch-case** control structure determines what action to take. If you add a **case** for 14 and 15 (see the codes in Figure 16.9), then the **saveToDRAM( )** and **loadFromDRAM( )** routines can be called when the user presses the appropriate keys.

ASSIGNMENT: Implement the routines presented in this exercise and verify that they work properly. Integrate the routines with the oscilloscope editor from Exercise 15. (As an alternative, you may choose to integrate with the LCD editor of Exercise 14, but you will have to adjust the I/O pin assignments.)

REVIEW QUESTIONS
1. What is the function of the RAS and CAS lines? Why do DRAM chips multiplex their address lines?
2. How can we use the same I/O lines for two purposes? What must be done to prevent conflicts between external devices?
3. Explain the requirements for refreshing a DRAM. Relate your explanation to Figure 16.4.
4. How can we pulse one line on an I/O port while keeping all the other pins stable?
5. Explain the formula for calculating the address in the **saveToDRAM( )** function.
6. Explain how the **loadFromDRAM( )** function converts the bits being read back into a word. Why is it necessary to set data to 0 in this routine?

7. Why must the **refresh( )** routine be placed in *both* the **wtkp( )** and **wtkr( )** routines?

8. Why does calling the **refresh( )** routine from within the oscilloscope routine make the refresh happen more often? Why is it unlikely that the **refresh( )** routine, when placed in the oscilloscope routine, will alter the timing for the scope display? If the time taken for refresh takes too long, then we can refresh *some* of the lines before each line is scanned on the scope. How can you implement such a solution?

Exercise 17
Controlling Multiple Motors

PURPOSE: The purpose of this exercise is to examine the problems and solutions associated with controlling 2 or more motors simultaneously.

OBJECTIVES: After the completion of this exercise, the reader should be able to:
- Discuss the problems associated with controlling multiple stepper motors simultaneously.
- Discuss the problems associated with controlling multiple dc motors simultaneously.
- Discuss the problems associated with controlling dc and stepper motors simultaneously.
- Implement solutions to all the problems mentioned above.
- Create a demonstration that manipulates multiple motors simultaneously.

THEORY: In several earlier exercises, we have examined how to control the speed and position of both dc and stepper motors. The programming solutions we examined in those exercises assumed that only 1 motor was being manipulated. If an application involves multiple motors, however, there is a good chance that situations will arise where 2 or more of the motors must be controlled simultaneously. A robot arm is a good example. Imagine how spastic the arm would appear if it moved each joint individually when trying to move the arm to a new position.

Let's begin our discussion by assuming that we have a robot arm with a shoulder motor and an elbow motor. For this example, let's also assume that both motors are stepper motors. If the desired position required the shoulder to move 200 steps and the elbow to move 100 steps, then we should move the shoulder 2 steps, the elbow 1 step, the shoulder 2 steps, the elbow 1 step, and so on, until the destination is reached. This is easy as long as we use nice round numbers like 100 and 200. If the steps required are 67 and 92, however, the methodology is not quite so obvious.

Fortunately, a simple algorithm does exist for handling this problem. To make the explanation of the algorithm more concrete, let's assume we will control 3 stepper motors, with the number of steps being 8, 5, and 2 for each successive motor. The algorithm requires first that we find the largest number of steps taken by any joint. Let's call that number N. In our example, N would be 8. We divide N in half and use the answer to initialize a counter for each motor. For our example, all 3 motors would start at 4.

Now all we have to do is perform the following operations N times. First, subtract the absolute value (the motors can be moving in reverse) of the number of steps each joint is supposed to take from the associated counters. If the resulting number is positive, then we continue with the loop. If the number is negative, then we step the joint in question and add the value of N to the counter

Loop	Joint 1	Joint 2	Joint 3
1	4 – 8 = –4 (step and add 8)	4 – 5 = –1 (step and add 8)	4 – 2 = 2
2	4 – 8 = –4 (step and add 8)	7 – 5 = 2	2 – 2 = 0
3	4 – 8 = –4 (step and add 8)	2 – 5 = –3 (step and add 8)	0 – 2 = –2 (step and add 8)
4	4 – 8 = –4 (step and add 8)	5 – 5 = 0	6 – 2 = 4
5	4 – 8 = –4 (step and add 8)	0 – 5 = –5 (step and add 8)	4 – 2 = 2
6	4 – 8 = –4 (step and add 8)	3 – 5 = –2 (step and add 8)	2 – 2 = 0
7	4 – 8 = –4 (step and add 8)	6 – 5 = 1	0 – 2 = –2 (step and add 8)
8	4 – 8 = –4 (step and add 8)	1 – 5 = –4 (step and add 8)	6 – 2 = 4

Figure 17.1: These calculations show how each motor is stepped the correct number of times.

for that motor. To help demonstrate this algorithm, Figure 17.1 shows the calculations just discussed.

As you can see, not only does each motor step the correct number of times, but the steps are spaced as equally as possible over the entire range. Figure 17.2 shows a code fragment demonstrating how to implement this algorithm in C. You might want to attempt to write your own version before proceeding. To make the calculations efficient, assume that the number of steps each motor will take is stored in an integer array.

The code shown in Figure 17.2 assumes that we have a tool function to handle some of the details. It assumes that we have a function to which is passed 2 arguments, the number of the motor to step and either a 1 or a 0 to indicate the direction to step the specified motor. This tool can be built in many ways. One simple solution is to **switch** on the motor number passed and create a **case** for each motor. This allows specialized code for each of the motors. This is especially valuable if the different motors use different pin assignments on different ports, making a general-purpose step routine difficult. Each case should use the second argument passed to determine the direction to step the motor.

Notice that the calling routine uses the comparison operator >= to pass a true/false condition and thus indicates the direction for the motor being stepped. Notice also how compact and efficient we were able to make the code because the data being manipulated is stored in arrays. The failure to organize data so that it may be processed efficiently is one of the most common mistakes made by novice programmers. There is a big lesson to be learned from this example. Don't take it lightly.

```
// assume that the number of steps each motor will take has been
//     stored in the array ns[ ]
// assume that the array mcount[nm] has been declared
// assume that nm is the number of motors
int n = 0, i, j;
// first find the maximum number of steps of any motor
for(i=0; i < nm; i++)
       if(abs(ns[i]) > n)
              n=abs(ns[i]);
// next initialize all the motor counters
for(i=0; i<nm; i++)
       mcount[i] = n/2;
// now perform the calculations n times
for(i=0; i<n ; i++)
       for(j=0; j<nm; j++)        // do the calculations for each motor
          {
          mcount[i] - =  abs(ns[i]);
          if(mcount[i]>=0)
             {
             mcount[i] + = ns[i];
             step_motor_number(i, ns[ i ] >= 0);
             }
          }
```

Figure 17.2: This code fragment implements the algorithm of Figure 17.1.

If the motors that we wish to control are dc motors, we must use an entirely different tactic. Recall from Exercise 12 that a potentiometer or count system can be used to indicate the position (and through calculation) the speed of a dc motor. If we need to move 2 dc motors to 2 destinations, we should start them at 2 different speeds using our best guess at what speeds might best accomplish the goal.

If we monitor closely the counters or potentiometers associated with each motor, we can easily see when the motor speeds need to be adjusted. For example, if we see that the first motor has reached 1/10 of the way to its intended destination before the second motor has reached 1/10 of the way to its final position, then we can either reduce the speed of the first motor or increase the speed of the second. If we continually adjust the speeds of the motors, the effect will be that each motor runs at exactly the right speed to ensure that both motors reach their intended destinations at the same time.

The key word in this discussion is *continually*. If motor positions are not monitored closely, then 1 motor can get so far ahead of the other that its speed will have to be reduced considerably, making the motion of that motor irregular at best. If the speeds of the motors are being controlled with software, as described in Exercise 10, it can be difficult to time the duty cycle of multiple motors simultaneously while monitoring their positions.

One way of solving time-critical problems such as these is to use interrupts to create a multitasking environment. Such a solution would have to be customized for different processors and different applications, so at least for this text, we need another choice. An alternative is to delegate some of the responsibility to hardware. Adding hardware may not be the most economical solution, but it is very easy to understand and implement.

The circuit in Figure 17.3 has 4 inputs that should be driven by an output port. The hardware shown will generate a duty cycle proportional to the number sent to the port. It works like this. The counter continually cycles from 0 to 15. When a 0 is detected, the F/F is set and remains set until the counter matches the number sent from the port. If the number sent from the port is 5, for example, then the F/F will remain on for 5/16 of the total count period. The output of the F/F is disabled during state 0 of the counter to ensure that a 0 sent from the port will never turn the output on. The output from this circuit attaches directly to the ON/OFF line in Figure 10.9. To achieve a reasonable frequency (50–100 Hertz) for this signal, we need to clock the counter in Figure 17.3 at about 1200 Hertz.

If we have a circuit like that of Figure 17.3 for each of the motors in our system, then we can establish the speed for each motor by simply writing a number from 0 to 15 to the I/O pins assigned to that motor. A separate bit would have to be assigned for each motor to control the direction. This circuit is an ideal candidate for implementation as a PLD if you have that capability.

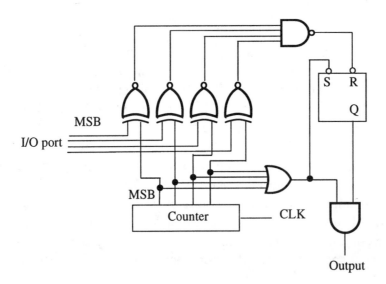

Figure 17.3: This circuit can control the speed of a motor without software intervention.

If we kept track of the position of each motor by monitoring the pulses generated by a shaft encoder, we would need to monitor the pulses from all the motors simultaneously. Although this isn't an impossible task, we can reduce the complications by again resorting to hardware. An obvious choice is to build a hardware counter for each motor and have that counter incremented by the output from the shaft encoder. If the output from each of the counters is connected to its own input port, then the software can clear the appropriate counter before a motor is turned on and then find its present position at any time by reading the present value of the counter.

Even a small counter of 5 bits or so can enable the software to monitor the movement of a motor over a fairly wide range of motion (32 pulses from the shaft encoder). If we needed longer sequences, the software can be programmed to keep track of how many times the counters have cycled and react accordingly.

With the ability to control the motors by sending the value of the desired speed to a port and with the ability to determine the location of any motor at any time by reading a port, we can easily coordinate the positions of 2 (or more) dc motors simultaneously. Let's assume that we want 2 motors to move to different positions at some speed stored in a variable we will call **sp**. Since the 2 motors will have to move at different speeds, our system will simply try to keep at least one of the motors operating at the requested speed. The software should clear all the counters (using an output pin connected to all the clears). It should set the speed of both motors to **sp**. To maintain the speed requested, the speed of one of the motors (for simplicity, let's assume we are discussing the first motor) is never changed.

The counts for each motor should be monitored continuously, which will be easy because the processor has nothing else to do. Each time one of the counters changes, the values of both counters can be compared to see if one or the other is moving too fast. Depending on the results of the comparisons, the speed of the second motor (and the second motor alone) should be increased or decreased. By keeping one motor constant and adjusting the speed of the other motor, we can maintain a speed close to the original requested speed. In this example, we kept the speed of the first motor constant. It probably makes more sense to keep the speed of the fastest motor (the one moving the longest distance) constant.

The only problem with using hardware to solve our speed and counter problems is that we will need far more input and output ports than we have been using for other exercises in this text. Examining a method for turning the printer interface into 4 8-bit output ports and 4 5-bit input ports can be a valuable exercise in itself. Figure 17.4 shows a method for doing just that.

The 4 output ports are made of 4 8-bit registers or latches. Any register can be used here as long as it latches on the negative edge of its clock. The data from the 8-bit output port of the printer interface can be directed to any of the 4 registers. The 4 input ports are simply tristates that can be addressed to enable the data from any one of them to be read by the standard input port of the printer interface. The 4-bit output port of the printer interface is used to control the access of the tristates and registers through the use of a 3-to-8 decoder, such as the 74138. When data is applied to the decoder, appropriate edges and levels are applied to the registers and tristate buffers. All we need is a set of tools for accessing these ports. To simplify the construction of these tools, we will use the printer port tools already developed.

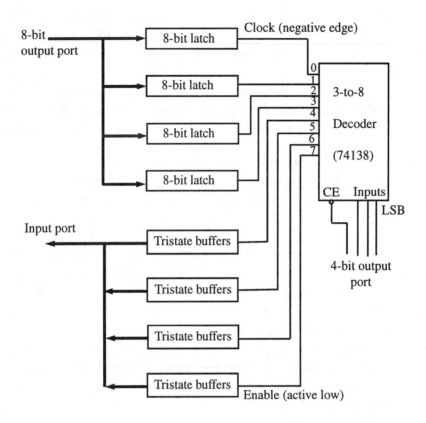

Figure 17.4: This hardware can turn a PC printer port into 4 input and 4 output ports.

The software for driving our expanded port system is not very complicated. It just needs to apply the proper signals in the proper order. Figure 17.5 shows the functions for accessing the new ports. Of course, if you construct this system, you may not use the older printer port functions anymore in your applications. All access of the new ports should be handled through the new tools.

The tool routines are well commented, so I don't think they need further explanation. They do assume the decoder is always left in the disabled state. If it should happen to be enabled by random data on the printer port, then the first access of any of the ports will leave the chip disabled so that future access cannot accidentally overwrite any of the registers.

All the projects in this text were designed so that they can be implemented using a minimum number of ports. With this expanded port system, you should be able to deal with more complex projects, even if you don't have additional I/O capabilities for your PC.

```
void output(int portnum, int data)
    {
    // the data provided is written to the port specified
    // send the port number to the decoder with CE high
    //    this will select the proper register when enabled
    out4data(8 | portnum);
    // apply data to all registers
    out8data(data);
    // enable the decoder and keep the input lines stable
    out4data(portnum);
    // disable the decoder while keeping inputs stable
    out4data(8 | portnum);
    // data is now latched into the selected register
    }

int input(int portnum)
    {
    int temp;
    // the proper inputs must be stabilized before enabling decoder
    // otherwise an accidental write might occur to a register
    out4data(8 | portnum);
    // now the proper tristate can be enabled
    out4data(portnum);
    // and the data can be read
    temp = inputdata( );
    // all done, so now return the chip enable high
    out4data(8 | portnum);
    // and return the information from the desired port
    return temp;
    }
```

Figure 17.5: These tools access the ports described by Figure 17.4.

So far we have seen how to control several stepper motors or several dc motors, but what do we do if we need to synchronize the movement of a dc and a stepper motor? Actually, the principles used for dc motors can apply here, with a little modification. Let's start by assuming we will step the stepper motor at the desired speed. We always know where the stepper is by keeping track of how many steps we have taken. Each time we take a step, we need to read the position (counter or potentiometer) of the dc motor (or motors). If the dc motor is ahead or behind where it should be relative to the stepper, we decrease or increase its speed accordingly.

ASSIGNMENT: This is a very unusual exercise because the material here depends greatly on the particular application under consideration. Even if you don't see an immediate need for this information, however, study the examples carefully. The principles discussed here can be applied to many other seemingly unrelated situations. (Knowledge is an interesting thing. Once it reaches a critical mass, it appears to grow exponentially as new information is added. This is true because the insights and perceptions gained from new data are not just related to the data itself but arise from its interaction with your previous knowledge.) To that end, the assignment for this exercise is open ended. After reading the examples in this exercise, choose a single, simple situation to explore. The only criterion is that it must involve the simultaneous control of 2 motors. You can control speed or position. You can use dc or stepper motors or one of each. Think of this as an experiment rather than an application. What you create does not have to perform useful work; it needs only to demonstrate a principle.

REVIEW QUESTIONS

1. Even if you have not completed the assignment for this exercise, choose a situation to explore as if you were ready to proceed. Outline the specifications for your choice and then discuss the personal reasons behind the choices you made.

2. The algorithm for stepping several motors is very effective and yet incredibly simple. Place yourself in the shoes of the original designer and try to imagine how you might have created it. How would you have started? What kind of activities or examples would you have explored? Is there any prior knowledge that you would have needed or that would have been a great help? Can you think of any other situations or applications that have similarities to the multiple stepper motor problem? What are they and how are they similar?

3. How can we use comparison operators to replace **if**( ) statements? If you cannot use the comparison operator method in Figure 17.2, show how you would have accomplished the same task.

4. The counters suggested for the dc motors were used to monitor the position of the motor relative to the time the counter was cleared. How can such a counter be used to provide information about the speed of the motor?

5. How many different speeds are available using the hardware described in Figure 17.3?

6. This exercise showed how the original 3 printer ports can be used to create 8 new ports. Couldn't we use those to create dozens of new ports and then those to create hundreds? What is the drawback to expanding our port system in this way?

7. When Figure 17.5 was discussed, it was emphasized that some lines had to be stable when another line was pulsed. Which lines had to be stable and why? Draw waveforms of the actions performed on the lines to aid your explanation.

Exercise 18
Ultrasonic Distance Measurement

PURPOSE: The purpose of this exercise is to explain how software control of ultrasonic pulses can be used to measure the distance to some object of interest. As the last exercise in this text, a secondary goal is to prepare you for the projects that follow in Part IV.

OBJECTIVES: After the completion of this exercise, the reader should be able to:
- Explain the principles of ultrasonic distance measurement.
- Describe the problems likely to occur when implementing an ultrasonic distance measurement system.
- Describe the methods required to calibrate an ultrasonic distance measurement system.
- Create an ultrasonic distance measurement system.

THEORY: Before we turn our attention to ultrasonic distance measurement, let's reflect on what we have accomplished. Previous exercises have demonstrated how to create tool functions for controlling and monitoring many types of devices. Each exercise has increased in complexity to the point that recent exercises have shown how numerous tools can be combined, using hierarchy-based designs, to handle reasonably complex situations.

Now you must test your skills and abilities by creating your own tools and solutions. Part IV of this text provides 11 general project descriptions to help you find an application that you will find interesting as well as challenging. The project descriptions lack specific detail and direction. They are meant only to trigger your imagination and get you started.

Don't be intimidated. As the exercises in this text became more complex, fewer details were given to you. Slowly but surely, you have assumed more responsibility for completing each assignment. If you have been successful up to now, I have no doubt that you will be able to handle the projects in Part IV. Even so, it doesn't hurt to help you through this transition period one last time. This exercise is designed to act as a bridge to the projects. It provides less detail than previous exercises, but more than you will get from the projects. I hope you find it helpful.

In this exercise, we will create a system that allows a computerized robot to determine how far it is away from a wall or other object in its path. The principle of our system is easy to understand. When our robot wishes to determine the distance to an object, it will generate a short burst of sound above the human hearing range that will be directed at the object in question. After the tone has been sent, the computer will listen and wait for the sound to bounce off the distant object and return. The amount of time it takes the echo to return can be used to determine how far the object is from the system.

Although we can create a burst of sound in the audible range, the continuous noise during normal operation of our system could be quite annoying. Instead, we will utilize a frequency above the human hearing range. This means, of course, that we cannot use standard speakers and microphones to generate and detect the signal. Fortunately, ultrasonic transducers are readily available for this purpose. They often come in matched pairs, one for transmitting and one for receiving. They are designed to operate at a specific frequency, the most common being 40 kHz.

First, we need a way of generating the tone. Although we can create it entirely in software, as we did in Exercise 3, we shall soon see that we will need the ability to adjust the frequency easily. Because of that, we will use the circuit in Figure 18.1 to generate our tone.

When the computer applies a logic 1 to the AND gate in Figure 18.1, the signal from the 555 will pass to the transistor, which drives the transmitting transducer. The 555 and the AND gate need to operate from a 5-volt supply. You can use a 5-volt supply for the transistor too, but I have experienced a much better range when I used 12 volts.

The 555 timer in Figure 18.1 needs to be adjusted to the resonant frequency of the transducers being used. Connect the receiving transducer to an oscilloscope. Turn on the transmitter and aim both transducers toward a wall or other large object that is a few feet away. Adjust the oscilloscope to see the received signal. Adjust the 555 frequency and watch how the amplitude varies on the oscilloscope. When the amplitude peaks, you have found the resonant frequency. Measure it with the oscilloscope and note it for later use. Aim the transducers at a wall about 8 feet away and make note of the amplitude on the oscilloscope.

Next, we need a receiving circuit. We need enough gain to convert the amplitude recorded above to at least 4 volts. The exact gain you will need will be based on your transducers, but something around 500 is not unreasonable. Such a high gain will certainly amplify noise as well as the desired signal, so a proper receiving circuit should look something like Figure 18.2.

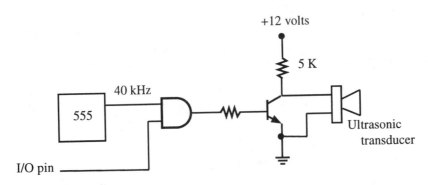

Figure 18.1: This circuit allows the computer to generate a 40 kHz burst.

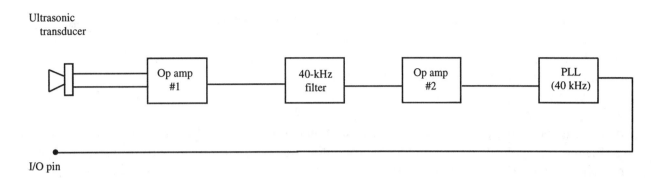

I/O pin

Figure 18.2: This circuit indicates the presence of an echo by toggling the state of an input pin.

The product of the gains of the 2 operational amplifiers as well as the gain of the filter should equate to the gain calculated earlier in this exercise. The filter should pass only 40-kHz signals and should have a bandwidth of only a few kilohertz at most. The phase lock loop (PLL) should be tuned to the resonant frequency of the transducers you are using. Make sure you are tuned to the fundamental frequency by monitoring the internal oscillator of the PLL, and not one of its harmonics. (I'm warning you because the harmonics have a much greater bandwidth and are easier to find than the fundamental.)

To test the operation of both circuits described so far, write a small program to produce a 2-ms pulse at a rate of 100 times per second. Apply that pulse to the transmit circuit. Aim both transducers at someone holding a notebook or other object so that it reflects the wave back toward the transducers. Connect the 2 channels of an oscilloscope to the output of the PLL and to the output pin controlling the AND gate. You should see the waveforms shown in Figure 18.3.

All the pulses shown in Figure 18.3 should be approximately 2 ms wide, but some variance is expected. The pulse controlling the AND gate indicates when the transmitter was enabled. The pulses labeled A from the PLL occur because the PLL triggers nearly immediately (it triggers so quickly because the 2 transducers are so close together), allowing the sound to travel the short path between the transducers.

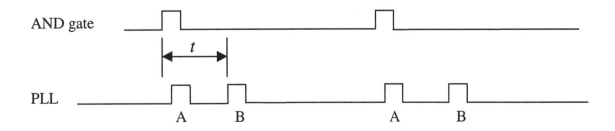

Figure 18.3: The waveforms above show how the distance can be determined.

The pulses labeled B from the PLL show when the echo was received. If the person holding the notebook moves further away, the time (labeled t) should increase. Likewise, if the person moves closer, the time t should decrease. If your system does not respond properly, you should examine the circuit of Figure 18.2 and determine the problem. Make sure that the time t is fairly stable before continuing.

Finally, you need to create a tool that will transmit an appropriate sized burst, wait until the initial signal (pulse A) dies out, and then measure the time period until the echo is received. How long should the transmit pulse be? The longer it is, the more power it will contain and the larger distance you will be able to measure. If the pulse is too long, however, you will not be able to measure small distances and your accuracy, even at reasonable distances, could suffer. Can you explain why?

How can you wait until the first pulse has subsided? Refer to Exercise 5. How can you determine the time of the echo? Refer to Exercise 9.

Although I have done a lot of the work for you, there is much left to be done. To complete the exercise, you will have to utilize information from courses you have taken or from library research. You will have to plan and organize. You will have to test and debug. That's what engineering is all about.

After you have completed this exercise, you will be ready to test your abilities on the projects in Part IV. I'll help you get started, but don't expect too much. Your trip with me is almost over. It's time you stepped out on your own. I hope you've enjoyed it as much as I have.

ASSIGNMENT: Implement the hardware and software described in this exercise. Use them to measure distances and display the readings with an appropriate method. If you find that your readings fluctuate a little, you might modify your tool so that it takes 5 readings, throws away the largest and the smallest, and returns the average of the other three.

REVIEW QUESTIONS
1. What choices did you have to make? Where did you find the information you needed?
2. What problems occurred during your implementation? How did you solve them?
3. What do you feel you learned from this exercise?

Part IV
Suggestions for Projects

Part IV provides descriptions of projects that can test the reader's ability to apply the concepts and principles that this text has explored. Hints and suggestions point the students in the right direction, but details, such as those provided by earlier exercises, are not provided. Even though the text provides sufficient background to enable most students to complete the projects described in this section, motivated students willing to perform additional research should be able to utilize the concepts presented here to develop elaborate projects.

Project 1
An Elevator System

PURPOSE: The purpose of this project is to design and build a model of an elevator system. As with all the projects in this section, the purpose of the text is to point you in the right direction. It is expected that you will conduct the experimentation and research necessary to bring this project to fruition.

OBJECTIVES: After the completion of this project, the reader should be able to:
- Describe a methodology for moving and controlling an elevator.
- Identify the strengths and weaknesses of using either stepper or dc motors.
- Create an algorithm for processing the floor and elevator buttons.
- Utilize your designs and the tool functions described in this text to create a working model of an elevator.

THEORY: Exercise 1 of this text described a simple elevator system and discussed a software model that can be used to control it. You should refer to that information because it provides a lot of background that will be helpful for this project.

Now that you have completed the exercises in this text, however, you should have the knowledge and experience to take the elevator in Exercise 1 to more realistic levels. The elevator of Exercise 1 moved from floor to floor as requested, but the user interface was far simpler than that of a real elevator. This simplification served its purpose at the beginning of this text, but at this stage, you should be able to go a lot further.

In Exercise 1, logically, there were really only 3 button inputs because the buttons *on the elevator* performed the same functions as the buttons *on the floors*. Furthermore, the algorithm in Exercise 1 created a situation where the buttons in the system would not be detected if they were pressed while the elevator was moving. In a real elevator, a button press can be detected at any time. The presses are immediately acknowledged by lighting a lamp in the button itself. The request made by the press, although detected and acknowledged immediately, may not be processed until later.

For example, a real elevator that is moving from the first to the third floor will not stop at floor 2 if the DOWN button on floor 2 is pressed. It will, however, process the request and move to floor 2 only after completing its movement to floor 3. If the UP button is pressed on floor 2, however, the elevator will stop while traveling from the first floor to the third. These actions certainly complicate the problem described in Exercise 1, but all we need is a plan.

Obviously, the system must have some way to detect keypresses while the elevator is moving. An easy solution is to place the detection code inside a module that can be called from the dc motor routine or anywhere else in the program that we need to monitor the switches. The detection software should not try to take any action in response to a button press. Instead, it should simply record the information so that other sections of the program can use it to control the actions taken.

A method for storing the switch button data needs to be devised. Since there are 7 switches total (3 in the elevator, 1 on the first floor, 2 on the second, and 1 on the third) the first method that comes to mind is an array that holds 7 integers. Any time a button is detected, its position in the array can be set to 1. When the button is processed, the processing routine will clear that position in the array.

The status of the buttons needs to be read on a regular basis, perhaps at least 10 times each second. Whenever your program has the possibility of staying in a loop for more than 100 milliseconds, it should call an update module that would scan the buttons and update the array. The scan routine might also illuminate LEDs to indicate that a button is pressed, a simulation of lighted buttons in a real elevator. Of course, each time a floor is reached, the software should check the button array and decide what action to take based on the current switch conditions.

If your computer system has interrupt capability, you might consider ORing the outputs from all the buttons together to create an interrupt signal. The interrupt routine could update the array and change the status of the LED indicators. This would be an ideal solution because the interrupt routine can accomplish its task so fast that other routines would not even notice and no calls to an update routine would have to be inserted in the code. Every routine would still have to monitor the button array, but none of the elevator routines would be responsible for keeping the array updated.

The elevator itself can be positioned using either a dc or stepper motor. A dc motor can typically move a heavier elevator. It can also move the elevator faster than a stepper motor. A dc motor requires that you have some means of determining when a floor was reached such as a mechanical switch or infrared beam at each floor. Another alternative is placing a slotted disk on the motor shaft so that incremental movements can be counted.

The stepper motor would be able to position itself to the correct floor by counting the number of steps taken. If you use a stepper motor, you should probably at least place a limit switch on the first floor so the system can move to the first floor and set the count to 0 when first turned on. The switch also allows the software to verify that no slippage has taken place by checking the status of the limit switch each time the elevator moved to the first floor.

If you really get ambitious, you might want to add a moving door to the elevator. Let me warn you, however, that this complicates the mechanics considerably. Without the door, nothing electrical has to be placed on the elevator. Adding the door means extra weight and having to deal with running wires to a moving object.

ASSIGNMENT: Define the specifications for an elevator that you wish to build. Be specific about how it should respond to user input. Implement your solution and test, troubleshoot, and debug the hardware and software until they perform according to your original specifications.

REVIEW QUESTIONS
1. What part of the design process did you find the most difficult? Why?
2. What problems did you encounter? How did you solve them?
3. Did your final implementation meet all the original specifications? If not, why? How do you think you could have overcome the limitations of your solution?
4. Was your final implementation accurate 100% of the time? What kind of situations caused it to fail? How do you think these situations can be dealt with?
5. What did you learn from this project that you feel was particularly valuable? How do you think it will help you in the future?

Project 2
Determining Colors

PURPOSE: The purpose of this project is to find a simple, inexpensive method for the computer to determine the color of an object. As with all the projects in this section, the purpose of the text is to point you in the right direction. It is expected that you will conduct the experimentation and research necessary to bring this project to fruition.

OBJECTIVES: After the completion of this project, the reader should be able to:
- Describe a methodology for allowing the computer to determine the color of an object.
- Identify the strengths and weaknesses of the final solution.
- Create a tool function that can return a numeric equivalent of the color of an object.
- Utilize the color-determining tool function in a program to demonstrate that it can successfully determine the colors of different objects.

THEORY: With today's technology, one method for determining the color of an object immediately comes to mind. If we have a large computer system (such as a PC instead of a single board controller or embedded microcomputer), we can purchase a video capture board, use it to take a picture of the object, and read the numeric value of the screen memory associated with the pixels in question. Such a method is certainly a possibility, but if you don't already have a video capture device or if you need a low-cost solution for a new product, it might not be a feasible solution.

To arrive at another solution, let's remember what causes objects to have a color property in the first place. When a white object reflects the light that falls on it, it reflects all colors relatively equally. A red object, on the other hand, will tend to absorb all colors except red. If we shine a white light (one that is composed of all colors) on a red object, most colors will be absorbed. Only the red light will be reflected, making the object appear red to our eyes.

If we shine a red light on a white object, it will still appear red to us because it reflects only red light (because red is the only light hitting the object). If we shine a red light on a green object, however, it will appear very dark or even black if our red light is the only light in the room. Obviously, if there is any white light in our room, our observations will be affected.

The above principle can provide us with the basis for a simple method for determining the color of an object. Let's start by connecting a photoresistor or other light-sensitive device to some form of A/D converter (refer to Exercise 9). If we use the 555 method, perhaps the photoresistor could be one of the two resistors that control the time periods of the generated waveform. If a more conventional A/D method is to be used, we can place the photoresistor in series with a fixed resistor of an appropriate size and connect a dc voltage across the 2 resistors. Since the 2 resistors will divide the voltage based on their relative resistance, the voltage across either resistor will vary based on the amount of light that strikes the photoresistor. If an A/D converter is used to read the voltage across one of the resistors (probably the one connected to ground) and if that resistor is the fixed resistor, then the number obtained should be proportional to the amount of light hitting the photoresistor. This is true because the resistance of most photoresistors decreases as the amount of light that hits them increases.

This alone does not allow us to determine color—only the amount of light hitting the photoresistor. Imagine, however, that we place several LEDs next to the photoresistor so that when they are on, the light they produce will be directed away from the photoresistor, but in such a manner that it can be reflected back to the photoresistor if an object was in close proximity.

Imagine further that all the LEDs are not the typical red LEDs. We can easily obtain yellow and green LEDs today and, for a little more money, even blue and white LEDs can be purchased. If only the red LED is turned on, for example, then the A/D reading is high only if the object being tested is red. Orange or purple objects show some red, but they show less than a pure red object. A green or blue object shows very little, if any, red.

By turning on different colors of LEDs (or even small flash light bulbs with color filters) and noting the amount of light reflected to the photoresistor in each case, we should be able to determine the color of the object reflecting the light. For example, if your subject is an orange object, you should observe that it reflects more light when it is illuminated by red and yellow light than by green or blue. It is important, of course, that we place the photoresistor and the lights in some small container that can be held up to the object being tested. This is to prevent room light from interfering with the measurements being taken.

It should also be obvious that, ideally, the photoresistor should be equally sensitive to different colors of light. It should also be obvious that we cannot expect to have such luck. A far more reasonable expectation is that some colors will affect the photoresistor more than others, even when they are of the same intensity. We can correct this easily.

For example, if the green LED, when pointed at a green object, generates an A/D value only half as large as the red LED when pointed at a red object, then we can use 2 green LEDs in parallel to generate twice as much light. Once we get the levels reasonably close to each other, we can mathematically compensate for any differences. If all the levels are too low, it might be necessary to increase the sensitivity of the photoresistor using a transistor or an operational amplifier.

We can use our system in several ways. If we want it to determine an absolute color, then we might want to determine the amount of each of the primary colors (red, yellow, and blue) being reflected. In such a case, we need to calibrate the levels for each of the colors as described in the previous paragraph.

Another potential application is for the computer simply to recognize which of several objects is presented to it, with each of the objects being a different color. In this situation, proper calibration is not critical. We don't really need to know what color each object is, we only need to know what color values (which we can determine through experimentation) certain specific objects generate. The known values can be stored in tables (arrays) and compared to a sample from an unknown object to see which is the closest match.

ASSIGNMENT: Define a color-related application that interests you and design the hardware and software needed to solve the problem. Implement your solution and test, troubleshoot, and debug the hardware and software until they perform according to your original specifications.

REVIEW QUESTIONS
1. What part of the design process did you find the most difficult? Why?
2. What problems did you encounter? How did you solve them?
3. Did your final implementation meet all the original specifications? If not, why? How do you think you could have overcome the limitations of your solution?
4. Was your final implementation accurate 100% of the time? What kind of situations caused it to fail? How do you think these situations could be dealt with?
5. What did you learn from this project that you feel was particularly valuable? How do you think it will help you in the future?

Project 3
A Light-Seeking Sensor

PURPOSE: The purpose of this project is to create a light-sensitive sensor that can rotate until it is pointed at a designated target, such as the brightest point in a room, or at a light flashing at a specific frequency, such as 2 pulses per second. Once the target has been found, the sensor should be able to use the positional information to perform some useful task. For example, the system could track and follow the source as it moves around the room. If 2 sensors were implemented, the system should be able to use the angles of each of the sensors to triangulate the position within the room of the target. As with all the projects in this section, the purpose of the text is to point you in the right direction. It is expected that you will conduct the experimentation and research necessary to bring this project to fruition.

OBJECTIVES: After the completion of this project, the reader should be able to:
- Describe a methodology for allowing the computer to locate a light source.
- Identify potential problems that might relate to tracking a light source.
- Design the hardware and software necessary for measuring the amount of light available as measured from different positional views of a sensor.
- Utilize your designs and the tool functions described in this text to create a light-seeking sensor.

THEORY: Detecting the intensity of a light source requires little more than a photoresistor and a suitable A/D converter, as discussed in Project 2. In this case, however, we might want a simple lens arrangement to make the sensor directional. At the very least, we need to place the sensor in the back of a small tube.

If the sensor and its directional apparatus is mounted to the shaft of a stepper motor, then we can rotate the sensor and take readings both to the left and right of the present position. If we remember the position of the brightest reading, we can return to that position and continue with the search. Making such measurements with a single sensor will require the stepper motor to move continually, taking readings of at least 3 positions before deciding if the object being tracked is moving and, if so, in what direction.

Rather than move the motor to take readings in 3 positions, you might consider constructing 3 sensors, each pointed a few degrees apart. Since all 3 readings could be taken without moving the motor, the system would be able to react much faster to a moving object.

You might also consider implementing 2 sensors, each with its own stepper motor and each placed at adjacent corners in a room. If the software moves each sensor to find the target, the angles of the 2 sensors can be used, along with a little trigonometry, to triangulate the position of the target. This idea is the basis for a simple navigation system. The accuracy of the system would be limited by the step angle of the motors, as well as the optical limitations of the sensors themselves.

In all these examples, we don't want the wires to the sensors to wrap around the motor shaft. To prevent this, we limit the movement of the motor to something appropriate to our needs: by mechanical stops, limit switches, or keeping track of the number of steps taken.

If a room has a lot of windows, the sunlight (even bouncing off a wall) can be brighter than a small light source such as a flashlight. A potential solution is to have your software look, not for the brightest light, but for a light that is pulsing at a specific frequency. If the light source is an incandescent bulb, the frequency should be very low, perhaps 10 Hertz or less, because higher frequencies will tend to create an average light level.

You might consider using infrared LEDs pulsing at a higher frequency, perhaps 40 kHz. The proper output from the sensors can be detected using a phase lock loop as described in Exercise 18. A tuned system might be necessary if your environment has either sun or fluorescent lights, both of which contain large amounts of infrared emissions.

A robot can use this method to aim itself toward a doorway or a nest that contains a battery charger. It is also easy to imagine a robot that can follow a light source (or you if you were wearing the light source).

ASSIGNMENT: Define the specifications for an application related to a light-seeking sensor and design the hardware and software needed to solve the problem. Implement your solution and test, troubleshoot, and debug the hardware and software until they perform according to your original specifications.

REVIEW QUESTIONS
1. What part of the design process did you find the most difficult? Why?
2. What problems did you encounter? How did you solve them?
3. Did your final implementation meet all the original specifications? If not, why? How do you think you could have overcome the limitations of your solution?
4. Was your final implementation accurate 100% of the time? What kind of situations caused it to fail? How do you think these situations could be dealt with?
5. What did you learn from this project that you feel was particularly valuable? How do you think it will help you in the future?

Project 4
A Line-Following Robot

PURPOSE: The purpose of this project is to create a simple mobile robot that can follow a line on the floor. As with all the projects in this section, the purpose of the text is to point you in the right direction. It is expected that you will conduct the experimentation and research necessary to bring this project to fruition.

OBJECTIVES: After the completion of this project, the reader should be able to:
- Describe a methodology for determining if a sensor system is on a line, to the left of a line, or to the right of a line.
- Identify potential problems that might relate to following a line.
- Design the hardware and software necessary for determining the position of a moving robot relative to a line on the floor.
- Utilize your designs and the tool functions described in this text to implement a robot that can follow a line on the floor.

THEORY: Before we begin our discussion of the sensors required for this project, let's look at the requirements for a simple mobile robot. Obviously, the robot needs drive wheels and some way to steer. To avoid the necessity of a steering system, the robot can be based on 2 motorized wheels and 1 or 2 casters. If both wheels turn in the same direction, the robot moves forward or backward, depending on the direction of rotation. If the 2 wheels turn in opposite directions, the robot turns left or right. The motors themselves could be dc motors, stepper motors, or even servomotors as described in Project 10 of this text.

You might want to visit a local toy store (or Radio Shack during the Christmas season). A small, motorized car or tank can probably be modified to meet the needs of this project easier than building a robot from scratch. Just be careful not to get something that moves too fast. Following a line, especially a curvy line at any reasonable speed, is a little more difficult than you might imagine. The mobile device should also be relatively small, unless you have a large area available. You might consider a line of black electrical tape on a white posterboard to get a consistent high-contrast image. The line should have gentle curves. Save sharp turns, forks in the line, and other complex situations until after you have a simple system working. If you decide to tape several posterboards together, tape on the underside so that you do not alter the reflective properties of the paper.

To keep the lighting conditions under the vehicle constant, a light source such as LEDs or a flash light bulb should be mounted under the vehicle near the sensors. Make sure the sensors are positioned and/or enclosed so they see only light that is reflected from posterboard and not directly from the light source.

The light sensors in this project differ from those in Project 3 because the sensors needed here do not necessarily need to detect how much light is being reflected. This means that the signal from the sensor could simply be a 0 when the sensor is over a black area (such as the tape) or a 1 otherwise. Of course, you can use the A/D method described in Project 3. With proper design and calibration, an analog sensor should be able to tell you additional information, such as how close to the edge of the tape the sensor is.

When you consider the algorithm for guiding the vehicle, remember that the line may be curved and that the program can easily find itself off the line without knowing for sure which side of the line it is on. The more sensors you have, the less likely the software will get confused.

I'd like to offer a suggestion for exploring the methodology required for this problem. You may think it sounds simplistic, but I urge you to try it before you pass judgment. Cut a piece of paper the size of your car or tank and punch holes in it where you plan to place your sensors. If you plan to have 3 sensors, then punch 3 holes. Number the holes so they can be identified.

Have a friend place the paper car on the posterboard so that the line is showing through at least one of the holes. Tell your friend to move the car in small increments by giving such instructions as "Turn right" or "Move forward." After each movement, your friend should tell you which holes show the line and which do not. If you plan on using analog sensors, you can be told what percentage of the hole shows the line, but nothing about whether the line is on the left or the right side of the hole.

Based on what you are told, you should try to give movement instructions to your friend that will force the paper car to follow the line. This process will take a lot longer than you would imagine, but it will give you great insight about how to write your program. Try changing the spacing and number of holes on your car. You might also determine exactly how far the car should move when you give a command. Proper planning at this stage will ensure success later.

ASSIGNMENT: Construct a simple robot and verify that your software can control its movements. Using posterboard and electrical tape, create a line that you wish your robot to follow. Use a paper robot as described in the text to develop an algorithm suitable for controlling your vehicle. Design and mount sensors on your robot based on your findings with the paper model. Implement your solution and test, troubleshoot, and debug the hardware and software until they perform according to your original specifications.

REVIEW QUESTIONS
1. What part of the design process did you find the most difficult? Why?
2. What problems did you encounter? How did you solve them?
3. Did your final implementation meet all the original specifications? If not, why? How do you think you could have overcome the limitations of your solution?

4. Was your final implementation accurate 100% of the time? What kind of situations caused it to fail? How do you think these situations could be dealt with?

5. What did you learn from this project that you feel was particularly valuable? How do you think it will help you in the future?

Project 5
Satellite Positioning

PURPOSE: The purpose of this project is to allow experimentation with problems associated with positioning a device, such as a satellite in space, where there is very little friction. As with all the projects in this section, the purpose of the text is to point you in the right direction. It is expected that you will conduct the experimentation and research necessary to bring this project to fruition.

OBJECTIVES: After the completion of this project, the reader should be able to:
- Identify the problems associated with positioning an object in the weightless vacuum of space.
- Describe the methodology for controlling the position of a device in space.
- Design a positioning system that can simulate, to some degree, the properties of a satellite in space.
- Utilize your designs and the tool functions described in this text to create a system that can move a simulated satellite to a desired position.

THEORY: Exercise 12 dealt with positional control, but the friction of the potentiometer should have dampened the movement to the point that the system stabilized relatively easily. If we need to orient a satellite in space so that it pointed in a certain direction, we would find a very different problem. Obviously, we cannot use conventional means for moving the satellite because we do not have anything to push against. The easiest solution is probably to expel gas from a compressed air tank. The reaction would move the satellite in the opposite direction from the point where the gas was expelled.

Once we get the satellite moving in a near frictionless environment such as space, there is nothing to stop it from continuing to spin forever (or at least for a very long time). If we want to experiment with such a problem, our first goal is to find a way to simulate the situation. Imagine that you have a circular piece of light wood (or other suitable material) mounted with a bearing (many types are available at your local hardware store) at its center so that the wood will spin freely in a horizontal plane. It's certainly not friction free, but a good bearing will serve our purpose. Recall how long a bicycle wheel will spin when not touching the ground. If you want to get really creative, mount the disk on a large cork and let it float in a bowl of water.

To move the wooden disk, we need to place cardboard vanes every 20 degrees or so. Each vane is perpendicular to the disk itself and situated so that if you blow on the vanes, the disk will move. Mount 2 12-volt fans so that 1 fan will blow the disk in a clockwise direction and the other fan will blow it in a counterclockwise direction. Interface the fans with the computer so that your software can turn on either fan as desired. We don't want to be able to control the speed of the fan. We must control the movement of the disk by controlling how long we turn a fan on.

Once the movement is started, the system should coast easily, making it overshoot its intended position. To stop the movement, we must turn on the opposite fan for the right amount of time. Research PID control, as discussed in Exercise 12, to help you design your program.

To implement a PID algorithm, the software must be able to determine factors such as the present position of the disk and its present speed. If we have slots or holes positioned around the outer edge of the disk, we can monitor how they make and break a light beam. By counting the number of pulses, we can determine the position of the disk, and if we measure the time between pulses, we can calculate the speed of rotation.

If your software is not smart, it might be difficult to tell which direction the disk is moving, especially if there is any oscillation around the destination. If you do a little research on optical encoders, you will see that using 2 beams with a proper hole arrangement can allow you to obtain both increment and direction information. You can also improve your accuracy by creating the pattern to break the beams with a CAD program and then printing it on a transparency.

ASSIGNMENT: Construct a hardware system for simulating a satellite in space and design a system for controlling its movement by turning on 2 fans. Implement your solution and test, troubleshoot, and debug the hardware and software until the disk can be positioned as requested to within the tolerance of your optical encoder. When compared to a real satellite problem, turning on a fan is analogous to using up gas in the compressed air tanks. Your goal is to position the system as fast as possible while turning on the fans in a minimum amount of time. If several people or several groups are engaged in this project, it can be used as a competition to see which solution is the most efficient. Each group should use the same hardware because systems with more friction will be easier to control.

REVIEW QUESTIONS
1. What part of the design process did you find the most difficult? Why?
2. What problems did you encounter? How did you solve them?
3. Did your final implementation meet all the original specifications? If not, why? How do you think you could have overcome the limitations of your solution?
4. Was your final implementation accurate 100% of the time? What kind of situations caused it to fail? How do you think these situations could be dealt with?
5. What did you learn from this project that you feel was particularly valuable? How do you think it will help you in the future?

Project 6
Audio Capture/Edit/Playback

PURPOSE: The purpose of this project is to create a system that can act as a digital recorder by capturing audio signals and playing them back as needed. Earlier exercises actually provided the software tools for recording and playing back the signals, so the emphasis here will be adding the ability to edit the recorded data. As with all the projects in this section, the purpose of the text is to point you in the right direction. It is expected that you will conduct the experimentation and research necessary to bring this project to fruition.

OBJECTIVES: After the completion of this project, the reader should be able to:
- Describe a methodology for providing editing capabilities to a digital recording system.
- Identify additional hardware needed to enable digital recording and playback.
- Research the necessary graphic commands and create a graphic interface to enhance the editing features of the system.
- Utilize your designs and the tool functions described in this text to create a digital recording system with playback and edit capabilities.

THEORY: In Exercises 8 and 9, we developed routines that captured analog data using an A/D converter and we saw how that data was stored in an array. We learned how to convert that data back to analog by copying the array to a port interfaced to a D/A converter.

For this project, you need to interface a microphone to an 8-bit A/D converter capable of at least 5000 samples per second. You need this minimum sample rate to obtain even a reasonable reproduction of an audio signal. A rate of 10,000 samples per second will give you telephone quality; 20,000 will start sounding more like your stereo.

A microphone will provide an ac signal, so if you amplify it with an operational amplifier or preamp chip, you will need an A/D converter capable of sampling ac signals. Another alternative is to add a dc offset to the microphone signal so that the final waveform will vary between 0 and 5 volts. Making these adjustments to the waveform is referred to as *signal conditioning*.

If you want to use headphones to hear the playback, you should be able to drive them from a single operational amplifier acting as a buffer for the D/A. If you want to use a speaker, you will need some form of power amplifier. You can choose which portions of the waveform to hear by deciding which portions of the array to copy to the D/A converter.

The basic idea of the editor is really simple. Imagine having several arrays to act as storage buffers for the sampled signals. The user should be able to record speech or other analog signals and store it in any of the buffers. The user should also be able to copy any portion of a buffer into any other buffer, starting at a specified position. If the program can graph these buffers on the screen, it will be easy for a user to specify portions of a buffer to play or copy by moving starting and ending cursors (small vertical lines on the graph) with the arrow keys. After the data in a buffer is finalized, the user should be able to save it to a disk. Saved files should be retrievable and the user should be able to place the data read from the disk into any buffer. Although the above actions are individually pretty simple, together they provide some powerful capabilities. Create the tool functions first, then assemble the system.

The challenge is to create a user interface that makes it easy to select which buffers and/or portions of buffers to use for editing operations. The graphs mentioned above do not have to graph every byte in the array, and they certainly don't have to have 256 levels of resolution. Scaling the amplitude to 20% of full scale allows several buffers to be displayed simultaneously on a PC screen. At 5000 samples per second, a 20,000-element array can hold 4 seconds of speech. Even a standard VGA screen is 640 pixels across, so the graph can display every thirtieth pixel or so, giving an edit resolution of about 130 milliseconds. If you want to get really fancy, you can mark a section of the buffer and have it expand to allow editing at a finer resolution.

The actual graphic commands needed for this project will vary based on what compiler you use, so they will not be discussed here in detail. A brief introduction to graphics is discussed in Appendix A, but you should visit your library or explore the help system that came with your compiler to get the details you need.

ASSIGNMENT: After you get the basic hardware and software working, thus allowing you to record and play back voices, define the specifications for a sound editing system. Pay particular attention to the user interface because the major goal is to make the system easy to use. Implement your solution and test, troubleshoot, and debug the hardware and software until they perform according to your original specifications.

REVIEW QUESTIONS
1. What part of the design process did you find the most difficult? Why?
2. What problems did you encounter? How did you solve them?
3. Did your final implementation meet all the original specifications? If not, why? How do you think you could have overcome the limitations of your solution?
4. Was your final implementation accurate 100% of the time? What kind of situations caused it to fail? How do you think these situations could be dealt with?
5. What did you learn from this project that you feel was particularly valuable? How do you think it will help you in the future?

Project 7
A Simple Logic Analyzer

PURPOSE: The purpose of this project is to create a simple logic analyzer that can sample 5 digital lines. As with all the projects in this section, the purpose of the text is to point you in the right direction. It is expected that you will conduct the experimentation and research necessary to bring this project to fruition.

OBJECTIVES: After the completion of this project, the reader should be able to:
- Understand the basic internal operation of a logic analyzer.
- Identify the need for trigger words and understand how they are implemented.
- Design software modules for capturing digital data, storing it in an array, and displaying it in a graphical format.
- Utilize your designs and the tool functions described in this text to create a simple logic analyzer.

THEORY: You probably have heard of logic analyzers and perhaps have even used one in the lab. Basically, a logic analyzer acts much like a storage scope except that it captures digital instead of analog information. One advantage of a logic analyzer over an oscilloscope is that the analyzer will typically have many channels, perhaps 32 or more. Another advantage of a logic analyzer is that the user can specify when to take the samples based on the patterns found in a trigger word or in the data itself. If you have never used a logic analyzer, do some research at the library or on the Internet until you feel comfortable continuing.

We can start building a logic analyzer by creating a routine that can sample an input port at various specified rates (such as every millisecond or every 100 milliseconds) and store the data gathered in an array. Once the data is gathered, another routine should be created that can graph the data. If you are using the 5-bit printer port, then your analyzer will be able to sample only 5 digital inputs and the graph of your data should be 5 waveforms showing the high/low patterns represented by each of the bit positions.

The actual graphic commands needed for this project will vary based on what compiler you use, so they will not be discussed here in detail. A brief introduction to graphics is discussed in Appendix A, but you should visit your library or explore the help system that came with your compiler to get the details you need.

Assume for a moment that you want to use your logic analyzer to sample the waveforms generated by a 4-bit counter. You can connect 4 lines from the input port to the F/F outputs of the counter. The fifth bit of the port can be connected to the clock signal that drives the counter. Your software should be able to sample all 5 signals at a specified rate. The rate at which you choose to sample would probably be based on how fast the counter is being clocked. For example, if the clock rate for the counter was 100 Hertz, then you might want to sample at 10 times that rate, or 1 kHz. To make graphing on a PC easy, let's assume that we always take 640 samples (one for each horizontal pixel on a VGA screen).

The 640 samples are taken in less than a second at the 1 kHz rate and display 4 complete count sequences of the counter when the data is graphed. Assume for a moment that the counter is faulty. You think there might be a noise problem when the counter transitions from state 14 to state 15. If you want to get a more detailed view of that portion of the count sequence, you can increase the sample rate to something faster, such as 10 kHz. At this rate, however, less than half of the entire count sequence can be viewed and you might have to take several sets of samples before you obtain a picture of what you wanted to see.

A logic analyzer solves this problem by implementing a trigger word. All this means is that we can specify when to start sampling by specifying a bit pattern for the system to watch for. Since we want to see the count transition from state 14 to state 15, we can ask the system to start sampling when it sees state 13. We might want to specify a condition for the clock line, or we might prefer to indicate that the clock bit is a don't-care bit. This allows the sampling to start when the other 4 bits matched our trigger word. If we want to get more sophisticated, we can design the system to allow the trigger conditions not only to include high, low, and don't-care, but also positive and negative edge transitions on any given bit position. Such a system allows the user to specify very precisely when to start taking the samples.

Real logic analyzers also allow the user to specify whether the data will be seen before or after the trigger event. The previous example was really a little misleading. The trigger word does not really tell the system when to start sampling. Instead, the system is always sampling (once it is enabled) and the trigger word simply tells the system when to quit sampling. If the system always takes 640 samples, the system might give the user a choice (pre or post) of stopping the sampling either 60 samples or 580 samples after the trigger word is found. When the sampling stops, the buffer will contain 640 samples with either 580 of the samples occurring after the match of the trigger word or 580 of the samples occurring before the match. This lets the user specify not only a sample rate and a trigger word, but also whether he or she is primarily interested in events immediately before or immediately after the trigger event.

Real logic analyzers have many other features and, as part of your research, you should try to operate a real analyzer. After doing so, reread the previous discussion and I think that the internal operation of an analyzer will become a little clearer. Implementing the features discussed in this project is relatively easy. Exercises in this text have shown you how to read information from a port at a specific rate and how to compare data bytes while masking out bits you are not interested in. We have also seen how to detect the edges of pulses, so with a little research and a lot of planning, you should be able to design your own analyzer and even have many of the features of commercial units, except perhaps for the high sample rates.

ASSIGNMENT: Decide what features you would like your simple logic analyzer to have and document them in a detailed specification. Think carefully about the user interface and try to make it as easy to use as possible. Implement your solution and test, troubleshoot, and debug the hardware and software until they perform according to your original specifications.

REVIEW QUESTIONS
1. What part of the design process did you find the most difficult? Why?
2. What problems did you encounter? How did you solve them?
3. Did your final implementation meet all the original specifications? If not, why? How do you think you could have overcome the limitations of your solution?
4. Was your final implementation accurate 100% of the time? What kind of situations caused it to fail? How do you think these situations could be dealt with?
5. What did you learn from this project that you feel was particularly valuable? How do you think it will help you in the future?

Project 8
A Plotting Arm

PURPOSE: The purpose of this project is to understand better the inner workings of commercial plotters by creating a robotic arm that can draw various shapes using a felt-tip marker. As with all the projects in this section, the purpose of the text is to point you in the right direction. It is expected that you will conduct the experimentation and research necessary to bring this project to fruition.

OBJECTIVES: After the completion of this project, the reader should be able to:
- Describe the advantages and disadvantages of various hardware configurations for building a plotting device.
- Identify potential problems that might relate to the drawing of triangles and circles.
- Design the hardware and software necessary to draw triangles and circles with sizes and positions being specified by a user.
- Utilize your designs and the tool functions described in this text to implement a robot system that can draw shapes according to your specifications.

THEORY: Plotters enable users of CAD programs to create large detailed drawings of anything from electrical schematics to plans for your new house. Internally, a plotter is nothing more than a computerized pen that can be moved to any point on a plotting surface. Commercial plotters can be very expensive because they need fast speeds, fine accuracy, and extra features like the ability to lift a pen or even change the pen to get different colors.

For this project, however, consider keeping the features simple so you can concentrate your efforts on motor control and software algorithms. The first thing you will need to do is decide on a configuration for your arm. Let's look at 2 possibilities.

The first choice is probably the most obvious. You can model the hardware portion of your arm after a standard *x-y* plotter or a flat-bed scanner. One motor can move the arm horizontally and the other motor vertically. Since we are looking at a positioning problem, stepper motors should be considered.

Another configuration for the plotter is a two-dimensional jointed arm. Imagine a shoulder and an elbow system that can lie flat on the paper. Your design can be simple because the arm does not have to lift anything, not even itself. You might even let the arm rest on Teflon slides to reduce the friction. If you use a pulley system between the motors and the joints, you will not have to mount the motors on the arm itself. This means that the arm can be very light and easy to move.

In both cases described above, you will need a method for attaching a pen or marker to the drawing portion of the arm. To keep things simple, consider gluing a brass or cardboard tube to the arm at the proper place. Choose a tube with a diameter such that a marker, when dropped into the tube, will fit snuggly. Your software can prompt you (using perhaps an LCD or even LEDs) when to insert or remove the marker from the tube. A felt-tip marker should work well because it won't need to be held tightly to the paper to get a good line.

Both options above have advantages and disadvantages when it comes to drawing, so you can choose either configuration primarily based on which is easiest for you to construct. For example, the x-y system will allow you to draw lines fairly easily, but it will have trouble drawing circles. To specify that the system must be able to draw both triangles and circles, it will be necessary to do some research and planning, no matter which system you choose to implement.

You should develop tool functions for moving your arm to any coordinate on the drawing surface, no matter where the arm is presently located. With the jointed arm, you will have to calculate the angles each joint should have for a given coordinate using trigonometry. You will also have to use trigonometry for the x-y arm when you determine the coordinates of points on a circle.

The tools should move both motors simultaneously to eliminate steps in the drawing as much as possible. Once the tools have been completed, the main program needs only to determine the location to which the arm needs to move to create the shape being drawn. The tools themselves will handle the details of how to position the arm using the motors.

Since precise positioning is of prime importance, stepper motors probably make the most sense, but the servomotors discussed in Project 10 are a reasonable alternative.

ASSIGNMENT: Define the specifications for a simple robot that can draw triangles and circles as specified by the user, and design the hardware and software needed to solve the problem. Implement your solution and test, troubleshoot, and debug the hardware and software until they perform according to your original specifications.

REVIEW QUESTIONS
1. What part of the design process did you find the most difficult? Why?
2. What problems did you encounter? How did you solve them?
3. Did your final implementation meet all the original specifications? If not, why? How do you think you could have overcome the limitations of your solution?
4. Was your final implementation accurate 100% of the time? What kind of situations caused it to fail? How do you think these situations could be dealt with?
5. What did you learn from this project that you feel was particularly valuable? How do you think it will help you in the future?

Project 9
Scrolling Signs

PURPOSE: The purpose of this project is to create a matrix of LEDs that allows messages to scroll from right to left, so it can be read like a sign. As with all the projects in this section, the purpose of the text is to point you in the right direction. It is expected that you will conduct the experimentation and research necessary to bring this project to fruition.

OBJECTIVES: After the completion of this project, the reader should be able to:
- Describe a methodology needed for multiplexing a matrix of LEDs so that they can display a pattern without flicker.
- Identify potential problems that might relate to displaying a single pattern or to sequencing a series of patterns to create the illusion of a scrolling sign.
- Design the hardware and software necessary displaying a scrolling message on a matrix of LEDs.
- Utilize your designs and the tool functions described in this text to implement an LED matrix sign that can scroll messages specified by the user.

THEORY: You have probably seen small scrolling signs used to get your attention in store windows. You have probably seen similar signs on the highway to tell you about traffic problems ahead. Perhaps you have noticed the gigantic television displays present in most of the stadiums used for professional sporting events. If you looked closely, you should have noticed that in all these cases, the display is made up of hundreds of light sources.

After working with the exercises in this text, it should be easy to see how we can use the computer to turn a light on and off, and it should be just as obvious that we don't want the expense of driving each light by connecting it to an individual I/O pin. Instead, we must reduce the cost by multiplexing the lights in some manner. We can learn more about how commercial signs work by creating a simple system composed of LEDs.

Let's assume that we start with a bank of 112 LEDs arranged in a 7-by-16 matrix. You can use individual LEDs to create your matrix or, with a little effort, you can probably find a suitable matrix to use as a building block. The Liteon LTP2057, for example, is a 5-by-7 matrix organized in a package about 2 inches tall by 1½ inches wide. You probably will want to settle for a 7-by-15 matrix if you use a display package such as this.

Uppercase letters and numbers can be formed easily with a 5-by-7 matrix, so our sign can display almost 3 characters simultaneously if we leave only 1 column of LEDs blank between the characters. One advantage of this size is that we can control it using only the ports available in the standard PC printer interface.

The 8-bit port can be connected to the rows of the matrix. The output from the 4-bit port can be sent to a 1-low 4-to-16 decoder whose outputs connect to the columns of the matrix. This means that each LED in the matrix has a row and a column connection. The anode of each LED is a row connection and should connect to one of the 8-bit port pins. The cathode for each LED is a column connection and should connect to one of the outputs from the decoder. This arrangement is shown below.

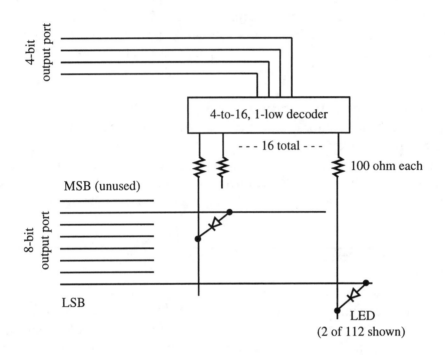

If a 0 is applied to the inputs of the decoder, then the first column of LEDs will all have their cathodes at ground potential. The voltage supplied by bits that are high on the 8-bit port will then illuminate the corresponding LED in that column. Since the cathodes of the LEDs in all the other columns will not be grounded, the data on the 8-bit port will not affect them.

Your software should select each column of the matrix by sending a number to the 4-bit port while sending the pixel data for that column to the 8-bit port. If a loop continuously illuminates each column for the proper amount of time, then the entire display will appear to be active.

To allow the sign to scroll pixel by pixel instead of character by character, it should be treated as a graphic display. The pixel data for an entire message should be translated first and stored in another array that is used to control the sign. You should create tools for displaying portions of the pixel array on the display matrix. The main portion of your program must select only sections of the array to be displayed. If the sections are sequenced properly, a scrolling effect will be generated.

Once you understand how the sign works, you might want to consider special effects or even animation of stick figures or simple shapes. Use your imagination.

ASSIGNMENT: Define the specifications for an LED-based matrix sign and design the hardware and software needed to solve the problem. Implement your solution and test, troubleshoot, and debug the hardware and software until they perform according to your original specifications.

REVIEW QUESTIONS
1. What part of the design process did you find the most difficult? Why?
2. What problems did you encounter? How did you solve them?
3. Did your final implementation meet all the original specifications? If not, why? How do you think you could have overcome the limitations of your solution?
4. Was your final implementation accurate 100% of the time? What kind of situations caused it to fail? How do you think these situations could be dealt with?
5. What did you learn from this project that you feel was particularly valuable? How do you think it will help you in the future?

Project 10
Using Servomotors

PURPOSE: The purpose of this project is to examine hobby servomotors and how they can be interfaced with a computer. As with all the projects in this section, the purpose of the text is to point you in the right direction. It is expected that you will conduct the experimentation and research necessary to bring this project to fruition.

OBJECTIVES: After the completion of this project, the reader should be able to:
- Discuss how hobby servomotors are controlled by pulse-width modulation.
- Identify potential applications where servomotors are appropriate.
- Design the software necessary for controlling one or more servomotors.
- Utilize software tools that you have developed to implement a solution using servomotors for a motor-based application.

THEORY: If you are building any of the projects in this text that require a dc motor, one of the biggest problems you might have is finding a suitable motor for your application. Hobby servomotors, like those you might find in a radio-controlled car or airplane, can sometimes be a good choice. They are inexpensive and powerful for their size.

Hobby servomotors have a 3-wire cable composed, usually, of red (+) and black (–) wires for power (typically 5 volts) and a third wire for control. If pulses are applied to the control wire, the width of the pulses controls the position of the servomotor's output shaft. Servos usually have a movement range of about 180 degrees. If the control pulse is approximately 1 ms wide, then the servo will position itself near the center of its range. As the pulse width is varied, typically from 0.5 ms to 1.5 ms, the position of the servo shaft will move proportionally from 0 to 180 degrees. The actual frequency of the control pulses is not critical. To get maximum torque, however, the pulse should occur at least 50 or 60 times per second.

After completing the exercises in this text, you should have no trouble writing a module that can create pulses of a variable width to control a single servo. If you need to control several servos, you must send each its own control pulses. As such, the 4-bit output port can control 4 servos. Even if each servo required a 2 ms pulse at 60 Hz, only a total time of 480 ms out of each second would be required. This leaves plenty of processing time to decide where the servos should be positioned for your application.

Controlling servos can be an interesting exercise and, because you can easily control their position, they can be used in many applications instead of stepper motors. What you can't control, at least not directly, is the servo's speed. Whenever you change the pulse width of the control pulse, the servo moves to the new position at its maximum speed. If you want it to move to the new position at a slow rate, you must change the pulse width slowly rather than all at once.

With this background and a little planning and research of your own, you should be able to create a set of tool functions that can manipulate multiple servos simultaneously. The decisions about what tools to create and what parameters they should be passed is as important to this project as how to write the actual code.

ASSIGNMENT: Select a motor-based application, perhaps from elsewhere in this text, and develop a solution using servomotors. Perform any research necessary and then develop the appropriate algorithms for your system. Implement your solution and test and debug it until it performs according to your original specifications.

REVIEW QUESTIONS
1. What part of the design process did you find the most difficult? Why?
2. What problems did you encounter? How did you solve them?
3. Did your final implementation meet all the original specifications? If not, why? How do you think you could have overcome the limitations of your solution?
4. Was your final implementation accurate 100% of the time? What kind of situations caused it to fail? How do you think these situations could be dealt with?
5. What did you learn from this project that you feel was particularly valuable? How do you think it will help you in the future?

Project 11
Simulations

PURPOSE: The purpose of this project is to create a computer simulation that can be controlled using the tools developed throughout this text. As with all the projects in this section, the purpose of the text is to point you in the right direction. It is expected that you will conduct the experimentation and research necessary to bring this project to fruition.

OBJECTIVES: After the completion of this project, the reader should be able to:
- Discuss the methodology associated with simulations and simulation design.
- Identify potential areas where simulations can be valuable and discuss the advantages of using simulations in those areas.
- Design the software necessary for creating a simulation.
- Utilize a simulation of your design and the tool functions described in this text to create a program to demonstrate the value of simulations.

THEORY: Throughout this text we have created programs to control physical devices such as LCDs, motors, LEDs, and keypads. In some cases, I suspect that the time it took some readers to procure appropriate parts and construct the physical circuits took longer than writing the associated programs. The value of the experience, however, is probably worth all the effort. In most cases, I have found the motivation manifested in students after they have written programs that interface successfully with the outside world far greater than anything exhibited from writing programs that search a database or calculate the taxes for a payroll check.

Even so, there is some value, in some situations, in the ability to jump right into a programming task. Sometimes the item we want to control is too large to store conveniently or too expensive to purchase, especially if we need one for each student in a class. In some cases, we might need to test the algorithms we develop before we construct the physical device that we want to control. At other times, we might find it motivationally valuable to get participants involved in a control project as quickly as possible, even if the device being controlled is only a simulation. In fact, if the simulation is good enough, it might create as much interest and enthusiasm as the real thing.

Let's look at a few simple examples. Imagine a simulated motor on the screen of your computer. Imagine also that the speed of the motor can be controlled by pulse-width modulating a real or simulated I/O pin. The simulated motor can simply show a spinning shaft connected to a pointer or colored disk to make the movement easier to observe, or it can turn a simulated pulley that winds a simulated string that lifts a simulated elevator. In either case, the simulation will be the most effective if we can control it just as we would with a real motor.

Creating a graphical simulation of a motor is a relatively easy task. If we want only a spinning pointer connected to a shaft, we can calculate in advance the endpoints of all the positions we will need and store them in an array. We can sequence through the array, drawing the pointer at its new position and erasing it at the old position. The delays we use to control the sequencing will be reflected in the speed of the simulated motor.

If our simulation is running on a dedicated PC, the program samples an input pin and stores a running set of samples in a circular buffer. The program uses the contents of the buffer to calculate the average duty cycle applied to the pin and sets the sequencing delay based on the present duty cycle. The net effect is that we have a control program running on one machine that can control the actions of the simulated motor on the other machine.

The most important feature in the above discussion is that the simulation can be controlled by *the exact same program* that can be used to control a real motor. With a little research, it would be easy to program inertia and mass for the simulation so that it becomes even more like a real motor. Someone controlling this simulation, however, can begin learning about motor control without building any circuits or destroying any transistors.

In this example, one computer is dedicated to the simulation, but the same effect can be created on one computer using interrupts to allow the simulation to execute in the background. This allows programmers to test their control programs at the office or at home and then later use the same program to control a real motor in the lab.

If the time-related physical aspects of a dc motor seem too difficult to simulate, consider other choices. If you really want to control movement, a stepper motor is far easier to simulate than a dc motor. Simulations don't necessarily have to be physical. Consider simulating an LCD complete with the ability to process commands such as clear screen and cursor movements. If simulated on a dedicated computer, the virtual LCD program can monitor an input port and actually perform its actions based on the status of the pins acting as the enable, R/W, RS, etc. Writing such a simulation can teach you a lot about interfacing.

If you wanted a less realistic simulation of an LCD, your program can interface to it, not at the port level but at the tool level. To do so you would need only to create new tool functions for **LCD_command**( ) and **print_character**( ) as described in Exercise 7. These new functions simply perform their actions on the simulation. Since all the other tools, such as **print_string**( ) and **print_number**( ), are based on **LCD_command**( ) and **print_character**( ), they control the simulation without any modification. Even the **editNum**( ) function discussed in Exercise 14 should work as written.

If the simulation versions of **LCD_command**( ) and **print_character**( ) are stored in one include file and the real versions stored in another, then any program that you write could control either a real LCD or the simulation by including the right header file.

ASSIGNMENT: Decide on a simulation that you would like to write and develop a detailed specification of exactly what should be expected from your system. Perform any research necessary and then develop the appropriate algorithms for your system. Implement your solution and test and debug it until it performs according to your original specifications.

REVIEW QUESTIONS
1. What part of the design process did you find the most difficult? Why?
2. What problems did you encounter? How did you solve them?
3. Did your final implementation meet all the original specifications? If not, why? How do you think you could have overcome the limitations of your solution?
4. Was your final implementation accurate 100% of the time? What kind of situations caused it to fail? How do you think these situations could be dealt with?
5. What did you learn from this project that you feel was particularly valuable? How do you think it will help you in the future?

Appendix A
Review of C and C++

Let me remind you that this text is not intended to teach you how to program in C or C++. It explores how to use C routines to control external devices connected to I/O ports, and it tries to do this so that even beginning programmers can benefit from the examples and applications. If you have no prior knowledge of C, you should expect to supplement this material with a general text on C and C++. Doing so will allow you to maximize the benefits you can get from it. Above all, don't get discouraged. Learning any language takes time. C is definitely a language that is worth the effort.

This appendix provides only a brief overview of C and it is intended to serve 3 potential reader groups. First, there may be readers who are familiar with C but need a short review because they have not used it in a while. Second, programmers experienced in other languages might find this overview sufficient if they have a reference manual or even online help available for their compiler. Finally, if this text is being used in a less rigorous introductory course that covers only Parts I and II, then this appendix might fill readers' needs. Having said this, let me emphasize once more that a previous background in C is highly recommended to get the most from this material.

Throughout this review, I will generally use the term C to refer to both C and C++. Most compilers today are technically C++ systems, but you can certainly use them to write C programs that don't take advantage of any of the extended features of C++. For the most part, the control applications discussed in this text do not need the features of C++. For continuity, a couple of the examples in the text are implemented as both C functions and C++ objects, but knowledge of C alone will be sufficient for most readers. For that reason, this review will not deal with object-oriented programming and class architectures.

The C language is often thought of as a difficult language to learn. Although there are a few features of C that make it complicated, those features add power and versatility not found in less robust languages. For the most part, C is not any more complicated than any other computer language. Why then has C gotten a reputation for being difficult?

The answer is that C is a language based on symbols rather than words. Figure A.1 shows a few of the symbols used in C and their associated meanings.

%	modulo divide
^	exclusive OR
&	bitwise AND
&	address of
|	bitwise OR
&&	logical AND
||	logical OR
~	bitwise NOT
!	logical NOT
+ +	increment
- -	decrement
> >	shift right
< <	shift left
+ =	increment by
- =	decrement by
{	begin a block
}	end a block

Figure A.1: These are only a few of the symbols used in the C language.

When a person does not know BASIC, Pascal, or nearly any other computer language, and tries to read (not write) a program in that language, he or she generally can understand most of what is read because most languages are based on words such as IF, SHIFT, AND, PRINT, and BEGIN. The use of such words makes many programming languages almost as readable as English with a little mathematics thrown in.

With C, if you don't know the meaning of the symbols, you have absolutely no idea of what the program is saying. To make matters worse, many of the symbols in C are made up of 2 other symbols, and even the same symbol can have several names and meanings depending on the context. If you think about it, this is a lot like English. Two words used together can mean something different than either of the two words alone (jumbo shrimp, hard drive, etc.). Many words have different meanings based on how they are used (read, tear, etc.). If you have trouble with C, you must familiarize yourself with its symbols. If you don't, you will find learning C as difficult as learning English without being told about the alphabet.

The C language is made up of self-contained modules or functions that can be given information (by other modules) to process. When the processing is complete, an answer is returned to the module that provided the original data. Figure A.2 shows an example of two modules in a simple C program.

```
float average(int a, int b)
    {
    float ans;
    ans = (a+b)/2.0;
    return ans;
    }

void main(void)
    {
    float x, y=2;
    x = average(y,7);
    // x will now have a value of 4.5
    }
```

Figure A.2: Properly organized C programs are composed of self-contained modules.

The two modules in Figure A.2 are named **average** and **main**. All C programs must have a *main* function. The order of the modules in the program is not important. Execution always begins with **main( )**, which can call on other modules to perform tasks as needed. Even these second-level modules can call other modules as a program gets larger and more complicated.

Let's examine the module **average( )** first. There are many types of variables in C, and this module refers to two of them. An *integer* variable can hold only whole numbers, while a *floating point* variable can contain numbers with fractional parts. In general, integers take up less memory than floats. Integer mathematics always takes less time than similar floating point calculations.

The first line in **average( )** looks like this:

float average(int a, int b)

The items inside the parentheses indicate that the values of two integers will be passed to this module. To be able to refer to those values while writing this module, the line above indicates that the names **a** and **b** will be used to refer to the passed data. The word **float** at the beginning of the line indicates that this module will return a floating point answer.

The beginning and end of a module is marked with braces, { }. Inside the module **average( )**, the first line creates a temporary variable **ans** of type float. The semicolon at the end of a line marks the end of the statement. In this case, *temporary* means that this variable exists only while this module is being executed. No other modules can refer to this variable. Even if the name **ans** is used elsewhere in the program, it would not refer to this piece of data. Variables of this type, those that are defined within a module, are referred to as *local* variables. Each time a module is called, the value of local variables must be re-initialized. Local variables may be declared *static* if there is a need for a module to keep a permanent copy of its data.

The only items that we can refer to inside **average( )** are **ans**, **a**, and **b**. The second line in **average( )** adds the 2 items passed and divides the sum by 2.0. Calculations in C always elevate all the items in an expression to the type of the item with the highest level. By using the floating point constant, 2.0, you tell the compiler to convert both **a** and **b** to floats, and floating point mathematics will be used for the calculation. The equals sign causes the floating point answer to be placed into the variable **ans**. If the sum had been divided by the integer 2, an integer divide would have produced an integer answer of 4, which would have been converted to 4.0 before being stored in **ans**.

The last line in **average( )** tells the compiler to return the value of **ans** to the module that passed the values of **a** and **b**. Let's look at **main( )** to see how that passing takes place. The first line of **main( )** uses the word **void** twice. Inside the parentheses the void indicates that nothing is passed to **main( )**. The void at the beginning of the line means that **main( )** will not return anything. In some systems, DOS, for example, items can be passed (if desired) to a program that is being run and the program, when finished, is expected to return a code to DOS to indicate if any errors occurred while it was executing. In most cases, if you are not sure what needs to be passed to and from **main( )**, you can assume **void**.

The first line inside **main( )** creates two floating point variables. The variable **x** is not initialized to any particular value, but the variable **y** will have an initial value of 2 (really 2.0). The difference between 2 and 2.0 is really only a matter of how the compiler stores the information internally and how it deals with the data when it sees it in an expression. Since **y** is a floating point variable in this example, the value provided will always be converted to a floating point format. The next line in **main( )** looks like this:

```
x = average(y, 7);
```

This line calls the function **average( )** and passes 2 numbers, the value of **y** and 7, to it. This means that when **average( )** begins to execute, **a** will have a value of 2 and **b** will have a value of 7. When **average( )** is finished, it returns its answer to **main( )**, where it is stored in **x**, as indicated by the comment in the code. C++ assumes that any line beginning with two slashes is a comment. Comments in C must begin and end with slashes and asterisks as shown below:

```
/*  this is a comment in C or C++  */
```

Unlike the C comments, C++ comments are terminated automatically at the end of the line. You can use C comments in a C++ program if you wish. In fact, because C++ is an extension of C, nearly everything available in C is usable in C++.

Let's get back to the call of **average( )** and look a little deeper. Remember, the compiler uses different methods for storing integers and floats. This means that the compiler must convert the floating point representation of the value of **y** to an integer representation before passing it to **average( )**. If this conversion does not take place, the data stored as the variable **a** in **average( )** would be interpreted incorrectly.

How does the compiler know whether or not to perform this conversion? The compiler analyzes the C program starting at the top and moves downward. Since it analyzed the module **average( )** before getting to **main( )**, it knows what **average( )** expects to be passed. This allows the compiler to process the call in **main( )** correctly. Don't confuse the *analyzing* and *processing* referred to here with the execution of this program. The C language is a compiler. It analyzes the source code that you write and translates it to machine code that can be executed directly by the computer hardware. The translation process starts at the beginning of the program and proceeds line by line until the end is reached. The execution of the translated code starts at **main( )** and, as we will soon see, can jump all over the place until it finally stops at the end of **main( )**.

The compiler can get confused, however, if a module is called before it is defined. Look at Figure A.3, for example. It is similar to Figure A.2, except that the positions of **main( )** and **average( )** have been reversed. When the compiler processes **main( )** and translates the call to **average( )**, it does not know what **average( )** expects to receive. This is true because the compiler started at the top of the code and it has not even gotten to the **average( )** module at the time it is processing **main( )**. To prevent confusion in C and compile errors in C++, the programmer must place a *function prototype* at the beginning of the program to tell the compiler that **average( )** will be passed 2 integers and will return a float. Notice that the prototype, like most statements in C, ends with a semicolon, while the line that defines a module does not. Notice also that the prototype does not have to mention any variable names. It needs only to declare the *types* that will be passed so the compiler can write the proper machine code.

C has many standard functions that can be called from the programs that you write. Having these functions available means that you don't have to reinvent the wheel when you write a program. To prevent the type of confusion just discussed, even standard functions that are integrated into a C compiler need to be prototyped.

```
float average(int, int);  // this is the prototype

void main(void)
    {
    float x, y=2;
    x = average(y,7);
    // x will now have a value of 4.5
    }

float average(int a, int b)
    {
    float ans;
    ans = (a+b)/2.0;
    return ans;
    }
```

Figure A.3: Prototypes can prevent confusion by indicating what variable types are passed to and from modules.

To make the prototyping of standard functions easy for the user, C languages use disk files, referred to as header files, that contain (among other things) the proper prototypes for functions. For example, the file **string.h** contains the prototypes for many string modules that make manipulating string data easier. The file **graphics.h** would have to be used if your program contains calls to graphic functions and **math.h** would be required if your program utilizes calls to complex math operations such as trigonometry functions. You can add these prototypes to your programs by placing statements like the following at the beginning of your source code.

```
#include <string.h>
#include <math.h>
```

If you do not include the proper header files, the compiler will give you an error when it tries to process a call to an internal function. Other items found in header files are defined constants, as demonstrated below.

```
#define PI        3.1415
#define TRUE     1
#define FALSE    0
```

Defined constants are generally written in capitals to prevent possible conflicts with defined words, which must be in lowercase. Header files contain a few other items, but you should consult a complete book on C or your compiler's documentation for more detailed information than space permits in this short review.

The ability to make decisions about what code to execute and what to skip is the basis for adding intelligence to any programming language. The C language uses an **if( )** statement to make decisions, as shown in Figure A.4.

When the compiler executes an **if( )**, it decides if the expression inside the parentheses is true or false and then executes one of two blocks of code, as indicated in Figure A.4. In this example, the statement will be true if the value of **a** is less than 6 and false if it is greater than or equal to 6. Internally, a *false* is represented by a value of 0 and *true* is represented by any nonzero value. This means that an expression like **if**(3) is always treated as true and **if**(0) is always treated as false.

```
if ( a < 6 )
     {
     // do the statements in this block if the if( ) is true
     }
else
     {
     // do the statements in this block if the if( ) is false
     }
```

Figure A.4: The **if( )** decision in C has many options.

Expression	Meaning
a	true if a has any nonzero value
a < 6	true only if value of **a** is less than 6
a < = 6	true only if value of **a** is less than or equal to 6
a = = 6	true only if value of **a** is equal to 6
a ! = 6	true only if value of **a** is not equal to 6
!(a = = 6)	true only if value of **a** is not equal to 6
(a>2) && (a<=5)	true only if value of a is greater than 2 AND less than or equal to 5
(a==6) || (a<b)	true only if value of **a** is equal to 6 OR value of **a** is less than value of **b**
!((a==2) || (b<6))	true only if value of **a** is not equal to 2 AND value of **b** is greater than or equal to 6 (DeMorgan's rule)

Figure A.5: These are examples of decision-oriented expressions in C.

The **else** portion of an **if**( ) statement is optional. Without the **else**, the system will do the indicated block for a true condition and skip the block for a false. The braces enclosing a block are also optional if the block contains only a single statement. Using the braces can often avoid confusion, however, especially with situations such as one **if**( ) inside one of the sections of another **if**( ). Figure A.5 shows examples of expressions that are valid arguments for an **if**( ) statement.

Loops are another important method of controlling what lines of code are executed. The basic loop in C is a *while* loop. An example is shown in Figure A.6.

The **while**( ) loop tests the expression and, if it is true, executes the statements in its associated block. Each time the block is completed, the expression is tested again to see if the loop should continue. The expression for the while loop can be any syntax that is valid for the **if**( ) statement. An important point to notice here is that if the expression is false when the loop is first encountered, none of the statements in the loop will ever be executed.

```
while (expression )
    {
    // perform the statements in this block
    // as long as the expression in the while( ) is true
    }
```

Figure A.6: Any expression that can be used in an **if**( ) can be used in a **while**( ).

```
do  {
      // the statements inside this block
      // will always execute at least once
      // then the loop will continue as long
      // as the while expression is true
      } while (expression);
```

Figure A.7: A **do-while( )** loop makes its decision to continue at the end of the loop.

Figure A.7 shows another kind of C loop known as a *do-while*. The **do-while( )** is similar to the **while( )** but performs its decision at the end of the loop instead of at the beginning. This means that the statements in the loop will always be performed *at least* once, since they are executed before the first decision is made.

You will notice in all the examples in this review that the code has been indented to show where blocks of statements begin and end. Indenting is not required by the compiler, but it makes reading the code easier for programmers. There are many acceptable methods for indenting C code. As you read through different books and programs, you can analyze what other programmers have found valuable and adopt what works for you. The important thing is to decide on how you will handle indenting and then remain consistent in your methods—unless of course your employer has an internal standard that you must follow. In that case, following the designated standard is probably your only option.

The final type of loop available in a C program is the **for( )** loop, which is really a simplified method for dealing with a typical **while( )** format. A **while( )** often needs to establish an initial value for a variable before the loop begins. After the statements inside the loop are executed, a variable might need to be incremented, decremented, or otherwise altered before the decision is made to continue the loop. Such an example is given in Figure A.8.

The actions of Figure A.8 can be accomplished more concisely by using a **for( )**, as shown in Figure A.9.

```
x = 0;    // initialize the value of x
while(x<10)
     {
     // place statements to be executed here
     x++;   // C shorthand for x = x + 1 (increment x)
     }
```

Figure A.8: This loop will execute its internal statements 10 times.

```
for( x = 0; x<10 ; x++)
    {
    // place statements to be executed here
    }
```

Figure A.9: The **for**( ) statement can handle certain formats concisely.

A **for**( ) has 3 separate fields separated by semicolons inside the parentheses. The first field executes prior to starting the loop, and the last field executes at the end of each pass through the loop. The middle field acts exactly the same as the argument in a **while**( ) statement.

Another control structure worth mentioning in a review is the **switch-case,** which is shown in Figure A.10. The **switch** can test the value of any integer (or character) expression and diverts the program flow to a matching **case** or to the **default** if no **case** matches are found. The **break** statements terminate each **case** and cause the program to continue at the statement following the **switch-case** block.

As mentioned above, the **switch-case** can work with integer or character variables. A character variable is really a small (8-bit) integer. Other than size, the only real difference in nonarray instances of either type is that integer variables default to signed and character variables default to unsigned. There are numerous variable types in C, including long, double, and Boolean, but one type we absolutely need to discuss in a review is pointer variables.

```
switch (x)
    {
    case 1:  // do these statements
             // if x is equal to 1
             break;
    case 8:  // do these statements
             // if x is equal to 8
             break;
    default: // do these statements
             // for any other condition
             break;
    }
```

Figure A.10: The switch-case control structure allows multiple comparisons to be made easily.

One of the advantages of C is that it allows you to refer to variables by their *value* and by *reference*. *Reference* simply means that we can refer to a variable by specifying the address in memory where it is stored. A pointer variable can hold the address to a piece of data rather than the data itself. We can declare a pointer variable **x** that can hold the address of an integer like this:

```
int * x;
```

The asterisk in this example indicates that the variable being defined is a pointer and the **int** indicates that the data being pointed to is an integer. If we have an integer variable **y**, we can place the address of **y** into **x** with the following statement:

```
x = &y;
```

In this statement, the ampersand is a symbol that means *address of*. The statement says, "Store the address of **y** into **x**." Let's look at an example to see how pointers can help us when we program. First, let's examine a fragment of code that can swap the values of 2 integers. This code fragment is shown in Figure A.11.

```
int a= 5, b=6;
int temp;
temp = a;
a = b;
b = temp;
```

Figure A.11: This code fragment swaps the present values of **a** and **b**.

The code in Figure A.11 works fine as long as it is present in the same module as the variables **a** and **b**. If we want to create a tool function that can swap the values of any 2 variables, however, this type of procedure does not work. If we pass the values of the variables to the tool module, then the module swaps only the values that it received. Since those values are only copies of the real data, the original data has not been swapped. The code in Figure A.12 shows how to create a working **swap( )** function.

The **swap( )** function in Figure A.12 is defined to receive the addresses of 2 integers and to return nothing (**void**). Notice that the use of the asterisks here is the same as before. They simply indicate the associated variables are meant to hold addresses of data, not the data itself. In the body of the **swap( )** function, the asterisks have a different meaning. Used in this context, they mean *contents of*. The line following the declaration of the integer variable **temp** can be read as "Copy the contents of the address pointed to by **x** into **temp**." The next line causes the contents of address **y** to be copied into the memory location pointed to by **x**. As you can see, this function can swap the contents of any 2 addresses passed to it.

```
void swap(int * x, int * y)
    {
    int temp;
    temp = *x;
    *x = *y;
    *y = temp;
    }
```

Figure A.12: This swap function exchanges the values of 2 variables whose addresses are passed to it.

```
#include <a:swap.c>

void main(void)
    {
    int a=23, b =67;
    swap(&a, &b);
    // a is now 67 and b is 23
    swap(&a, &b);
    // a and b are now back to their original value
    }
```

Figure A.13: If the **swap**( ) code is placed in a file, it can be used in other programs.

Since the module in Figure A.12 is really a tool that can be used any time by any program that needs to swap the value of 2 integers, let's assume that we save this code in a file as swapcode.c. We can then include this file in any program and use it as needed. The example in Figure A.13 shows how to utilize the **swap**( ) tool in another program.

This example assumes that the **swap**( ) file is stored on drive A. The path should be altered in the include statement so that the system knows where to look for the file. Notice how the & operator is used to pass the addresses of the variables **a** and **b** to **swap**( ). As you can see, address pointers provide interesting capabilities for programmers.

Pointers are also associated with arrays. We can define an integer array in C with the following statement.

```
int a[10];
```

In this case, the array **a** will be large enough to hold 10 elements that can be referred to as **a**[0] through **a**[9]. It is important to remember that C does not perform any boundary checks on array operations. If your program tries to store data in element **a**[100], C will decide where that location would be if the array was that big, and then place the data there (without any regard for what that location might really be used for). As the programmer, you should make sure that all accesses of the array elements are within range.

We can use the ampersand operator to find the address of an array element just as easily as we can a simple variable. The expression &**a**[9], for example, is the address of the last element in the 10-element array **a**[ ]. We can use this method to find the address of the entire array by finding the address of element 0, the first element in the array. The C language gives us an even better method. When your program refers to the name of an array without using any brackets, then C interprets that to mean you want the address of the array. Let's see how this can be useful to us.

First, however, let's see how we can find the average of an array. Look at the code fragment in Figure A.14. When it declares the array, it also shows a method to provide initial values for the

```
void main(void)
    {
    int i, a[5] = {4, 12, 6, 78, 3};
    float ans = 0;
    for(i=0; i<5; i++)
        ans = ans + a[i];  // could also be written ans + = a[i];
    ans = ans/5;            // could also be written ans/=5;
    // ans now contains the average of the array
    }
```

Figure A.14: This code finds the average of an integer array.

elements. A **for**( ) is used to sum the values and the total is divided by the number of elements. Since **ans** is a float, we do not have to use 5.0 to make the answer a float.

The code in Figure A.14 has severe limitations. For example, it can find only the average of the array **a**[ ] and only if the array is composed of exactly 5 elements. Figure A.15 shows how to create a tool for averaging the elements of an array.

In the **average_array**( ) module in Figure A.15, you can see how to use C syntax to indicate that the address of an array is to be passed. Actually, the first line in the **average_array**( ) module can just as easily be written as follows.

```
float average_array(int *a, int num)
```

```
float average_array(int a[ ], int num)
    {
    float ans = 0;
    for(i=0; i<num; i++)
        ans = ans + a[i];  // could also be written ans + = a[i];
    ans = ans/num;             // could also be written ans/=5;
    // ans now contains the average of the array
    return num;
    }

void main(void)
    {
    int x[5]={34,15,2,7,9};
    int y[7] ={14,1,8,6,12,14,9};
    float ans1, ans2;
    ans1=average_array(x,5);
    ans2=average_array(y,7);
    // ans1 and ans2 now hold the averages for the 2 arrays
    }
```

Figure A.15: This code shows a module that can find the average of any integer array.

As far as C is concerned, both methods are simply different ways of saying the same thing. Both mean that an address is being passed. The C language sees no real difference. To illustrate this point further, imagine an array created as shown below:

int x[10];

We can access element 3 (the fourth element in the array) using array syntax with the following statement. It copies the value of element 3 into the integer **y**.

y = x[3];

It is equally valid to access the same element using pointer syntax, as shown below:

y = *(x+3);

In the above line, **x**, as you remember, is simply the address of the array. By adding 3 to this base address, we get an address that points to the fourth element in the array. The asterisk *dereferences* this address, giving us the contents of it. The C language makes great efforts to make such expressions easy to use. For example, if **x** is the address for an array of characters that require 1 byte for each element, then **x+3** evaluates exactly as it is written. If **x** is an array of floats that requires 4 addresses for each element, then **x+3** really evaluates to **x+(3*4)**. The compiler has this ability because it knows the *size* of the items being pointed to.

No discussion of arrays in C is complete without a discussion of strings. Unlike most computer languages, C does not implement a string data type. Instead, strings are simply arrays of characters with a binary 0 or null character terminating the string. If we want to create an array that can store the word HELLO, we can do so like this:

char x[6] = ('H', 'E', 'L', 'L', 'O', 0);

The single quotes tell C these items are characters and should be converted to an 8-bit unsigned integer representing the ASCII codes for each specified character. Notice the numeric 0 in the sixth element of the array. Notice also that the string is only 5 characters long, but it must reserve 6 memory locations due to the required null. Without the null, this string really is just an array of characters and not a string. An easier way to initialize a string is shown below.

char x[6] = "HELLO";

Double quotes are the C syntax for a string and tell the compiler to place a null at the end of the characters stored in the array. C++ compilers often provide a string class that makes the manipulation of strings as easy as languages that have string data types. Before you decide to abandon the original C strings made from character arrays, you need to know that the original C strings have a tremendous speed advantage over the class version. This makes the original strings very appropriate for embedded controller applications such as those described in this text.

```
int isupper(char c)
    {
    if(c>='A' && c<='Z')
        return 1;      // indicate a capital
    else
        return 0;
    }
```

Figure A.16: This module decides if a character passed to it is a capital letter.

Let's look at an example of how we can deal with C strings and characters. Let's start by creating a tool function that can determine if a character passed to it is an uppercase letter. The code for this example is shown in Figure A.16.

The module in Figure A.16 returns true if the character passed to it is a capital letter and false for everything else. If you understand how this routine works, it is a good time to demonstrate how efficient C can be if we are willing to give up a little readability. Figure A.17 shows another version of the **isupper**( ) function.

In Figure A.16, the code was really saying "If this expression is true, return true. If the expression is false, return false." As you can see in Figure A.17, we can return the value of the expression and eliminate the **if**( ). If you examine well-written C code, you will see this type of methodology (as well as many other efficient shortcuts) used as standard practice. I certainly endorse this type of code and encourage you to study the coding styles of professional programmers whenever possible. On the other hand, I don't want readers of this text to get so bogged down trying to understand the syntax that they fail to see the algorithms I'm trying to demonstrate. To that end, I will generally try to make the code in this text as readable as possible. Occasionally, however, I will throw in a little efficient code with the hope that it will add to the value of this text, especially if I don't overdo it.

If you understood the **isupper**( ) module, you should be able to create an **islower**( ) using the same principles. Let's see how we can use an **islower**( ) to help us create a **toupper**( ) module that can return the capital of any lowercase letter passed to it. Figure A.18 shows the code for such a module. Notice that if the letter passed is not a lowercase letter then it is returned unchanged.

The information you need to understand this module is the fact that the ASCII codes for lowercase letters are exactly 32 greater than ASCII code for their uppercase counterparts. Notice

```
int isupper(char c)
    {
    return (c>='A' && c<='Z');
    }
```

Figure A.17: This version of Figure A.16 is far more efficient.

```
char toupper(char c)
    {
    if(islower(c))
        return(c-32);
    else
        return(c);
    }
```

Figure A.18: This module will return the uppercase version of any lowercase letter passed to it. Any other character passed is returned unchanged.

also that C can perform mathematical operations on characters just as if they were integers. In fact, if you keep in mind that everything inside a computer is represented by a binary number, then this makes perfect sense. Many languages try to protect the programmer from his or her own mistakes and do not allow these types of operations.

One of the reasons that C is so powerful is that it does not prevent the programmer from doing things that don't make sense on the surface. The compiler might warn you when things look strange, but if you want C to do something, in most cases it won't get in your way. Of course, with this power comes enormous responsibility. If you tell C to do something really outlandish, it will do its best to oblige.

You should be able to build a **tolower( )** module using the principles shown in Figure A.18, but it's not really necessary. The standard C libraries include versions of **isupper( )**, **islower( )**, **toupper( )**, **tolower( )**, and many other functions. I should mention for the sake of accuracy that these functions are often implemented in the standard libraries as macros. There is no reason to go into macros here, however, because you can treat them as if they were normal functions. If you want to use these modules in your C programs, all you need to do is include the file **ctype.h**.

To demonstrate many of the principles discussed in this review, let's look at one more string example. The code in Figure A.19 creates and uses a tool that can capitalize the first letter in every word in a string.

```
#include <ctype.h>

void capitalize_words(char *string)
    {
    int i;
    // this module capitalizes any character preceded by a space
    // the first letter has no space, so it must be handled separately
    string[0]=toupper(string[0]);
    for(i=1; string[i]; i++)        // i moves through string until the null which
        if(string[I–1] = = ' ')     //    tests false
            string[i] = toupper(string[i]);
        else
            string[i] = tolower(string[i]);
    }

void main(void)
    {
    char x[50] = "heLLo 85 cat doG tEst";
    capitalize_words(x);
    // the string now reads "Hello 85 Cat Dog Test"
    }
```

Figure A.19: This program demonstrates many of the principles discussed in this review of C.

One of the things that I hope you noticed in Figure A.19 is that the program is created from a series of nested routines. Exercise 1 of this text explores this principle in some detail. If you are new to programming, read Exercise 1 and then study this appendix again.

Until now, we have not had any means of entering data from the keyboard or displaying data on the screen. The C language does not have any native input or output commands. Instead, all I/O is performed by library functions. Standard C uses functions such as **printf**( ), **puts**( ), and **putch**( ) to display data on the screen. Input from the keyboard is obtained with functions such as **getch**( ), **gets**( ), and **scanf**( ).

With C++, I/O became easier to use because of the addition of **cin** and **cout**. In Windows-based C compilers such as C++ Builder and Visual C++, all I/O must be performed using Microsoft's foundation classes or other tools that manage dialog boxes, menus, etc. If you wish to be a thorough C programmer, you certainly should study all these alternatives.

In this text, however, no video output or keyboard input will be required. This text explores controlling external devices such as keypads, LEDs, LCDs, motors, D/A converters, and more. All necessary interactions with the user will be performed by the devices being controlled. This is a realistic situation for a book about hardware interfacing. After all, how many microwave ovens or telephone answering machines have you seen with a full-sized keyboard or VGA display?

Most versions of C come with a complete set of graphic routines that allow you to plot points, draw lines, fill areas, and so on, on a VGA monitor. While the exercises detailed in this text do not use graphics of any kind, some of the application projects recommended for continued study can certainly benefit from a compiler capable of graphics. Because graphic commands are not standardized, I will leave it to the readers to study the documentation provided with their compiler if they wish to attempt an application that requires graphics. Even so, it is worth providing a simple introduction to graphics at this time.

Nearly all compilers with graphic capabilities will have a function for drawing lines similar to the one below:

```
line(x1, y1, x2, y2);
```

This function draws a line from one set of *x*, *y* coordinates to the next. The maximum values of the coordinates depend on the screen resolution. A typical size is 640 pixels horizontally and 480 pixels vertically. The graphics on many systems are implemented as a fourth quadrant system with the 0, 0 position in the upper left-hand corner of the screen. Let's see how we can use the **line**( ) function to graph some data. Figure A.20 shows a simple program for graphing a sine wave.

```c
#include <graphics.h>
#include <math.h>

void main(void)
    {
    int x;
    float angle, y[640];

    // initialize the graphics mode here
    // 640-by-480 resolution is assumed

    // calculate 640 y values
    // start both x and angle at 0
    // increment angle so that after 640 operations it will reach 2 PI
    //  (the sin( ) function expects the angle to be in radians)
    for(x = 0, angle = 0; x<640; x++, angle += 6.28/640)
        {
        y[x] = sin(angle);  // value will be between −1 and 1
        // now scale the values to be between 100 and 200
        // −50 is used to invert the signal for fourth quadrant graphing
        y[x] = y[x]*(−50) + 150;
        }
    // now graph the data
    for(x=0; x<639; x++)
        line(x, y[x], x+1, y[x+1]);
    }
```

Figure A.20: This program creates the graph of a single sine wave.

The values to be plotted are stored in an array as they are calculated and scaled. Changing the 50 will increase or decrease the overall amplitude of the waveform, while changing the 150 will move the waveform up or down on the screen. The loop that draws the graph simply connects adjacent points 2 at a time until the end of the array is reached. You will have to do a little research to determine what functions your compiler uses to initialize the graphics mode for your system and to insert the proper statements in the code at the position indicated by the comments.

The process of programming can be thought of as 2 activities. The first is the design stage where the programmer examines the problem and creates a plan or algorithm for solving it. After a conceptual solution has been prepared, the second phase is entered where the plan is coded in the desired language. Generally speaking, you can reduce the entire time for a programming project by spending more time on the design phase.

For many people, the design phase of a program is somewhat abstract and difficult to visualize. For some of these people, flowcharts make the visualization easier. Flowcharts provide a way to organize your thoughts about what a program must do to accomplish its tasks. In addition, they can make it easier to see potential errors in logic. Exercise 1 of this text discusses flowcharts in more detail. For those readers who might not be familiar with flowcharts, however, let's look at a few examples.

Normally, when statements are executed in a program, they execute in sequential order. For example, look at the statements below:

```
x=3;
y=x+4;
```

If we want to visualize these 2 statements in a flowchart format, they might look like Figure A.21. Two simple statements were shown here because the purpose of this example is to show the sequential nature of the blocks. In actual practice, the contents of the blocks would probably be more general. For example, a block in the flowchart might state a concept that has to be accomplished without going into details of exactly how it will be done. If the flowchart described a teacher's gradebook program, for instance, a block might have a stated objective such as "Find the class average."

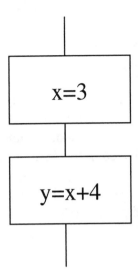

Figure A.21: This simple flowchart shows how to indicate that 2 actions must be accomplished sequentially.

If the action or activity being described by a block is complex, it probably should be implemented as a separate module or function that can be executed with a call. If you expect to implement a flowchart block as a function, it should be drawn as shown in Figure A.22.

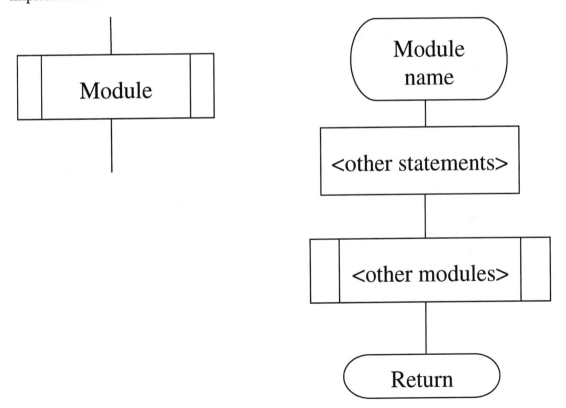

Figure A.22: Modules are the building blocks of a well-organized program.

The left side of Figure A.22 shows how to indicate that a complicated process will be implemented as a separate module. The right side of the figure demonstrates how a separate and complete flowchart can be used to describe the internal actions of the module on the left. Notice that even modules can call other modules.

Ovals are used to indicate the beginning and end of programs or modules. In Figure A.22, the top oval states the name or action of the module and the bottom oval indicates that program execution returns to the point where the module was called. If some value, such as the class average, is to be returned, then that can be reflected in the termination oval.

Decisions can be implemented in a flowchart, as shown in Figure A.23. The letters **A**, **B**, and **C** represent actions or C statements that are to be performed.

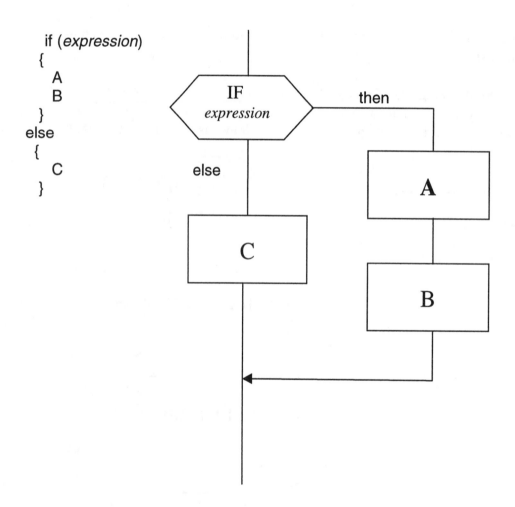

Figure A.23: This flowchart describes the decision code on the left.

```
while (expression)
    {
      A
      B
    }
```

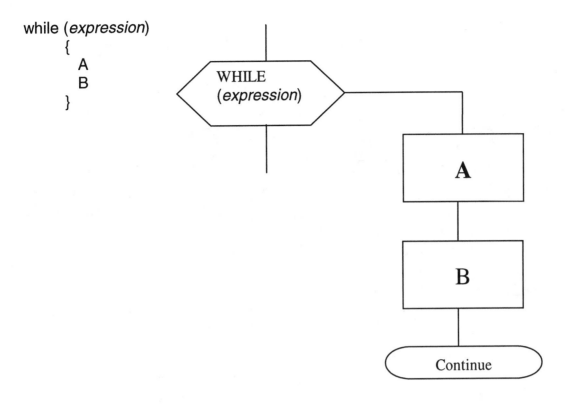

Figure A.24: This flowchart describes the **while( )** loop on the left.

Figure A.24 shows how a flowchart can be used to describe a **while( )** loop. The termination oval indicates that the loop should continue at the beginning.

Other loops can be described in similar fashions. Figure A.25 shows a code example for a **do-while( )** loop and how it can be illustrated with a flowchart.

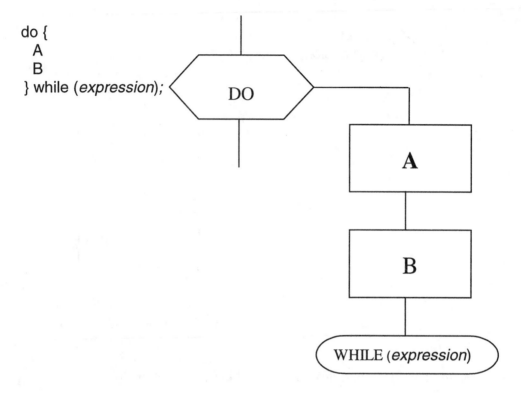

```
do {
  A
  B
} while (expression);
```

Figure A.25: This flowchart describes the **do-while**( ) code on the left.

It is difficult to see the value of any of these charts when they are shown individually. Figure A.26 shows a simple example that demonstrates how an entire program can be described with a flowchart. The program described is taken from Figure A.15. For many people, the flowchart makes it easier to visualize the actions taken by the program.

I contend, however, that programs organized properly are as easy to read and visualize as flowcharts. For that reason, most of the exercises in this text will not provide flowcharts. To help readers who have grown dependent on flowcharting adapt to my methods, however, Exercise 1 will show both code and flowcharts.

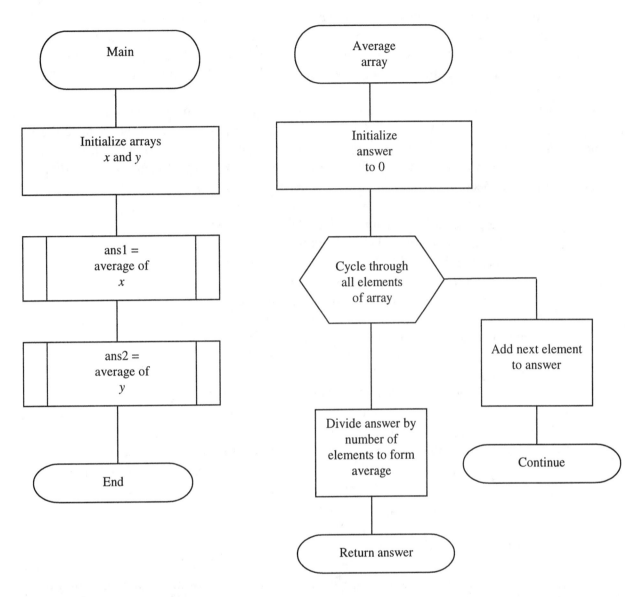

Figure A26: This flowchart describes the program in Figure A.5.

I suspect that some readers of this text will implement the exercises, not on a PC, but on a single board computer built around a microcontroller such as the Motorola 68HC11 or the 8051 from Intel. Many versions of C, including public-domain versions of Small C, are available for these and other small processors. Small C has many limitations. Even some of the commercial compilers available for microcontrollers are subsets of a full C compiler. Study the documentation provided with your system carefully if you have any problems. The examples in this text *should* run without problems on most systems, but there are too many variables to ensure 100% success.

Small C is usable, but it is far from a complete version of C. I would not recommend it for any substantial project. It is free, however, which makes it worthy of consideration in some situations. I have tested many of the examples in this text with public-domain Small C compilers with reasonable success (subject to the following comments). Unfortunately, some versions of Small C have undocumented differences (some cannot really be called bugs) from standard C.

To assist readers that might want to use such a compiler, Figure A.27 lists some of the discrepancies that I have found. This does not mean that all public-domain compilers have these problems, or even that these are the only problems you can anticipate. I recommend, however, that you write a few test routines if you use a public-domain compiler and your programs don't seem to operate as expected.

> Floating point variables cannot be used.
> > FIX: Use integers and characters for everything.
> Functions that return data larger than 8 bits are unreliable.
> > FIX: Consider using global variables.
> The decisions expressions <= and < work in reverse.
> > FIX: Use < when you mean <= and vice versa.
> Functions must be defined with the old-style argument declarations.
> > FIX: Use the old style instead of standard C syntax.
> All functions return integers (or in some cases, characters) and may not
> be declared as void or character or integer.
> > FIX: Don't declare a return type; for a void function, just don't return anything.
> Variables cannot be initialized when they are declared (all types).
> > FIX: Variables must be set equal to a value after being declared.
> No error is given when a variable is not declared (address 0 is used in the code).
> > FIX: Always declare all variables used.
> Only 1-dimensional arrays are supported.
> > FIX: If you need int x[3][10], use int x[30] and substitute x[a*10+b] for
> X[a][b].

Figure A.21: These problems have been known to occur in some public-domain Small C compilers.

Remember, this review is far from a comprehensive study of C. I have tried to touch on everything needed for this text. If you are completely new to C, additional reference material is highly recommended.

Index